IN THE MIDST OF THINGS

In the Midst of Things

The Social Lives of Objects in the Public Spaces of New York City

Mike Owen Benediktsson

PRINCETON UNIVERSITY PRESS

PRINCETON AND OXFORD

Published by Princeton University Press
41 William Street, Princeton, New Jersey 08540
99 Banbury Road, Oxford OX2 6JX

press.princeton.edu

All Rights Reserved

ISBN: 978-0-691-17433-4
ISBN (e-book): 978-0-691-18906-2

British Library Cataloging-in-Publication Data is available

Editorial: Meagan Levinson and Jaqueline Delaney
Production Editorial: Jenny Wolkowicki
Jacket design: Chris Ferrante
Production: Erin Suydam
Publicity: Kate Hensley and Kathryn Stevens
Copyeditor: Maia Vaswani

Jacket art: Shutterstock / M. Unal Ozmen

This book has been composed in Adobe Text Pro

10 9 8 7 6 5 4 3 2 1

For Slevy

CONTENTS

It is the structure of the city which first impresses us. . . . this vast organization which has arisen in response to the needs of its inhabitants, once formed . . . forms them, in turn, in accordance with the design and interests which it incorporates.

—ROBERT PARK (1915)

We shape our buildings, and afterward, our buildings shape us.

—WINSTON CHURCHILL (1943)

While I was writing the concluding chapter of this book, a deadly new virus made its way from Asia and Europe into the United States, where it would wreak havoc on the bodies, livelihoods, and social lives of Americans for years to come. The coronavirus, or Covid-19, pandemic, as it has come to be known, transformed life in New York City practically overnight. It swept through the metropolis in spring 2020, killing more than twenty thousand New Yorkers and compelling previously unthinkable changes in the daily routines of the city's residents.

Many of these changes were related to some of the central themes of this book. The virus transformed the way we interact with one another in public, the objects we use, and how we use them. We were forced, abruptly, to become self-conscious in our urbanism, thinking carefully about how we move through public space. Marks on the pavement appeared on the city's sidewalks and on the grass lawns of its parks, indicating the proper spacing of human bodies. The informal proxemics of the street gave way to formal recommendations endorsed by public health agencies. An array of strange new objects appeared in public places, and took up long-term residence. New Yorkers accustomed to the nuisance of unwanted closeness now found themselves separated by plexiglass panels, disposable rubber gloves, cotton masks and plastic face shields, and, whenever possible, six feet of open space. The subway became a ghost town.

The New York City that appears in this book is a place that existed prior to these changes. In this bustling city of the recent past, congestion was a bigger concern than contagion. It has taken two full years for reminders of that city to reappear. In recent months, the city's public spaces have reclaimed some, if not all, of their previous vitality. New Yorkers have reasserted their characteristically brash, unselfconscious use of the sidewalk and the subway platform. Restaurants are no longer empty. Vaccine cards are checked at the door, allowing a semblance of normalcy inside. Experts have repeatedly suggested that the end of the pandemic is in sight. But the city is not the same. In addition to the inanimate objects, laws, and social norms that guide behavior in public, there is another factor at work—a living thing that wields invisible power over the places where strangers congregate, creating anxiety and hesitation even when it does not produce sickness.

It is not clear at present what the future holds for New York City. Perhaps some of the changes forced by the virus will become permanent features of the urban landscape. Or maybe there will be a "post-pandemic" New York in which public space is, once again, governed primarily by laws and social norms that have little if anything to do with protecting public health against an infectious disease. In either case, it has become clear to me in the past eighteen months that the themes in this book will continue to be relevant, even if the book itself describes a city that no longer exists. As long as the residents of New York and its suburbs are relaxing on a lawn in a waterfront park, taking a moment to sit and watch the world go by in a public plaza, holding subway doors for one another, occasionally dodging traffic on divided highways, or talking to the vendor at their local newsstand, the public objects in this book will still be relevant, their lessons vital. Their stories, and the stories of the people, places, and spaces around them, will still be worthy of a closer look.

Introduction

If you look around at your home, or office, or wherever you happen to be reading this, your eyes will settle on countless manmade objects. This is not a risky speculation. They literally surround us at all times. In cities, they typically occupy our entire field of vision. What we generally do not see, however, is that these objects have ideas in them. Ideas about us. The chair in which you sit makes assumptions about you. Some of these might be correct, others incorrect. Your height and weight, the length of your legs, and the width of your torso—your chair has ideas about all of this. Your chair also has ideas about how you might like to sit. Erect or recumbent; rigid or relaxed. It may even contain ideas about how you *should* sit, imposing its own normative standards upon your posture. If you happen to be seated in a classroom, then your chair is probably a bit uncomfortable. This is intentional. It wants you to stay awake.

Sometimes, the ideas that are designed into objects are oriented on individual human users. Other times, they involve social norms or relationships, and here things get complicated. A dining-room table gathers, but not quite like a television does. A bathroom door separates, sometimes imperfectly. The window in the kitchen reinforces a gendered division of labor.[1] A rifle next to the door reflects the natural order of the universe.[2] Our material possessions, it turns out, are sociologically complex and fascinating things.

But this book is about a different class of things. When you leave your home and venture out into your community, you will encounter objects that do *not* belong to you, and that come together to constitute what is commonly referred to as public space. Let's call these things "public objects." These objects have ideas about you as well, but to them, you are only one of many—part of a collectivity. They will lump you together with the hundreds, or thousands, or perhaps even millions of other people who routinely occupy the same environment. The "public," in other words.

Outside your door, you may be lucky enough to find a sidewalk. If you do, it will probably assume that you (now plural) prefer to walk in straight lines, rather than in sinusoidal patterns or circles. A public stairway will anticipate that you might need a handrail for support, or textured surfaces for added traction. A street sign will imagine your native language, your level of literacy, and your attention span. The great majority of public objects are humble things. Their purpose is to facilitate everyday life, and if they do their job well, we repay them by ignoring them completely. They are the small talk of the material world: if we find them to be a little boring, this is a feature, not a bug. At the same time, this class of objects is deceptively interesting, just like the objects in your home. As it turns out, the material landscape outside your door is not just a physical space. It is a densely significant cultural product, embodying countless assumptions regarding who you are, how you think, and how you should behave. And these assumptions can be massively important.

Unlike the artifacts in your living room, public objects are meant for use by the public. This means that they have to imagine who, exactly, that public might be, what it might want, and what it might need. Sometimes, the ideas designed into public objects are idealistic, expressing hope for a more just, inclusive, or joyful society. Other times they are practical, aspiring to greater efficiency or safety. And still other times, they reflect cynicism, mistrust, or a desire for hierarchy or domination. Not far from my home, a crosswalk has been painted the colors of the rainbow, to signify public support for the LGBTQ community. Several blocks away, a short stone wall is crowned with sharp, daggerlike rocks, to prevent people from sitting on it. One object expresses hope and inclusiveness, while the other embodies territoriality and suspicion. In fact, the ideas behind these objects have really only one thing in common. They are ideas about society itself—how it might be, or how it must be.

These ideas are not trivial, uniform, or universal. They always reflect a specific social context. The objects around us have much to say about the political and economic forces that prevail in our communities. The material world serves as a sort of sociological connective tissue, expanding outward from each individual; upward to political, economic, or cultural institutions;

and backward through time. Social scientists often attempt to understand how "micro" and "macro" are linked, striving to identify the mechanisms that connect the small-scale world of the individual with the large-scale world of the society as a whole. Public objects compose such a mechanism. They tie our subjective, moment-by-moment experiences to those of many others. They guide our thoughts and movements along channels that reflect economic interests, bureaucratic routines, and cultural or political ideologies. When we leave our domiciles and move through public space, we have no choice but to use objects that were shaped by these forces. In doing so, we come into a fairly direct type of contact with the forces themselves. We engage them with our very bodies. Perhaps we resist their invisible propulsion. Or maybe we go with the flow.

This book examines the social lives of six material things found in the public spaces of New York City and its suburbs. Each of these public objects has a story to tell about the social and economic changes sweeping through New York City and its environs. And each of these stories illustrates an important but widely unappreciated fact of urban life—that material objects constitute a primary point of contact with the broader social and political currents that swirl around us. A newly built lawn on the Brooklyn waterfront reflects a competitive struggle between different conceptions of the public good, each drawing on a distinct ideological tradition. A low cement wall on a divided highway in New Jersey speaks of escalating suburban poverty and the demise of the postwar American dream. A metal folding chair on a patch of asphalt in Queens tells us of the political obstacles that face attempts to make the city more livable and sustainable.

Starting with a close look at these objects, and then expanding my focus to include the people, places, and spaces around them, I argue that social life occurs "in the midst of things" in two respects: we are surrounded by a material world that constrains and shapes our experience; and, through this experience, we come into direct contact with a much larger set of "things"—ideas, laws, markets, policies, and so on—that together constitute the broader ongoing narrative of social change.

Material Sociology: Affordances and Programming

This book employs an approach that is far from "paradigmatic" in the Kuhnian sense.[3] Material sociology, pardon the pun, is not really a thing. There is a good reason for this and a not-so-good reason. The good reason is that the material world does not seem to explain many of the things that are of interest to social scientists. The early twentieth-century sociologist Georg Simmel famously suggested that buildings and other material objects "fix the contents" of society. According to Simmel, objects anchor social processes in space, offering longevity to social formations that otherwise might dissipate with time. But, he acknowledged, they typically do not make things happen on their own.[4]

Obviously, objects enter into our social consciousness practically every day. They are useful metaphors—they make abstract social categories and processes more concrete. We communicate using an everyday poetry that links material things with our social world, without thinking about why these linguistic shortcuts work. We know that the "white-collar worker" or the "pencil pusher" is different from the "blue-collar worker" or the "hard hat." The "latte sipping" elitist is different from "Joe six pack." The "white tablecloth banquet" is different from the "brown bag lunch." Social structure is not something we can easily see or feel, so we refer to its material correlates, in a form of metonymy.

Even more fundamentally, our daily social routines are closely linked to material things. Our lives are, in fact, impossible to describe without frequent reference to objects. "Taking out the trash," "going to the bank," and "getting the car washed" are cultural rituals that involve the routine care of material possessions. They make sense only if we assume that the material world exerts a constant power over our social reality. Nevertheless, material artifacts often seem trivial compared with the large-scale social forces that drive human behavior on a broader scale. The things that really matter—inequality, deviance, racism, rationality—can be said to take place *through* the material world, not *because* of it.

But if we are too quick to dismiss the causal significance of objects, we run the risk of failing to understand how they work. If objects "fix the contents" of the social life of the city, how exactly do they do this? This is one of the questions that I seek to answer in the pages that follow, occasionally drawing on concepts from several distinct fields of social research and theory.[5] In the interest of doing so clearly and directly, it might be helpful to identify and define a couple of important ideas, right from the beginning. Throughout this book, I make use of the terms *affordances* and *programming*. Both concepts are vital for thinking about indirect consequences of design and planning and, by extension, the social control capacity of public objects and places— what they do (and don't do) for specific groups of people in specific settings.[6]

Affordances are, generally speaking, the ideas that objects have about us. More precisely, they are the behavioral possibilities that are endorsed by an object or place.[7] Affordances can be embedded in the design of an object, as well as the sign and rule systems that apply to an object's use.[8] But they are real only to the extent that they are recognized by an actual human being. In this sense, affordances do not exist inside of an object, but in the relationship between an object and a person.[9] *Programming* is the act of embedding affordances in an object or place. Programming can be used to suggest not just what could be done with a thing, the essence of an affordance, but what *should* be done (or not done) through the imposition of prescriptive programs of use.[10] Programming takes three forms: material, symbolic, and institutional. I'll take a moment to discuss each one in turn.

Once programmed into the *material* surfaces of an object or a place, affordances can become physically coercive in their control over human behavior. The steel and plastic contours of playground equipment offer carefully selected affordances—*slide here*—while negating others—*do not jump from here*—seeking to guide children's behavior in a way that provides both fun and safety. Subway turnstiles, speed bumps, and airport security checkpoints engage in similar sorts of behavioral engineering, coercing human action in specific directions in order to preserve the rule of law or to derive profits, as the case may be. But not all material programming is intentional. Some is coincidental, emerging from the unintended ways in which material form shapes human behavior. An industrial refrigerator is too large and too heavy to be carried in your pocket, but this is not to prevent theft or misplacement. Many restroom keys, on the other hand, are tethered to large and cumbersome objects for this exact reason.

The affordances implicit in design are often combined with signs, labels, and symbols that reinforce or modify the intended pattern of user behavior. This *symbolic programming* generally offers a cheaper and more flexible way of suggesting how users should behave. It would be tremendously expensive to design a parking space that physically exists only at certain times of day, but a cheap piece of pressed aluminum, mounted on a signpost, can advertise the local parking regulations and perhaps have a similar effect.

A third way in which public objects stabilize social life is through the institutional assignment of specific uses to objects. Unlike physical and symbolic programming, this *institutional programming* is typically invisible. The formal laws and informal norms that apply to a given object may be written down somewhere or advertised through signage, but in some cases, they are simply known, residing in the background knowledge of users.[11]

Also unlike material or symbolic programs, institutional programs imply a "third party"—perhaps an anonymous stranger, a neighbor, or the federal government—who recognizes appropriate and inappropriate uses of an object and provides incentives or sanctions. In the case of privately owned objects and spaces, the most important third party is the owner, who often has wide leeway in dictating how an object should be used. Within the home, informal norms and sanctions typically take over. Many parents of young children, myself included, uphold a de facto anti-graffiti ordinance that is enforced not by the local police but by an inconsistently applied system of time-outs and television privileges. In public settings, on the other hand, an equally comprehensive authority may reside with the state, and institutional programming may consist of a complete legal code for public behavior. Sidewalks, because they are public, are institutionally programmed, or regulated, in a way that one's living room is not.

Through these overlapping material, symbolic, and institutional means, public objects confer structure, regularity, and a degree of predictability to the social life of the city. Paradoxically, when they do this job effectively, they disappear into the background, permitting us to go about our lives without wondering which objects to use, and when, and how. Theorist Bruno Latour famously referred to material objects as "the missing masses," an army of actors who remain invisible when we fix our eyes on the social realm.[12] For Latour, objects are the sociological equivalent of dark matter: rarely observed but vital in explaining observable patterns of behavior. They are, in a sense, the most ancient of social media, helping us concretize and transmit our interests, ideas, and mental states. And to the extent that they are successful, social scientists (and people in general for that matter) are free to focus on what people do and why they do it without being distracted by the things they do it with.

When Objects Make Trouble: Appearance, Disruption, Disappearance

So, things fix or stabilize society. This is the good reason for ignoring material objects. The not-so-good reason for ignoring them is an assumption that the social world is stable all, or even much, of the time.[13] New things are constantly appearing on the scene. Old things deteriorate, vanish, or simply fail to function as planned. During these moments, objects "make trouble," disrupting social order, to repurpose a term used by sociologist Harold Garfinkel.[14] When they confound our expectations, objects emerge from the background of social life into the foreground, becoming more visible to us. Theorists have offered some clues concerning when we can expect this to occur, highlighting three discrete phases of an object's lifespan: when it first appears in a social setting, when it disrupts desired patterns of action, and when it gradually or abruptly disappears.

The first moment in which objects typically make trouble is when they first appear. For designers and architects, this occurs during the innovation phase, when the technical properties of objects remain unsettled and their social capacities are not yet taken for granted.[15] For the public, objects generally appear a bit later, when introduced for the first time into an uncontrolled social environment. At these times, designers, planners, and ordinary users scrutinize the form of a new public object, a process that can expose the social implications of design decisions.

Designers and architects generate affordances during the earliest stage of an object's life course, imagining patterns of social use. When they design physical structures, writes Thomas Gieryn, they "theorize" about society. "To some degree, every blueprint is a blueprint for human behavior and social structure, as well as a schematic for the 'thing' itself."[16] Design professionals have no choice but to make assumptions, not simply about the physiological or psychological traits of users but also about their sociological and cultural backgrounds, their lifestyles, or their personal histories.[17] Through these inferences, they translate social context into material form, theorizing a social universe in which their object is rational, profitable, virtuous, and so forth. According to John Chris Jones, designers "are obliged to use current information to predict a future state that will not come about unless their predictions are correct."[18] The subject matter of urban planning, design, architecture, and engineering, in other words, is a fictional future that must be extrapolated, imperfectly, from the sociological present and then conjured into being through material means.[19]

Along the way, architects, designers, and planners construct hypothetical users whose qualities are defined in relation to the characteristics of the artifact under consideration. Even when based on deep knowledge of the social context around a proposed public object or public space, these users are fictional constructs. Unlike the protagonists of books and films, however, they bear little resemblance to actual human beings; they do not have complicated backstories, idiosyncratic personalities, or ambiguous motives. They are assembled out of implicit or explicit assumptions concerning how an object will be used, or a space inhabited. And, as fictional people, they continue to haunt a material artifact long after actual users appear on the scene. The resistance offered by a restroom door tells us about imaginary users' strength, which has been programmed into its mechanisms; the mirror on the restroom wall tells us of their vanity; the stalls convey their desire for privacy. These physical and cultural traits do not belong to the actual users of a restroom, but their imagined counterparts, who remain imprinted upon the space's surfaces and mechanisms, even after a living, breathing person has taken their place.

Occasionally, designers explicitly and earnestly describe the users they have in mind for a given object. When these moments occur, they are crucial, bringing the social implications of design to the surface. But typically, they do not occur in public. The social calculations involved in design generally take place on password-protected computer networks or behind closed doors. In the case of consumer goods, private corporations hide their market research in order to protect their designs from competitors, or to paint their products in a flattering light. Imagined users may appear later, in product marketing campaigns—a child on the box, whose job is to show that a toy is suitable for toddlers with small hands, an athletic young man hiking toward a distant ridge, who illustrates the appropriateness of a pair of pants for an outdoorsy lifestyle, or a pixelated human who lounges, admiring a computer-drawn sunset in an architectural rendering, offering intentional clues to the social programming of a proposed public space.

As material artifacts make their first appearance in uncontrolled social settings, these imaginary people are replaced with real ones. When a new foreign object is introduced into an existing social world, there is no guarantee that its users will react as designers intended. After an object or a built space is constructed, the well-behaved, imaginary people who appear in blueprints and designs are replaced by a more unruly and less predictable collectivity: actual human users. The "potential environment" envisioned by designers and planners is supplanted by the "effective environment" created through human use, to use a pair of terms coined by sociologist Herbert Gans.[20]

At these fascinating moments, the affordances incorporated into new public objects can emerge sharply into view, through their contrast with the needs, desires, values, expectations, habits, or routines of a human population. In some cases, new social norms prove necessary. According to Claude Fischer, the home telephone was seen as a rude and socially intrusive object at first—much like a neighbor who barges in without knocking. The object compelled its users to decide on an appropriate greeting from a range of equally plausible options. (It turns out there was nothing natural or inevitable about "Hello.")[21] Focus groups, surveys, and prototypes provide an initial test of how an object will be received, but the real test comes when it is introduced into the sociological wilderness of unpredictable everyday life.

Luckily for us, material things rarely exert absolute control. They are used in ways that are unforeseen by their makers all the time. A paving stone can be thrown at the police. A book can be used to stabilize a wobbly desk. As Terrence McDonnell argues, the social contexts in which objects are used impose a degree of "entropy," producing new meanings that were unforeseeable by their designers.[22] Things that were originally functional—for example, the "Green Monster" in Boston's Fenway Park baseball stadium—can take on profound symbolic meanings that supersede their utility, as Michael Borer has shown.[23]

These new meanings may turn out to be far more significant than the old ones. The Blarney Stone, a limestone block embedded in a castle battlement in Ireland, was designed to stop arrows and crossbow bolts, and perhaps, once upon a time, it did. But it is now an object of rare celebrity, kissed by thousands of tourists who desire to be more eloquent in speech. Once devoted to fortification and defense, its current social function is to deliver "likes" on Instagram when paired with an appropriate hashtag. Central to the spectacle is the blunt humility of the stone, its own ineloquent silence, and the physical contortions necessary to kiss its underside. When artifacts are used in unforeseen or counterintuitive ways, the ideas that inspired their design are brought into relief, through their contraposition with new programs of use.

A second type of moment when the material world emerges into the foreground occurs when an object disrupts a desired or habitual course of action. The immediate causes of disruption can vary. Sometimes, an object breaks down, or malfunctions, failing to provide the service that it was designed to offer. Repair or redesign become necessary, bringing into view the object's affordances.[24] Other times, it is the user who deviates from the object's expectations, imposing new and unanticipated demands. Objects are frequently incorrect about us, as any left-handed person knows. When their assumptions are wrong, they force themselves into our consciousness. Often, we anthropomorphize the disobedient object in question, as if its resistance were personal. These moments reveal the extent to which we mentally blur the lines between people and things. We yell at the computer when it refuses to respond to our keystrokes. We kick the door when it jams, to punish it for being incalcitrant. We repeatedly jab at a lit elevator button, as if this expression of our frustration meant anything at all to its impassive circuitry.

Moments of disruption are particularly revealing in the case of public objects, because they elicit reactions from the people and organizations who hold power over things. In response to changing social or physical conditions, the affordances of a public space can be altered—*reinforced*, or *adapted*. And, again, this takes place through material, symbolic, or institutional means. Consider a large flowerbed positioned near the entrance of a public building (say a library) that, due to its position in between the sidewalk and the library entrance, has come to serve as an informal pedestrian route, resulting in a defined pathway, barren of vegetation.[25] A knee-high wrought-iron fence can be erected around the flowerbed, making it physically awkward to cut through the flowers on foot; a small sign can be planted, asking visitors to stay on the sidewalk; or library security guards can be tasked with keeping an eye on the flowerbed during their rounds, and asking patrons not to intrude. In these three hypothetical scenarios, the initial affordance (*flowerbeds are for admiring, not for walking through*) has not been altered, but instead reinforced physically, symbolically, or institutionally.

Now consider a fourth possibility. A landscaping company is hired by the library to create a formal path where there was previously an informal one. They remove the crushed daffodils in the place where people have chosen to walk, and line the resulting pathway with paving stones, while leaving the surrounding flowerbed untouched. The social meaning of the space has been changed. Formerly ornamental, the area is now functional. In this case, its affordances have been physically *adapted* rather than *reinforced*. Crushed daffodils might seem a trivial matter, but often the stakes are higher. As theorist Langdon Winner famously argued, objects are political—their materiality allows them to reinforce social hierarchies or advance specific interests.[26] By suggesting affordances, or programs of use, they become charged with normative significance—they guide and constrain human activity in ways that are rarely directly coercive, but that establish the parameters of user behavior, empowering some users and marginalizing others. Their ability to gently nudge us toward one course of action is just as political and consequential as their ability to prohibit, punish, or exclude alternatives.

Finally, a third scenario in which material artifacts emerge into the foreground of human events occurs when they *disappear*, revealing the degree to which habitual patterns of action depend upon overlooked artifacts and technologies. Just as a misplaced set of keys highlights all of the routine activities that require locking or unlocking, some public objects—bridges, churches, monuments—reveal their broader importance to a community when threatened or removed.[27] The affordances of these objects, perhaps taken for granted, become conspicuous when the object disappears.

At these moments, the capacity of material things to recede into the background of human action and passively stabilize society has a paradoxical effect, as social action can be destabilized in unpredictable ways in their absence. For some New Yorkers, the twin towers of the World Trade Center were functional as well as symbolic landmarks—large objects, visible from a great distance, which helped pedestrians find their bearings in dense Midtown or Downtown Manhattan streets. After the World Trade Center fell on 9/11, their psychological disorientation was overlaid by moments of literal disorientation—for example, when emerging from a subway station in an unfamiliar part of town.

When appearing for the first time, disrupting our desired or habitual behavior, or disappearing, things make trouble, revealing their importance within the dynamic and uneven social landscape of the contemporary city. But these moments have received little attention from mainstream social science. Traditional sociology offers little guidance on how and when material objects are contested, modified, and adapted, a topic that has only recently begun to generate concerted interest.[28] This book is motivated by a series of speculations. What if, rather than looking past objects, we place them at the center of the analysis? What if we direct our attention to the occasions when public objects first appear, when they disrupt our behavior, and when they disappear—moments when the material world emerges into the foreground of individual thought and social consciousness? By shifting focus away from individual human actors or social groups—conventional "units of analysis" in the social sciences—to the objects that they use, perhaps we can learn something new about how people relate to the material world around them in the public spaces and places of the city.

Public Space and Place

All of the objects in this book are found in *public space*. In fact, the public space in and around New York City is not just the setting but, to a lesser degree, the subject of the chapters that follow. At a philosophical level, public space is important because it is the material embodiment of the public *realm*—a theoretical arena in which open cultural expression and unencumbered social contact may occur.[29] Rarely, if ever, does actual public space live up to this ideal. But public space is nonetheless vital to a wide range of social processes that depend upon interaction and communication. It is where the members of a society come together, if they come together. It is where democracy happens, if it happens. It is where we encounter strangers, and people whose backgrounds differ from our own. Public space is where social movements mobilize and conflicts erupt. For these reasons, it is central to discourse and collective social action. Some people consciously participate in public life by volunteering at a soup kitchen, supporting a professional sports team, or voting on election day. However, by a qualitatively different standard, we are all public actors whenever we are *in* public. It is partly by sharing meaningful forms of contact with the material world outside our doors that we become a society.

In less abstract terms, public spaces differ from private spaces in that public spaces are seen as providing public (non-exclusive) benefits. This role is institutionalized in formal laws and ordinances that seek to insure that the objects found in public space are both publicly accessible and for public use, a consideration that limits the authority of any one private person or organization over the built environment. In other words, the material form of objects and rules about how objects are to be used are both central to the publicness of public space. Gramercy Park, on Manhattan's East Side, is a manicured green space surrounded by a tall iron fence and locked gates, to which local property owners have the key. The park is a private space. It is not just legally but visibly and tangibly private, and it has objects to thank for this. Manhattan's Central Park, in contrast, is accessed via gateways and openings that were designed to be welcoming. Central Park is a public space. It is not just legally but visibly and tangibly public, and it owes this, in part, to material objects.

Some public spaces are publicly owned and managed by the state. But increasingly, they are privately owned. And more generally, across the United States, parks, plazas, and other public spaces are encroached upon by private interests and private enterprise.[30] Nevertheless, the areas in and around New York City still contain great expanses of public space, and much of this terrain is intensively used. This is a book about public objects, but it is also, necessarily, about public space, which is constituted, embodied, and realized by such objects.

Place is another concept that is important to this book. Place is different from space. Space, including public space, is inherently abstract, emptied of its specific contents in order to gather together social processes that do not "take place" in the same place. Places, in contrast, are tangible, meaningful, and unique. According to a definitive essay by sociologist Thomas Gieryn, all places have three ingredients: a location, a configuration of material things, and a set of meanings that people attach to both the location and the things involved.[31] Although social life occurs within and across space, it is situated and immersed in place. In other words, we do not consciously live, work, study, or spend our leisure time "in space," we do these things in places—discrete locations that have their own identities, and that, importantly, are composed of specific combinations of material objects.[32]

Places are invested with meaning. Sometimes the meanings involved are sacred, sometimes they are profane. A concert hall, a prison yard, and a vacant lot all might qualify as places, although they carry starkly different connotations. The way we think about places is crucial to their ability to shape and structure our social lives. Places anchor the everyday interpretations that are necessary for any action or interaction—the basic, usually unspoken set of assumptions that sociologists who study interaction refer to as "the definition of the situation."[33] For this reason, behavioral norms are place specific. We do not usually throw parties in a graveyard or brush our teeth at the post office.

Just as public objects are vital to public space, they are central to place. Things are given meaning by the specific locations in which they are found. A urinal mounted on the wall of an art museum is to be treated differently from the one in the bathroom. The vertical steel poles found in a subway car are materially identical, but sociologically different, from the ones found in firehouses, which are, in turn, different from the ones found in strip clubs, although all three poles look and feel the same. By the same token, objects help to define and create specific places. When we walk into an ambiguous place for the first time—a new store or restaurant, or, for that matter, a neighbor's house—we tend to find ourselves asking, "what happens here?" Objects provide our first clue, and in many cases, the only one we need. In thinking about material objects, place directs our attention to how objects are used and perceived by people in specific locations. Considerations related to the possession of objects, or the distribution of objects in space, or across space, though important in their own right, run only through the background of this book. In the foreground is the question of how objects are used (or misused) at specific places and times.

Programming the City

All of the case studies in this book are set in New York City or the surrounding area. This is not coincidental. The city has become a veritable petri dish for an approach to urban design and planning that raises the profile of mundane public objects. In recent decades, city agencies have focused on improving quality of life through increasingly public interventions in the small-scale environments of the city. This strategy has transformed small, quotidian things that were formerly supporting actors in the drama of city planning, objects such as park benches, bike racks, and apartment building entryways, into leading players in their own right.[34] Public objects, the centerpieces of this book, have become battlegrounds for competing ideas about what kind of city New York is, and to whom it belongs.

It was not always this way. In the early twentieth century, city planners prioritized housing and infrastructure projects that were massive in physical scale, and legitimized their material interventions in the landscape of New York by invoking the economic and social prospects of the city as a whole. Older neighborhoods inhabited by immigrants or people of color were regarded by city planners such as Robert Moses not simply as expendable but as blights on the landscape of the modern city. Informal urbanism—the ostensibly chaotic street life of the city—was a problem to be solved through the application of technocratic expertise.[35] Public benefit was construed broadly in this process, superseding concern for the specific communities that were most directly affected. The needs of a particular neighborhood were only rarely invoked to justify the design of federally subsidized public housing, for example, or the drastic expansion of the city park system or highway system.[36]

During this time, the authority of city planners and urban designers increased in accordance with the size and ambition of their projects, insulating them from the public they served. But during the second half of the century, the scope and ambition of urban development began to change.[37] A mounting chorus of influential critics condemned urban planning as a high-handed enterprise, indifferent to the needs and concerns of local communities. In New York City, the writing and activism of journalist Jane Jacobs helped to trigger a sea change in urban design and planning.[38] During a series of high-profile battles, community-based social movements forced public authorities to modify or abandon major interventions in the urban landscape. These defeats helped to change both the culture of urban planning and its legal and regulatory context, as community stakeholders were increasingly granted input into the siting and design of local public spaces.

In the case of large-scale projects, this input became a required element of the public review processes required by city, state, or federal law.[39] In other cases, community actors were involved in the planning or design process from the outset, a practice known variously as community-based or participatory planning and design.[40] As a result, city planners have become more susceptible to political pressures and arguably more receptive to community-level concerns. Not coincidentally, contemporary city planners are far more likely to emphasize the importance of what sociologist

William H. Whyte called the "social life of small urban spaces"—the informal patterns of thought and behavior that develop at street level in the city's parks and plazas and on its sidewalks.[41]

In a 2006 essay, roughly at the start of the period covered by this book, Amanda Burden, a New York City planning commissioner under Mayor Michael Bloomberg, acknowledged these changes in plain terms, suggesting that Jacobs "prevailed" in her struggle against Robert Moses by influencing the context in which planners now operate. "While no one person changed the physical landscape of New York as much as Robert Moses, Jane Jacobs' legacy and her influence is much more deeply rooted and felt widely by urbanists, planners and elected officials," Burden wrote. The centralized planning and "broad brush" plans of the Robert Moses era, according to Burden, were "a thing of the past": "Planning today is noisy, combative, iterative, and reliant on community involvement. Any initiative that does not build consensus—that is not shaped by the give-and-take of the public review process—will be an inferior plan and, deservedly, will be voted down by the City Council, and die."[42]

In the first two decades of the twenty-first century, the Bloomberg administration extensively reworked the urban fabric of the city, using policy and planning to spur private development, transform transportation infrastructure, and modify public space. These sweeping changes reflected a complex and conflicted set of objectives for the city, enhancing environmental sustainability and public safety, while simultaneously converting urban space into an asset intended to attract affluent residents and tourists to the city and spur real-estate investment.[43] When Mayor Bill de Blasio took Bloomberg's place, he made only sporadic efforts to deviate from his predecessor's approach to public space, largely preserving, if not expanding, Bloomberg's legacy. Contemporary New York City, where public space is both valued and locally contested, is an ideal environment in which to take a close look at the social role of public objects. In this place and time, small, humble things found out in public—bits and pieces of infrastructure, components of green space, the odd assortment of objects that planners refer to as "sidewalk furniture"—emerge as sites where competing ideas about social life come into visible conflict.

Methods and Organization of the Book

Many fascinating books have been written that explore the social role of things. Several of these books pursue a single material object across breadths of time and space.[44] Other similarly excellent books have looked at how a new object is interpreted or used by different members of a community, or across a society.[45] Still others have examined all of the objects found in a given home, or on a particular block, in a sort of material census.[46] This book attempts something different. The chapters that follow provide a close look at routine interactions between people and things. Their guiding assumption is that these interactions contain valuable information—clues that help us to uncover new insights about how the social world and the world of things are intertwined, more generally. To paraphrase this book's epigraphs, the built landscape is shaped by an array of social forces, and this landscape, in turn, shapes us, guiding our thoughts and actions. For this reason, public objects are Rosetta stones, whose stories help us to decode the sociology of urban and suburban life, revealing the links between our subjective experience of the city and the invisible factors at work in a given place and time.

Each of the chapters that follow begins with a detailed look at the social life of a public object, drawing on my fieldwork in New York City and the surrounding suburbs. I then gradually expand the focus to include the people and places, and, eventually, the political, economic, and cultural forces that surround the thing in question. By zooming in on a single object, and then zooming out to bring its social and historical context into the frame, I try to gain a better understanding of how the material realm mediates between our individual, subjective experiences and the larger social world we inhabit.

The six objects featured in this book were chosen because they share two traits in common. All of the objects are found in public space. And all of the objects, in one way or another, make trouble. They are, or have been, controversial—focal points of social and political friction or debate. As noted above, the social role of material objects is invisible under most circumstances. It emerges into the foreground when objects problematize life as usual, offering new affordances or taking away old ones in ways that create tension or conflict. Understanding the sociology of public objects means getting to the bottom of this trouble.[47] As I progressed through the case studies in this book, I chose my research methods based upon the kind of trouble that the objects caused. I obtained county medical records in order to study pedestrian deaths in the suburbs. I scanned the minutes of public meetings and combed through hundreds of media reports to trace the political controversy provoked by the design and planning of Brooklyn Bridge Park. I used ethnographic fieldwork and interviews to sketch out the widely divergent meanings and interpretations attached to the plazas created by the New York City Department of Transportation (NYC DOT). And so on.

This omnivorous approach to research produced evidence that falls in four general categories. Along with a constantly shifting team of graduate and undergraduate research assistants, I engaged in extensive participant observation in the settings described in this book, generating hundreds of pages of notes, photographs, and illustrations. As part of this ethnographic work, I observed the object at the start of each chapter for an extended period (between six and nine hours) on a single day, in some cases repeating this "day in the life" approach over two or three days. This laborious method resulted in perhaps the best kind of data on the way objects and spaces are used, producing rich and detailed descriptions of interactions between people and things. The second category is spatial and demographic evidence. I used quantitative data gathered by the Census Bureau and other government agencies to situate the objects in their socioeconomic and demographic context. Thirdly, I talked to city planners, designers, community members, and users of the objects and spaces discussed.[48] Finally, I relied heavily on a wide variety of archival sources, including newspaper articles, blueprints and other technical documents, advertisements, medical examiners' reports, and so forth. With these data in hand, I proceeded in an inductive, rather than a deductive, fashion. Rarely did I have clear hypotheses to test. Instead, I used the sources at my disposal to extend my ethnographic perspective and map out the larger spatial and historical context for each object and the place where it is found, moving outward until a pattern or trend emerged that provided fresh perspective, or an insight that felt unobvious. There was never a clear and definite endpoint to this process: in the case of each object in the book, I concluded my research when I felt as if I had learned something new, and when, for practical reasons, I simply needed to move on.

This book is separated into three parts. Each part focuses on one of the important moments in the social life of a material thing. The first part, "Appearance," describes the design process and the introduction of new artifacts into an existing social context. In chapter 1, "The Public Lawn," I tell the story of a sloping lawn in a controversial new public park on the Brooklyn waterfront. Through interviews and archival research on the design process, I excavate the origins of several debates that threatened to cast a shadow on what elected officials and city planners heralded as a rival to the city's great urban parks. When the coalition that initially supported the park fractured, a variety of competing objectives for the space emerged. In advocating for specific designs and defending or criticizing the plan to place housing in the park, community members constructed the park's users, imagining various publics who would benefit from the space.

Chapter 2, "The Folding Chair," tells the story of a blue folding chair in a newly created public plaza in Jackson Heights, Queens. In 2008, as part of a broader program of infrastructural renewal, NYC DOT launched a plan to convert dozens of underutilized spaces across the city into pedestrian plazas, citing new urbanist principles, public health, and environmental sustainability. This initiative has extended deep into the outer boroughs, creating plazas in neighborhoods that vary widely in their demographic and socioeconomic mix. The prospect of open, flexible urban space and informal street life embodied by the folding chair was not universally welcomed, and served as a sort of Rorschach test revealing the unique aspirations and anxieties at work in different areas of the city. By examining in detail several plaza projects that met different fates, the chapter reveals the way attempts to foster urban quality of life are shaped by the local political and social contours of a heterogeneous city.

The second part of the book, "Disruption," describes attempts to modify objects in response to changing social conditions and social norms. Chapter 3, "The Traffic Divider," moves from New York City to its suburbs, where a growing low-income population occupies a built landscape designed for the last century's middle class. In recent years, the state of New Jersey has confronted a rapid deterioration in pedestrian safety—the result of a growing suburban population that lacks access to an automobile and is forced to improvise dangerously in a sprawling landscape of strip malls and divided highways. The objects that populate this landscape, cement traffic dividers and dusty strips along the sides of arterial roadways, take on different functions and meanings for different classes of users. After investigating pedestrian deaths on two roadways in Atlantic County, Black Horse and White Horse Pike, I describe the potentially serious human cost of a condition I refer to as programmatic conflict—a disjunction between the needs of users and the design of built space. I then show that inequality within and between suburban communities shapes the ways in which they seek, through design and regulation, to bring public behavior and the programming of built space back into sync.

In chapter 4, "The Subway Door," I take a detailed look at a particularly controversial and problematic object in New York City's transportation infrastructure. Since the first subway stations opened, just after the turn of the twentieth century, the transportation agencies that manage the New York City subway system have grappled with passenger behavior in and around the points of entry for individual subway cars. The subway relies not just on the formal infrastructure, comprising the material technologies and human employees who work for the Metropolitan Transportation Authority (MTA), but on something I call *informal infrastructure*—systems of passenger etiquette that are not simply polite or pleasant but vital to the functioning of this formal infrastructure. By blocking the doors, pushing on board an already crowded train, or holding the doors open, subway riders violate this etiquette, compromising the reliability and efficiency of service. In recent years, these breaches of informal subway etiquette have become increasingly common, compelling the MTA to seek behavioral engineering through a variety of means.

The third and final part of the book, "Disappearance," looks at the social consequences of removing objects from urban public space. Chapter 5, "The Newsstand," analyzes the social consequences of an object's gradual disappearance from landscape of the city. The sidewalk newsstand is an iconic New York City artifact designed to house a person and to mediate social interaction in specific ways, facilitating the exchange of money, goods, and information. The formal social functions of these kiosks, however, obscure their informal social functions, which include the monitoring of public space and the fostering of everyday sociability among New Yorkers. In telling the story of these disappearing artifacts, I flesh out these informal social functions, illustrating the costs of losing material artifacts that provide stability, security, and social interaction in otherwise anonymous urban space.

Finally, the concluding chapter looks at a sixth artifact, a humble bench in Midtown's soaring Trump Tower that disappeared temporarily, only to be begrudgingly restored by the well-known owner of this eponymous skyscraper. By looking at the controversial history of this final object, I attempt to bring the book up to date, pull together the threads that run through the previous chapters, and summarize some general findings about how people relate to the objects and public spaces of the city. But first things first. We start with two stories about when public objects first appear on the scene . . .

PART I

Appearance

1

The Public Lawn

FIGURE 1.1. Harbor View Lawn.

Harbor View lawn is perched on a pier extending into the East River. It slopes gently downward, toward the skyline of Downtown Manhattan and the Statue of Liberty. What is this thing for? It offers very few clues. An aggregation of stone, soil, and millions of blades of living grass, interspersed with clover and the occasional dandelion, a lawn is typically not regarded as an object at all, but an open space—an outdoor environment that lends itself to a range of social uses.[1] But let's take a moment to consider its material qualities. The main defining feature of this particular lawn is its gradient, which carries it gradually downward, toward the sparkling blue water of the harbor. The slope is gentle, but assertive enough that a beach ball might roll down it without being kicked. Placing a plastic cup of wine on the lawn would be slightly precarious. Sitting facing uphill would feel just a little bit unnatural. What does the lawn want from us? It wants us to sit facing the harbor and admire the view.

And who, exactly, are "we" in this line of speculation? In the fading sunlight of a late summer evening in 2014, the lawn seemed to belong to many people at once. People who tend to occupy distinct niches in the ecology of New York City came together in this place, in order to do a variety of things. An excerpt from my fieldnotes reads as follows:

> At the top of the lawn, where it is flattest, a young woman sits cross-legged, reading a picture book to two toddlers. Over by the shrubs on the south side, a pair of teenagers is huddled together, engaged in low-level PDA. Sitting close to them, maybe on a double-date, is another young couple, just chatting. Further down the lawn, a middle-aged man is dancing by himself, humming tunelessly to nobody in particular. He seems to have chosen the geometric center of the lawn for this performance, as he could have done it almost anywhere else. The sun has dropped behind lower Manhattan, and the view from the lawn is a postcard.

Some lawns are surrounded by barbed wire, others by ornamental filigree. The undulating lawns of a European estate, or a contemporary office park, clearly belong to someone or something, whether there is a fence or not. Other lawns are technically open to the public, but offer telltale clues that they are reserved for specific uses and functions. It would be socially awkward and physically risky to cast a picnic blanket on the fairway at a public golf course. Bocce and badminton are not welcome in the green spaces adjacent to national monuments, or places of worship. These spaces are physically open, but sociologically closed, earmarked for certain kinds of rituals.

The lawn on the pier seems to have been designed with a different agenda in mind, one with openness at its heart. According to the famous nineteenth-century landscape architect Frederick Law Olmsted, a large, public lawn exemplified the single most important benefit provided by an urban park: "[escape] from the cramped, confined, and controlling circumstances of the streets of the town; in other words, *a sense of enlarged freedom*."[2] The lawns of his iconic parks were intended to provide a pastoral backdrop for a "gregarious" form of recreation that served to "counteract the evils of town life." An unobstructed expanse of green turf, Olmsted argued, had a way of bringing out the best in the urban public, gathering the diverse residents of a modern city, while removing the obstacles that confine and separate them.[3]

References to the landscape designs of Olmsted and his partner, Calvert Vaux, seem to be almost mandatory when discussing urban parks, particularly those in New York City, but in this case they might be appropriate. The lawn on the pier is part of Brooklyn Bridge Park (BBP), a massive public space along the Brooklyn waterfront, which officials have compared to Central Park and Prospect Park. BBP is similar to these spaces in physical scale. If its advocates are to be believed, it will be comparable in its impact on the lives of New York City residents. And, to be fair, when sitting on Harbor View Lawn, enjoying a cool marine breeze that flows up the East River from the harbor, this public space does seem to offer the psychological benefits that Olmsted and Vaux saw in their own parks.

But the question bears repeating: whose lawn is it, exactly? In the case of this particular public object, and, for that matter, the rest of the park, the answer turns out to be complicated, the target audience unclear. The park has been subject to competing demands from neighboring communities. It was constructed using revenue from private apartment buildings, which currently finance its maintenance. As a result, its publicness has been called into question from the start. A pervasive ambiguity crept into every aspect of its design, public symbolism, and regulation. Who would the park serve? Neighboring residents? The borough of Brooklyn? The world?

These kinds of questions should be asked of any public object found in contemporary New York City. They should be asked of the public places and spaces of American cities in general—an urban landscape in which territoriality and privatization have increased in tandem with social inequality. In the case of the lawn, basic intuition provides some clues concerning where to look for answers to such questions.[4] Are there physical barriers surrounding the lawn, or hostile design elements intended to intimidate and exclude? Are there legal restrictions on who may enter? Is anyone under a legal or moral obligation to pay for entry? The answer, in every case, is *no*.

But the lawn, like every other element of the park and the built environment beyond, embodies a type of ownership in its material form. Even an object of such apparent simplicity reflects a set of tradeoffs, which become visible when we look closely at the process of planning and design. A subtly inclined plane of grass, tilting toward a pleasant view, the lawn seems to be the most innocuous of landscape features. If we find politics in this public object, surely we will find them everywhere. It turns out that the lawn embodies a fairly specific conception of how humans should relate to nature in an urban environment. It was designed for an imagined public, whose needs and desires were informed by a centuries-long history of humans using expanses of grass for leisure, recreation, or aesthetic pleasure. Other possible publics vied for supremacy over the design of this place, propelled by a set of political and economic interests that exist in the here and now, and that exerted influence over the lawn's creation.

This chapter tells the story of the lawn's origins, shedding light on the contentious process through which a public object was conceived, designed, and brought into being. Over a period of several decades, a diverse set of adjacent neighborhoods, each one demographically and economically distinct, jostled to impose their own visions on the park's material design. As a result, design decisions that often remain hidden were made in plain sight. Elected officials, designers, community members, and other stakeholders debated elements of the park's design. And they did so publicly, and vociferously. Like the other public objects in this book, the lawn has much to tell us about its place and time, exposing one of the most pervasive questions affecting New York and other cities in the twenty-first century. When officials, city planners, developers, or residents propose that an object or a place will serve "the public," who exactly do they mean?

Focus Groups, Lawsuits, and Towers in a Park

In the early 1980s, decades before Harbor View Lawn was opened to the public, a lumberyard and a collection of large, rusty storage sheds occupied a series of piers on the Brooklyn waterfront. The Port Authority of New York and New Jersey had shut down shipping at the site, and initiated plans to sell the property to commercial developers. In keeping with the agency's policy of consulting local civic leaders when such decisions were made, the Port Authority contacted the Brooklyn Heights Association (BHA) a powerful group representing the adjacent neighborhood of Brooklyn Heights. Members of the organization's leadership saw high-rise development on the site as a threat to the neighborhood's aesthetics and quality of life, and marshalled their formidable legal and political resources to influence the process.[5] At first, green space was an afterthought for the burgeoning movement, but it proved popular with residents and civic leaders from surrounding communities, who were strategically brought on board. Eventually, a formal coalition advocating for a waterfront park was formed.

The sale of the land was put on hold, but the coalition was weakened by internal divisions. In a sign of things to come, representatives of different neighborhoods along the waterfront had different priorities, and divergent visions for the site. Meanwhile, the state required that any development plan pay for itself, and the coalition ultimately failed to convince officials that a park could be funded on the site. Over a roughly fifteen-year period, the piers sat in quiet neglect, as local support for a waterfront park repeatedly foundered. Finally, in 1998, recognizing that community involvement in the redevelopment plan was inevitable, but needed renewed focus and momentum, Brooklyn elected officials created a local development corporation (LDC) and provided $1 million for the body to gather community input and draft a plan for the waterfront. The LDC took seriously the job of overseeing a broad, participatory planning process. Over the next year, several dozen community meetings involving thousands of neighborhood residents were held to develop a set of guidelines that would shape the design and financing of the park. Out of this series of public town-hall-style meetings and planning charrettes held in nearby community centers, a set of principles for the design and administration of the public space emerged. The park would incorporate areas for active recreation as well as passive forms of leisure such as strolling and picnicking. It would be financially self-sustaining, relying on commercial development (a hotel and several restaurants) to cover operating costs, in place of ongoing government expenditure. Residential development and office space were discouraged as sources of revenue. In 2000, the first master plan for the park was published, implicitly endorsing these guidelines.

At the inception of the park's planning, then, neighborhood associations representing the residents of surrounding communities were integral to the design process. As a result, different interests and distinct underlying conceptions of leisure and recreation were injected into the design from the very beginning, when the park was still just an idea. This attribute of the design process led a *New York Times* reporter to a wry observation regarding the community planning meetings that preceded the drafting of the master plan:

This atmosphere is far different from the conditions that prevailed when Frederick Law Olmsted and Calvert Vaux created their two 19th-century masterworks, Prospect and Central Parks. At the time, the areas around those parks were sparsely populated, the designers enjoyed a basic public agreement about what parks were supposed to be, and they had the space to make compromises. . . . [W]here planners of old began designing a park with a country walk and a drafting pen, planners today begin with a focus group.[6]

To be sure, this description of the design of Prospect and Central Parks is heavily romanticized. The reporter neglected the contentious politics surrounding both projects and, most egregiously, the displacement of African American landowners and other residents from the Central Park site.[7] But the article captured a key difference between nineteenth-century and twenty-first-century urban design and planning. The requirement that surrounding communities be consulted on the design of BBP meant that the landscape architect on the project would have to reconcile the needs of these communities. The complex social context around the park—the history, demographics, and socioeconomics of surrounding neighborhoods—entered into the park's design from the very beginning, and imposed competing demands from within.

When Michael Bloomberg came into office, he gave a boost to park advocates' cause. City and state agencies had made it clear that they did not want to pay for a public park. But the Bloomberg administration saw a connection between city revenue and waterfront green space—an amenity that would attract desirable young white-collar residents to Brooklyn and retain them when they started families.[8] In late 2004, the development corporation announced a decision that was consistent with this model, but that further politicized the design process, unveiling a new plan that sharply contradicted the spirit of the original, community-based guidelines. New residential buildings would be situated within the park, and the residents of these buildings would make payments in lieu of taxes to cover the park's expenses. This would render the park almost entirely financially self-sustaining, with private-sector financing of capital as well as operating costs. Instead of the commercial spaces that neighborhood advocates initially suggested, the project would be funded by "a-park-ments," as a local news outlet described them: residential towers built inside the park's footprint.[9] The communities along the waterfront would get their green space, but they would have to share it with the residents of these towers.

The new plan provoked public anger and a lawsuit from community members involved in the original planning process, but survived intact.[10] Nevertheless, elected officials representing the surrounding area refused to endorse the plan, and their approval became necessary in 2010 when the city government sought to take full control of the project and ensure that it would be privately financed. In a concession to these officials, the development corporation again held a series of hearings and solicited alternate funding proposals from the public. But in spite of successive rounds of public input, much of it hostile to housing as a source of park revenue, the apartment towers remained in the plan. Public park space would share the land with four apartment buildings, in addition to a hotel, a marina, and several restaurants.

Although the inclusion of luxury housing in a public park was unprecedented in New York City, it represents a variation on a dominant theme in local governance. Since the fiscal crisis of the mid-1970s, city officials have increasingly looked to privatize the provision of public goods to keep public spending low. Two other parks in the city, Hudson River Park and Bryant Park, already relied upon private funding streams. In the case of Bryant Park, neighboring property owners paid a levy to support the park's operations, not unlike the payments in lieu of taxes that would be made by the buildings in Brooklyn Bridge Park. The BBP plan represented a logical extension of this strategy, placing market rate, luxury apartment buildings in the actual footprint of the park. In doing so, it rendered the park itself a marketable amenity that would increase the value of this new real estate. In 2008, the first luxury condominiums in the footprint of the park were put on the market, and quickly set records for apartment sale prices in the borough. Apartments in a second building later were sold for unprecedented amounts, with condominiums purchased for upwards of $11 million. In 2015, the most expensive apartment in the history of Brooklyn, with an asking price of $32 million, went on sale. It was a triplex penthouse in a building inside the park.

But the funding plan for BBP created an added layer of controversy, problematizing the question of who the park was actually for — the public, or the residents of new luxury condominiums in the park. This ambiguity was embedded in the very legal structures on which the new park would be built. BBP would not technically be a New York City park. It would be managed by a public benefit corporation, or a "not-for-profit entity," as the corporation describes itself, rather than the New York City Parks Department. And rather than city parkland designated for public use, the park would lie on land that would be leased to the managing corporation by a subsidiary of the Empire State Development Corporation, another public benefit corporation. In both respects, the park would belong meaningfully to quasi-private organizations created by the government. These organizations are mandated to act in the public's benefit, but they are exempt from the transparency and accountability requirements that pertain to government agencies. The park would be directly managed by a corporation funded by the residents of the park—that is, a small population of wealthy condominium owners. Even if it were designed to serve the public, in legal and economic terms, the park would not belong to the public.

The ambiguous publicness of the park helped to catalyze an ongoing debate over the park's design that percolated in public hearings, community board meetings, and on the pages of neighborhood blogs virtually nonstop over a fifteen-year period. To be clear, this debate was necessary in part to assuage neighboring communities and convince them to support the new public space. Deeper into Brooklyn, the boosters of another large plan, to build a basketball arena and a series of high-rise apartment buildings on top of the Atlantic rail yards, had neatly sidestepped local elected officials and an extensive community review process, but the project was subsequently bogged down by lawsuits targeting the state's use of eminent domain. Meanwhile, the economic recession of the late 2000s eviscerated the plan's financing, leading the developer to drastically scale back the project. BBP would not suffer the same fate, partly owing to a design and planning process that was more transparent and more participatory from the start.

But democratic engagement did not lead to consensus. Throughout the planning process, a variety of stakeholders contested the park's design. As they envisioned the physical form that the park would take—its material design features and spatial configuration—they applied divergent views of the kinds of human activities the park should accommodate. These programs, or affordances, were linked to different conceptions of the public that the park would serve. The individuals and groups involved in the project rhetorically constructed fictional populations of park users that varied in origin, age, and socioeconomic status. In other words, when they formulated expectations for *what* the park would be for, they debated *whom* it should be for, unknowingly drawing upon politicized conceptions of leisure and recreation that extend back to the nineteenth century and beyond. At the heart of these debates was perhaps the simplest recreational space imaginable, but also one of the most ideologically fraught: the lawn.

A Front Lawn for Brooklyn Heights

Brooklyn Heights is an affluent neighborhood of narrow streets lined with towering London plane trees, perched high on a natural bluff overlooking the Brooklyn waterfront and beyond it, the East River and Downtown Manhattan. The guardian of this stately aesthetic environment is an old and powerful civic association. In the community-based movement in support of a waterfront park, the BHA staked out a central role, advocating for the creation of public green space on the piers.

The organization took an interest in the waterfront redevelopment plan for an obvious reason—the site's location in relation to Brooklyn Heights. When the Port Authority initially planned to sell the site to commercial developers, residents of Brooklyn Heights saw a threat to their neighborhood's quality of life, and, importantly, its most cherished aesthetic asset: its view of the Brooklyn Bridge and Downtown Manhattan. In the 1940s, the BHA had helped to convince Robert Moses to route the Brooklyn–Queens Expressway along an escarpment on the neighborhood's western edge. For its trouble, the neighborhood received a cantilevered public promenade above the roadway that offers a sweeping vista of the Manhattan skyline. Anything built on the waterfront would be visible and possibly audible from this historically and aesthetically significant space. On a fall morning in 2011, I visited the promenade. At this point, only a single small part of the park had been constructed and opened to the public—the rest of the space remained hypothetical. But in an excerpt from my fieldnotes, the affordances of the space for the neighborhood were clear:

> As I emerged from a narrow street onto the promenade, the orderly density of a wealthy nineteenth-century neighborhood—limestone and brownstone townhouses, sycamores, filigreed ironwork—gives way to a space that is the civilized equivalent of a cliff's edge. A couple stands near me, their arms crossed on the wall, admiring the panorama. The visual effect of the view reminded me instantly of a trip to the Grand Canyon, where a plateau abruptly drops away, producing a similar, but vertically inverted version of the sensation one feels when walking into a cathedral. My eyes were drawn outward, to the skyline of the city, which appears strangely near. In the foreground is the park, or where the park will be.

The park would be part of the neighborhood's sensory environment, and, through its adjacency to the promenade, inevitably linked with the neighborhood's public image and iconography. In this context, a low-lying, calm green space devoted to passive recreation, much like a typical suburban front lawn, held an obvious appeal. At an early point in the community planning process, the BHA advocated for the park to have a "heart of green" that would not merely protect the promenade's historically landmarked vista from obstruction, but actually improve the view.

In pushing for a low-profile, unobtrusive landscape on the waterfront, the organization linked the material design of the space with a program of

FIGURE 1.2. The view from the promenade in Brooklyn Heights. At the center of this view is the park's Pier 3, which features a lawn and a labyrinth of low-lying shrubs. This pier provides the "heart of green" that Brooklyn Heights community groups advocated for—a landscape devoted to passive recreation that would enhance the view from the promenade.

use. But the overriding concerns were the sensory aesthetics of the park for those situated *outside* of it—how it might look and sound from a distance. By this logic, one of the park's most important publics would not have to enter into the park to be affected by it.[11] This was made clear in a 2005 letter in which the organization responded to the *General Project Plan* for the park. The letter fleetingly acknowledges that a skating rink, ball courts, and other spaces for active recreation had been removed from the plan and replaced by residential buildings, a substitution that rankled other community organizations near the park. Instead of objecting to this measure, the BHA saved its strongest wording for recommendations concerning the height of these buildings, the direction in which the park's lighting should face (away from Brooklyn Heights), the sound it would generate, the motorized and pedestrian traffic to and from the park, and the capacity for any new construction in the park to obstruct desirable "view planes."[12] In practical terms, the park appears in this document less as a public space to be inhabited and used than as a potential nuisance situated in plain view just beyond the neighborhood's borders. Given this perspective, which framed the park as a visible and audible landscape feature, it followed that the BHA favored quiet, unobtrusive uses, or, in landscape design parlance, "passive recreation"—winding pathways, seating areas, and open green space, such as the sloping lawn described at the beginning of this chapter. In other words, the organization wanted the park to be a front lawn.

But if we look behind the metaphorical uses of an object, we often find its affordances. The cultural significance of a thing typically reflects a set of assumptions concerning what it does and how it is to be used. In this case, the logic behind BHA's design preferences echoed both the material and the ideological considerations that led to the institutionalization of the suburban front lawn across the country. The lawn in its original, European context was reserved for elegant estates, where it served as a marker of exclusivity and privilege, and these cultural associations are embedded in the object's material traits. Lawns are historically costly to maintain, requiring labor, as well as material resources such as water and fertilizer, and are typically visible from outside of a property. When translated into a suburban setting, a luxurious carpet of green grass externalizes and manifests socioeconomic status. It is a class marker, not just for the individual homeowner but for the entire neighborhood. For this reason, the city and neighborhood beautification campaigns that swept the suburbanizing nation in the 1920s emphasized front lawns and communal green spaces as reflective of a community's standing.[13]

The park, by virtue of its adjacency to Brooklyn Heights, would serve as the neighborhood's figurative front lawn, occupying the entire field of view from the Brooklyn Heights promenade and thus affecting the aesthetic experience of this iconic space and, by extension, its continuing prestige. The affluence of the community, translated into a set of aesthetic and symbolic concerns, was then further translated into a set of material qualities that the park should embody. A design that favored passive recreation and open green space would reflect well on Brooklyn Heights, doing nothing to devalue the aesthetic of its historic brownstones and landmarked public space.

This type of design drew additional support from Brooklyn Heights residents for a separate reason. Visitors to the waterfront would be likely to cross through the neighborhood to get to the park, as the nearest subway stations to the waterfront lie in the interior of the neighborhood. In the public hearings that took place during the initial community planning stages, neighborhood residents expressed fear that the park would generate disruptive noise and traffic. "I'd rather see a Costco or a Target down there than see this neighborhood overwhelmed by people from somewhere else," said a resident quoted in the *New York Times*. Other residents expressed fear that the neighborhood's social order would quickly give way to graffiti and marauding bands of teenagers as soon as the park was opened, or that the crowds walking down Joralemon Street to access the park would be like "'Napoleon's Grand Armée invading Russia in 1812.'"[14]

The social programming of built space can inspire hope, but it can just as easily incite fear, warranted or otherwise. Repeatedly during the planning process, Brooklyn Heights residents expressed concern that the park might prove *too* popular—that hordes of disruptive visitors from further into Brooklyn would flock to the waterfront, clogging local streets and sidewalks, if the park were made too attractive for their specific needs and desires. The people in question were, of course, purely imaginary at this point—fictional users, whose taste in public space and whose proclivity for noisy or unruly behavior satisfied an immediate rhetorical objective, dramatizing a set of inchoate fears concerning what the wrong design would bring. Although specific design recommendations discussed in Brooklyn Heights included overtly exclusive measures (gates or bollards blocking park access points from within the neighborhood), a less direct approach was to configure the material spaces within the park to help constrain and regulate the public it would serve.[15] This approach was evident long before the park plan was being given serious consideration. Anthony Manheim, an investment banker and former president of the BHA, eventually became a crucial advocate for waterfront public space, spearheading the coalition that fought for the park in the late 1980s and 1990s. But his initial vision for the site was an "executive training center . . . with gardens, athletic fields and a swimming pool, a whole resort of the type we see in Beverly Hills and Florida, a type of community that would cater predominantly to the Wall Street market."[16] This description, brimming with class signifiers, shows how a concern for attracting the right kind of public can be translated into material amenities.

Later, affluent homeowners around the park settled on pastoral green space for passive recreation as the preferred design. Lawns, trees, and plantings were preferable to indoor recreation centers and concert venues, as they would be less likely to draw noisy crowds from central Brooklyn through quiet neighborhood streets. Here, advocates drew upon a logic of social class that extends back more than a hundred years. In nineteenth-century debates over leisure and recreation, the enjoyment of natural, pastoral landscapes was codified as part of an Anglo-Protestant tradition, brought to the United States by way of New England. Among New York City's elites, appreciation of unblemished nature was understood to be inculcated via upbringing and formal education, while the lifestyle and the tastes of working-class New Yorkers were better suited for the enjoyment of commercial pleasure grounds, racetracks, and amusement parks.[17] When evaluating plans for Central Park, Manhattan's elites looked to landscape architecture to set the tone for the public space and to "insulate" the park, as social historians Rosenzweig and Blackmar put it, from "the unpredictability of the streets." What this meant was including pastoral lawns and formal promenades, while "excluding inappropriate alternatives, implicitly any view of the park as a public space that would accommodate and celebrate the aesthetic variety and the unpredictability of the city itself."[18]

In a similar fashion, the argument for a "heart of green" on the waterfront had social implications that homeowners in adjacent neighborhoods could get behind. Not only would green lawns and flowerbeds draw fewer visitors to BBP, they would draw a better class of visitors—quieter, less chaotic, and less disruptive in their use of surrounding streets and access points. This vision, like all of the programs advocated by the stakeholders in the park's design, carried with it an extended web of hypothetical reasoning that linked the material form of the park with an imaginary public. In place of the overt exclusion and control that iron gates would offer, green spaces like Harbor View Lawn promised a sort of selective inclusion—a set of social affordances for the space that would draw some Brooklynites to the park, but not *all* Brooklynites.

A Backyard for Condominium Owners

Directly presiding over the sloping lawn in BBP is "One Brooklyn Bridge Park," the first residential building to open in the park—a converted warehouse offering luxury lofts, private rooftop cabanas, a billiard room, a virtual driving range, and an array of other upscale amenities. On a warm summer evening in 2012, a second imaginary public for the park was readily visible in the ground-floor windows, where a series of posters advertised space in the building from my fieldnotes:

The posters depicted fictional residents created by the building's owners, or more likely an advertising consultant. Invariably young, stylish, and white, they inhabited a simulacrum of the surrounding environment, with short captions telling their stories. "Frank couldn't catch a ball, but his restaurant choices were always home runs," reads one caption, next to a man in a white suit drinking a glass of wine at a café table. "Shopping was Marcia's second favorite pastime," reads another. "Jump serves on the sand volleyball court were her first." The advertisements paint a flattering picture of the building's prospective residents, offering carefully crafted identities that, in every case, allude both to the park's outdoor activities and to the residents' upscale tastes. In doing so, they define the space culturally and socioeconomically, assigning something less than ownership—"usership" perhaps—to a hypothetical community for whom the amenities of the space are uniquely suited.

Frank, Marcia, and the other potential residents of the park's luxury apartment buildings composed the most salient and controversial imagined public that emerged in the design debates. Until 2008, when the first apartments in One Brooklyn Bridge Park were sold, this group of users remained purely imaginary in nature—their socioeconomic and psychological traits open to speculation. In general, however, their stake in the material design of the park was regarded by community activists on both sides of the debate as analogous to that of Brooklyn Heights. Both communities would be directly adjacent to the site. And by virtue of this adjacency, they would share an interest in the park as an aesthetic and sensory environment. But One Brooklyn Bridge Park and the other apartment buildings were inside the park itself and literally surrounded by public parkland. If the park would be a front lawn for Brooklyn Heights, it would be a backyard for the residents of these buildings.

Online advertisements by the developers of One Brooklyn Bridge Park supported this line of reasoning, implying exclusivity while never fully suggesting that the park was private space. An animated video advertisement features a young man in a sweater vest, who is handed a cocktail by his female companion while he surveys the Manhattan skyline from inside a spacious loft. A young, female voice narrates over music: "Vanessa insisted on high ceilings in a full-service building brimming with amenities. Steven needed a skyline view from inside the park, a quick commute, and a fine, aged cognac. No compromising was necessary. Life. Surrounded by eighty-five acres of park."[19] In the voiceover, a slight upward lilt draws attention to the word "inside" ("*inside* the park"), subtly highlighting the building's location in the interior of BBP as a central component of the exclusivity and prestige that is (not-so-subtly) signaled throughout the remainder of the advertisement.

FIGURE 1.3. An imaginary public for the park. In the windows of One Brooklyn Bridge Park, avatars representing the building's future inhabitants were used to advertise the suitability of the location for a lifestyle that combined athleticism with highbrow consumption. The precise relationship between this public and the surrounding space was somewhat murky, in part because advertisements like this one framed the park as a private amenity.

In another ad, a fit young man with a volleyball under his arm stands in front of the skyline while describing his "backyard staycation" in the park. These advertisements frame the park as an exclusive private amenity—they discursively transfer ownership of a public space in order to sell the apartments inside of it.

It is not uncommon for someone to colloquially refer to a public park as a community's "backyard." The metaphor conveys a certain familiarity and domesticity, and alludes to the wholesome social functions that supposedly occur in these sheltered green spaces. Again, the material characteristics of this space explains its cultural associations, while making these associations durable and portable: a backyard is situated behind the home, and is thus concealed from the public spaces of street or sidewalk. This material fact has led to the social categorization of the backyard as intimate and private space, for the use of family and close friends. Backyards are exclusive and proprietary spaces—venues for what anthropologist Constance Perrin called "selective association," where the only people one sees are those who were invited over.[20] Initially utilitarian in function, containing outdoor privies, wells, vegetable gardens, and the like, backyards emerged as recreational areas during the postwar suburban housing boom. They became an open-air living room—an outdoor extension of private domestic space.[21] The cultural connotations of the backyard, passed down through history, reflect a sense of privacy and intimacy that directly stems from the material and spatial relationship of a backyard to a dwelling.

With this in mind, the condominium advertisements at One Brooklyn Bridge Park commit the equivalent of a Freudian slip, alluding to the precise relationship (i.e., a proprietary one) between the proposed luxury apartment towers and the surrounding public space that most worried critics of the revenue plan. In public meetings and community planning sessions, these critics repeatedly raised the concern that the apartment towers would make the park feel like a private amenity, leading visitors, particularly working-class ones, to feel unwelcome in what would nominally be public space.

In response to these concerns, supporters of the plan cast the sense of ownership that the residents might feel over the park's public spaces in a positive light, appropriating the urban theory of Jane Jacobs in suggesting that private housing would provide "eyes on the park."[22] In a public hearing, a resident of Brooklyn Heights suggested that the residents provided a "strong constituency" for the space, offering a benign territoriality with regard to the park's lawns and walkways.[23] At the same hearing, the BHA president made a parallel argument:

> On a separate note, for those of us who regularly experience the park, it is clear the residents of One Brooklyn Bridge Park Condominium have not coopted the park and claimed it as their private backyard. Rather, our good neighbors' presence has enriched and enlivened the park. We do not fear the presence of additional neighbors living adjacent to this magnificent park. They will merely join the tens of thousands of us who, every day, are in awe by the wonders of this magical place.[24]

In the apartment buildings, the BHA saw "neighbors," underscoring the extent to which the two communities shared a similar relationship to the park. Both were immediately adjacent, and by virtue of this adjacency, they shared a preference for a material design that would emphasize passive recreation and ornamentation over skating rinks, ball courts, and concert venues that might draw a broader population into the park. But the two communities—one historically landmarked, the other brand new—also had affluence in common. And their socioeconomic status would open up this design agenda to charges of elitism as the debates unfolded, politicizing the argument for passive recreation and attractive landscaping in the park—design choices that, on the surface, appear innocent of any exclusionary intention.

A Spectacle for the World

In February of 2010, Michael Van Valkenburgh, the chief architect of the park, addressed the BHA in a maroon tie and a rumpled black cardigan, looking more like an affable college professor than a celebrity landscape architect. Indicating an oval-shaped lawn on a map of the park, he pointed out that the lawn's axis was oriented toward the Brooklyn Bridge. He sketched the social program of the site, narrating a visitor's imaginary experience: "When you're sitting on it you're looking at this magnificent piece of infrastructural architecture. That is a rather specific view. A rather bounded view. And it's a view that says 'sit here and let the majesty of that structure inform the scenery that you see.'" On the screen behind Van Valkenburgh, an architectural rendering appeared: park visitors sitting on the lawn gazing up at the Brooklyn Bridge. "This gives you a sense of how easy it is to . . . use the majesty of the circumstances around the context of the park setting to make certain kinds of park spaces." When Van Valkenburgh described what the view "says" ("sit here and let the majesty of that structure . . ."), he outlined an affordance, or a suggested program of use, as did the architectural renderings in the slides. Pointing to the sloping lawn described at the start of this chapter, he offered another hypothetical scenario:

> This is something we all find in the city, and this is why people like the [Brooklyn Heights] promenade so much, is because you go up there and even though the day hasn't been so great, the sun is going down and the beautiful Staten Island ferry orange is on that blue water. This is a version of that where you actually get to sit on the lawn.[25]

Van Valkenburgh had begun the presentation by invoking Frederick Law Olmsted's canonical designs for Central and Prospect Parks. In the same way that Olmsted's pastoralism was meant to counteract the appalling living and working conditions of the industrial city, Van Valkenburgh suggested, Brooklyn Bridge Park would offer a healing retreat from urban life—a physical and psychological escape at the end of a day that "hasn't been that great." The park's program, according to its chief architect, would involve reveling in sensory delights that would distract harried urbanites from their surroundings, offering a form of psychological renewal that came with marveling at awe-inspiring views and connecting with the natural and manmade environment.

Implicitly, this program identified Brooklyn residents as the imagined public that the lawn would serve. In other public appearances and interviews, Van Valkenburgh made this claim more explicit, describing the park as a "gift to Brooklyn" and repeatedly invoking an experience that authenticated and particularized this gift. At one of the community planning sessions in the early stages of the park's design process, according to Van Valkenburgh, an elderly woman and longtime Brooklyn Heights resident expressed a desire to walk down to the waterfront park at night, put her feet in the water and "see the reflection of the moon."[26] For Van Valkenburgh, this anecdote encapsulated the desire of locals to "touch the water," an affordance that he frequently returned to, and that eventually informed the park's design.[27] As a rhetorical device justifying material elements of the park—specifically, beaches, floating boardwalks, and other features that allowed park visitors to enjoy unimpeded contact with the East River shoreline—the anecdote tied the park's sensory delights to a powerful and authentic user: a lifelong Brooklynite, fulfilling a longtime hope. The right design would permit Brooklyn residents, for the first time, to enjoy a more intimate relationship with their natural surroundings, a worthy goal for Van Valkenburgh's team, and one they embraced.

But where Olmsted's lawns were meant to fade into the background, gathering and reframing social interactions between New Yorkers, the lawns and public spaces of BBP would offer escape by inspiring awe. In a departure from Olmstedian principles, the design of the park itself was meant to attract attention. When the *General Project Plan* emerged in the mid-2000s, it included features that would showcase innovative engineering and inspired design. Like the attractions at the world's fairs of the late nineteenth and early twentieth centuries, these elements were meant to produce a twofold sense of wonder, deriving from a new sensory experience and, simultaneously, from the impressiveness of the technological and artistic means used to achieve it. A "perched wetland" built entirely on a pier extending out into the river would invite exploration on meandering gravel pathways; an enormous berm, described by Van Valkenburgh as a "wave of green," would be constructed from repurposed stone excavated from the Second Avenue subway tunnel and would block the highway noise from the Brooklyn–Queens expressway.[28] A spiral-shaped jetty would allow visitors to

FIGURE 1.4. A world-class attraction. The park has hundreds of benches, in addition to raised viewpoints and lawns situated to offer views of the skyline and the Brooklyn Bridge. These features are central to the programming of the park as a viewing platform for the awe-inspiring, iconic architectural landmarks of lower Manhattan and the harbor—an affordance that was meant, in part, to attract foreign and domestic tourists to the site.

launch kayaks and paddle in currents artificially calmed by a system of "wave attenuators" and floating boardwalks. An architecturally unique, elevated pedestrian walkway would carry visitors from Brooklyn Heights down into the park. Most of all, the park would feature, at every turn, lawns, promenades, and walkways that would serve as viewing platforms for the majestic sights of the harbor, the skyline, and various architectural landmarks surrounding the site. As Van Valkenburgh's presentation for the BHA suggested, providing these sightlines would be the most significant architectural principle guiding the design.

In these respects, the predecessor for BBP's design would *not* be Central or Prospect Park, both pastoral refuges in the city, meant to hide the ostentatious human works of the surrounding cityscape. Instead, the park would be more similar to two other types of leisure space that Olmsted and Vaux scorned: the commercial pleasure ground, a horticultural amusement park containing landscaping elements (e.g., hedge mazes and fountains) that were intended to provide thrills to jaded city dwellers, and the continental European park that featured works of engineering, architecture, and sculpture as its focal points, offering visitors the experience of viewing manmade objects that were impressive in scale and ingenuity.[29]

To be fair, the target audience for these design elements was less likely to comprise Brooklynites than visitors from outside of the borough. While local elected officials praised the park for "taking back the waterfront" for Brooklyn residents, city and state officials instead emphasized the capacity for the park to serve as an attraction, drawing users from across the city and tourists from around the world. In the public statements, ribbon-cutting ceremonies, and press releases that marked progress toward the completion of the park, these stakeholders, more than other parties to the design and planning process, repeatedly emphasized the "spectacular," "sweeping," and "majestic" views afforded by the location, as well as the "world-class" attractions within the park. In 2009, when the park's development corporation leased the waterfront space from New York State, prior to the construction of the park, Brooklyn Borough president Marty Markowitz made illustrative (and typically hyperbolic) comments, referring to the park as an "urban emerald" with "spectacular views!" while City Councilman David Yassky, in a more sober tone, welcomed the opportunity to "transform the waterfront into a world-class destination that attracts businesses and economic activity."[30] The park's ability to serve as a world-class destination followed from its spatial location and material form, which were conducive to spectacle. A design for the park, a set of social affordances, and an imagined public were constructed in unison, one presuming the other.

That the park would serve international visitors was a virtual certainty, given its proximity to the pedestrian access to the Brooklyn Bridge, one of the city's most popular tourist attractions, and its visibility from the span. But it imposed a distinct demand upon the park's design—one consistent with the approach taken by Van Valkenburgh. For Brooklyn residents, the park's value would lie in its potential as an everyday or perhaps every-week amenity, visited after work or on weekends. In contrast, design elements meant to attract visitors from across the country and overseas had to be sensational enough to generate coverage in city guidebooks, travel media, and online reviews, and needed to offer a sensory experience compatible with the tourist experience. In this light, the Harbor View Lawn, which asks users to sit and look out at the Statue of Liberty, is appropriate in its behavioral demands. It orients the user's experience of the space on passive appreciation of an iconic landmark that is associated with the city's cultural identity across the globe. In an age when tourist itineraries are never complete without visits to landmark sites, now heavily documented on social media, the lawn is Instagram ready, waiting for visitors to arrive, selfie sticks in hand. To revisit the question posed at the start of this chapter, *who* would the lawn belong to? The design of the lawn itself provides an answer. It would belong to tourists, or, in the more euphemistic language preferred by some of the park's most prominent boosters, it would belong to the world.

A Playground for Brooklyn

Finally, a fourth public for the park was promoted by a different group of stakeholders involved in the park's planning: the residents of several neighborhoods whose borders extended to points adjacent to or near the corners of the site. Inhabitants of Cobble Hill, DUMBO, and Carroll Gardens, each represented by active neighborhood associations, found common ground with their Brooklyn Heights counterparts early in the process, but became divided from their neighbors when housing was introduced as a revenue source.

A bone of contention for the residents of these neighborhoods was the degree to which the park would afford active recreation. This, in turn, was a program consistent with the neighborhoods' spatial position in relation to the site. In contrast to Brooklyn Heights, DUMBO and Cobble Hill do not overlook the park, instead abutting the park at its northerly and southerly extremities. The site was not a front lawn or backyard, in these terms, but more of a proximate neighborhood resource. The aesthetics of the space were secondary to its ability to accommodate a set of desired social activities—namely, organized team sports and active outdoor activities such as biking and skateboarding.

In support of these activities, Cobble Hill residents alluded to a version of the public that was demographically specific, arguing that local children and teenagers required facilities for active recreation, such as playgrounds, athletic fields, skating rinks, and ball courts. In the initial community planning sessions and the housing hearings a decade later, Cobble Hill residents stressed the large population of young families in the neighborhood.[31] "There are more young families every year, and enormous demands for recreational spaces from all ages and during all seasons," one resident remarked. "We feel that the park should contain only such uses as can be utilized by all park visitors." Another resident linked the needs of families and children with the needs of the borough as a whole: "Our children are obese. They suffer from asthma at a rate unequaled in the nation. It's time we invested in our children. Maybe it is time the park focused on what is important to Brooklynites, not thinking about [a] world-class park, but what is important to Brooklynites."

These comments associate hypothetical park users with a specific geographic scale, delineating between a design consistent with a "world-class park" and one that meets the needs of "Brooklynites." In calling for spaces devoted to active recreation, Cobble Hill residents repeatedly referred to a potential public for the park that was specific with regard not only to age, but to place of residence. They drew a sharp contrast between the passive recreation and manicured landscapes favored by their wealthier neighbors to the north and the recreational needs of a broader, more diverse, and less exclusive cross section of Brooklyn residents. "It's inherently unfair and unjust to build a high-rise to pay for maintaining the landscaping in front of Brooklyn Heights," a Cobble Hill resident complained in the housing hearing. Another argued, "It is a park for the people. It's not an enclave. It's not a community. The community is outside of the park. The community visits the park."

As these comments suggest, the most authentic public for the park, according to activists from Cobble Hill and other nearby neighborhoods, resided outside of the park's immediate vicinity, but not *too* far outside. In short, they were residents of Brooklyn—contrasted on the one hand with residents of Brooklyn Heights and the apartment buildings in the park, who were depicted in this formulation as a local constituency with narrowly defined interests in the space, and on the other hand with tourists, or "the world." Roy Sloane, a community activist from the neighborhood, repeatedly called for a commercial recreational facility, suggesting that it would serve young people from throughout Brooklyn. In the 2010 hearings, he made representative comments:

> Our vision is for a much more active use of Pier 6 and its upland that would be an attractive destination to those of us who do not live immediately adjacent to the park, which is basically 99.99 percent of all of the residents of Brooklyn. . . . We need a real park, not just a place we visit when our relatives are in town. We want it to be part of our lives. . . . We need activities particularly for teens and adults.

These comments warrant a close reading. Sloane dismisses the preferences of those "immediately adjacent" to the park as selective and irrelevant, representing only a tiny percentage of Brooklyn's residents. But he then pivots and suggests that the design features appealing to tourists—or out-of-town relatives—are also irrelevant, as the public with the right to the park is the borough's residents, particularly its young residents.

For neighborhood advocates from Cobble Hill, the public with the most legitimate claim to the park space was defined not only by place of residence and age, but by socioeconomic status. Their criticisms of alternate park designs were typically loaded with class connotations. Activists from Cobble Hill and Carroll Gardens appropriated and redeployed a programmatic metaphor favored by Brooklyn Heights residents and the developers of the park's apartment towers. They used the term "backyard" in their arguments no fewer than ten times in the 2010 housing hearings to delineate between the interests of wealthy park residents and those of middle-class borough residents.

Brad Lander, a city council member, worried that the park would "come to feel like the backyard of a few wealthy Brooklynites." A Cobble Hill resident made a parallel argument: "What you are proposing is not the park that the community designed, as you've heard over and over again, but luxury housing with a spectacular backyard that will be uninviting to the public at large." Another compared BBP to Gramercy Park, a gated park in an affluent area of Manhattan. He described a dystopian future for the park, in which private development led to a narrowing of the social programs permitted in the space:

> That's what's going to happen . . . before you know it, not just I won't be allowed in there, but people won't be allowed in there with their kids after five, and won't be allowed to play soccer after six and they won't be able to listen to music at all. It's not a public park anymore.

As this comment illustrates, activists from Cobble Hill, DUMBO, and Carroll Gardens saw the condo owners' interest in the material design of the space as running contrary to the need for active recreation. Another Cobble Hill resident illustrated the logic behind this assumption:

> One other point I'd like to make is that when condos came into the park, all of the year-round recreation came out. Landscaping replaced the two pools. The indoor recreation center, the ice rink that the community had worked so hard for decades to get . . . Landscaping sells the condos while baseball fields do not.

In other words, landscaped lawns and open green space would boost the sale prices of the condominiums, providing a sort of amenity to the apartment buildings. In contrast, swimming pools and ice rinks would draw crowds from the interior of Brooklyn. These practical arguments reflected a concern that the apartment buildings in the park would create a class divide within the park's users, compromising its value as a public space. In fact, this anxiety had been running below the surface of public debates since the funding plan for the park was first announced. Back in 2005, a park activist based in Carroll Gardens had suggested that the buildings' residents would "become resentful about the 'unwashed masses' using their parkland."[32] For some local stakeholders, the recreational needs of proximate neighborhoods would inevitably be threatened by the elitist, exclusionary tendencies of a population that, as of yet, did not exist.

In this vision, like the others summarized above, arguments for specific material features of the park relied upon a desire for a set of social affordances, or programs of use, and these, in turn, implied an imagined public for the park. In some cases, these fictional user groups were fairly precise, extrapolated from a mixture of demographic statistics and other sources of data on the social structure of surrounding Brooklyn neighborhoods. In other cases, they were vaguely defined or aspirational—Brooklynites who wanted to touch the water, or "the world" awaiting to visit the park from afar. However, regardless of their empirical specificity, it is important to stress that these publics were rhetorical constructs—they existed only in relation to proposed material elements of the park's design. International tourists and nearby families with young children were demonstrably real, but as users of the park they were still chimeras, waiting to be conjured into being by the right combination of material elements. That they would come to the park, and bring to life the social visions outlined by various stakeholders in the contentious design process—this could not be assumed. At least, not yet.

Programming the Park

In the 2000s, as they worked with the development corporation to create a master plan for Brooklyn Bridge Park, Van Valkenburgh's team faced a formidable challenge. The design was densely and overtly political, as several distinct agendas would compete for primacy within the footprint of the space. In his keynote address to BHA, Van Valkenburgh acknowledged, in slightly euphemistic fashion, how these agendas would influence his work. The difference between his task and Olmsted's, he suggested, boiled down to "expectation of program." While the designs of Central and Prospect Parks were driven by the social and aesthetic vision of their designers, "this park is really driven by a very complicated and very conflicted set of aspirations regarding active and passive recreation." The final design would require "a complicated set of program offerings" within the site.[33] Van Valkenburgh and his team would have to broker a material compromise between the different publics to be served by the park, while also finding room to make an impressive statement of their own.

In order to incorporate the competing demands that arose during the design debates, Van Valkenburgh had segmented and compartmentalized the park's territory into a mosaic of smaller spaces, each programmed for a specific activity. Strategically arrayed at the foot of the luxury apartment buildings in the park and directly in front of the Brooklyn Heights promenade would be an undulating landscape of walkways, lawns, and plantings. These features would offer an appealing, low-profile appearance from those viewpoints. Further south, Van Valkenburgh devoted an entire pier to soccer, and another to basketball, handball, racquetball, and a skating rink, offering spaces for the active recreation desired by activists in Cobble Hill and the Farragut houses. This programmatic specificity extended down to the design and placement of objects in the park. Picnicking and barbecuing were assigned to an array of stationary picnic tables bolted into place, near a marina and a small jetty designated for kayaking. Fishing would be permitted along a specific rail on Pier 5, equipped with a bait-cutting table. The classic playground design, featuring an array of different types of equipment, was deconstructed and separated into a series of spaces, each devoted to a specific form of play: "slide mountain," "sandbox village," a "swing valley," and a miniature water park. The design sought to appease all of the stakeholders in the design debates, providing each group exactly what it wanted, while sacrificing the flexibility, adaptability, and informality that would have been granted by a more open program.

Meanwhile, the landscape architecture firm did not compromise in its intention to create a world-class attraction. The design featured an array of unique sensory experiences and inventive physical features. Along the waterline, visible and material barriers between walkways and the river were minimized. Van Valkenburgh placed only a thin, steeply sloping edge of boulders between park visitors and the water. An innovative bouncing pedestrian bridge would connect the Brooklyn Heights promontory to the park. An "exploratory swamp" featuring artificial mist generated by fog machines would be wedged between sand volleyball courts and the park's

Atlantic Avenue entrance. Every pathway in the park was oriented to offer majestic sightlines of the monumental urban structures beyond the park's borders. Throughout the park would be more than six hundred benches, the majority of which, like the lawns, invited users to admire the view of the harbor and the distant skyline.[34] Taken as a whole, the material features of the park endorse what might be regarded as a kind of sociomaterial pluralism. The space would be an attractive, green front lawn for Brooklyn Heights, a neighborhood park with athletic facilities and playgrounds, and a place of sensory wonders that would draw visitors from around the globe.

Starting in 2010, a single pier of Brooklyn Bridge Park was opened to the public, followed sequentially by other piers over the ensuing decade. At the core of the political struggles over the park's design was the question of whom the park would serve. The first few years of the park's existence offered some preliminary answers to this question. When journalists, bloggers, and online reviewers visited the park in the early 2010s, they found a demographically and geographically diverse population using the park. Visitors included school groups from predominantly Black and Hispanic public schools in northwestern Brooklyn, as well as families from Hasidic and Orthodox Jewish, South Asian, and Hispanic neighborhoods further into the borough.[35] User surveys conducted by the park's administration corroborated these anecdotal accounts of diversity.[36] Between 2011 and 2014, the space consistently drew between a quarter and a third (29–33 percent) of its users from the zip code in which it is located, a roughly equivalent percentage of its users from other areas of Brooklyn (26–34 percent), and a slightly larger share (32–43 percent) of its visitors from outside the borough. Park users, though predominantly White, were also more diverse than some observers predicted. In 2014, 49 percent of the park users self-identified as White, 14 percent as Black, 9 percent as Asian, 10 percent as racially mixed, and 16 percent as Hispanic (omitted from the other categories).

These numbers are consistent with the geographic distribution of visitors to the park—in demographic terms, the users were neither as homogeneous as the census tracts immediately adjacent to the park, nor as racially diverse as the borough as a whole, but somewhere in between.[37] The diversity of the park's users assuaged fears among observers in the media that the space would serve, in the words of the *New York Times* architecture critic, as a "glorified front lawn" for a corner of Brooklyn that already enjoyed an embarrassment of literal and figurative riches.[38] To the extent that the design was intended to draw a diverse combination of visitors, it was a success.

From Imagination to Reality

When a public space is opened to the public, designers' social theories about human behavior are put to the test. In the case of Brooklyn Bridge Park, the controversy surrounding the design raised the stakes significantly. The first few years after the park opened would show whether the park's visitors and its material artifacts would behave as expected. In spring and summer of 2015, I sent a team of undergraduate researchers to observe, categorize, and quantify the behavior of park visitors. In general, the results of this exercise were unsurprising—they revealed that park visitors tend to follow the rules, acting in accordance with the implicit programming of the park's many distinct environments. On five separate visits to Harbor View Lawn, they observed a total of 541 people, the majority of whom were sitting and looking out at the harbor. Picnickers and ballplayers were observed, but only in one particular area of the lawn (the top), where the incline was conducive to these activities. Elsewhere on the lawn, the gentle slope did its magic, encouraging single visitors and groups to sit facing the harbor. On two of these visits, the proportion of harbor watchers was overwhelming—89 (96 percent) of 93 visitors were sitting looking at the harbor on one occasion, 110 (89 percent) of 124 on another.

Other material objects were initially reluctant to function as the designers expected. When the first of the playgrounds in the park opened, an array of metal domes became dangerously hot in direct sunlight, seriously burning several toddlers. The sand on the beach in the park quickly eroded when exposed to the river's powerful currents, leaving a series of sharp, rusty metal pilings exposed. The bouncing pedestrian bridge bounced more than was pleasant or safe, and had to be closed for lengthy repairs. The boulder-strewn shoreline, which was meant to provide a naturalistic waterline and offer visual connection to the water, proved irresistibly tempting to children intent on climbing down to the river, some of whom fell between the boulders, or into the turbulent waters of the East River. A site visit to the park in summer of 2014 revealed the park officials' response: constant vigilance by the NYC Parks Department officers assigned to the site, as well as dozens of small yellow signs instructing visitors not to climb on the rocks. The signs were ironic in light of the designers' intent to connect visitors to the water—the design of the waterline apparently made the river too available, and had to be rectified by the symbolic programming of the site.

FIGURE 1.5. Programming and counterprogramming. Sometimes, the affordances of a place work too well. Van Valkenburgh minimized barriers between the park and the river, expressing a desire for the park to invite Brooklynites to connect with the water of the East River. When people took this invitation to heart, the park had to be posted with dozens of small yellow signs prohibiting the unsafe use of boulders, retaining walls, beaches, and so on.

It is tempting to read these cases as basic engineering mistakes. A failure to anticipate the physical capacities of inanimate objects seems to be at work: the tendency of metal to collect and conduct heat, the tendency of sand to wash away in powerful currents and tides, the frequency and amplitude of a suspension bridge's vibration when subjected to heavy use. But as the preceding discussion has shown, behind even these technical miscalculations lie sociologically meaningful tradeoffs. The design of these unique features, intended to attract visitors to the park and conjure a sense of imaginative escape and surprise, conflicted with their usefulness. Nonvibrating bridges were possible, as were mundane playground standbys (stainless-steel monkey bars, aluminum slides) that have been proven safe under a wide variety of climatic conditions. That these elements were not chosen speaks of the political and economic context in which the design of the park took place. They reveal a conflict between one program and another, pitting novelty against utility, or at least predictability.

In still other cases, the park's design proved conducive to uses that were entirely missing from either public discussions or architectural renderings. On a prematurely chilly late September evening, three unhoused people, two men and a woman, huddled behind a tall hedge that sequestered one small, irregular lawn in the perched wetland from another. With the help of a large cardboard box that once held a flat-screen television and several trash bags, they found in Van Valkenburgh's unique landscaping a wind-break, as well as a measure of privacy and concealment from the Parks Enforcement Patrol officers tasked with enforcing the rules of the park. Perhaps thirty yards away, several evenings before, I had ventured into the exploratory swamp and startled a young man in a small clearing who, upon seeing me, quickly made his way into the brush. A weary looking NYPD (City of New York Police Department) officer whose cruiser was parked on a walkway nearby offered one possible explanation, noting that the labyrinthine design of this section of the park made it a near-ideal place for people attempting to avoid surveillance. "The way this is designed, it's a perfect place for homeless guys and teenagers smoking weed." Concealment of illegal activity is a use clearly unintended by the designers, but was anticipated by critics of the park's design, who argued that the physical isolation, opportunities for concealment, and lack of attractions to draw nighttime use would make parts of the park "magnets for negative activity."[39]

In spring 2015, this possibility gained broader exposure. On a Wednesday afternoon in mid-April, a teenager pulled a gun on the Pier 2 basketball courts, firing two shots at nearby players and missing with both, then fleeing the scene. An ensuing NYPD investigation found the shooting to be gang related and planned ahead of time, as the shooter read a social media post indicating that his targets would be at the Pier 2 courts and went with the intention of attacking them, factors that seem to indicate that he thought the park would be an advantageous place for the shooting.[40] The incident highlighted an unanticipated facet of the park's design. A field visit the following Wednesday at roughly the time the shooting had occurred revealed a practically deserted pier, with only a handful of athletes playing under the watchful gaze of two police officers, whose cruiser was prominently parked at the pier's entrance.

Back to the Lawn

These unanticipated patterns of use are likely to be followed by many more over the decades to come. The park's publics will change, asserting new demands, at least some of which will have been unforeseen by any of the stakeholders in the park's design. In Rosenzweig and Blackmar's sweeping social history of Central Park, they offer a vivid and comprehensive analysis of this process as it unfolded in the case of that space, and the story they tell may hold clues concerning what is in store for BBP. As dense urban development enveloped Central Park, new constituencies challenged the pastoral aesthetic prized by its creators. Concert spaces, commercial activity, and restaurants were permitted. A new playground drew thousands of working-class children. The reservoir became a squatter's camp. The Great Lawn became a protest site. In perhaps the greatest insult to Olmsted's aesthetic legacy, baseball backstops were installed on the park's pastoral "meadows" by then parks commissioner Robert Moses.[41] The ability of Central Park to serve a changing public required substantial deviations from its initial social programming. Parks must, as Stewart Brand suggests of old buildings, "learn" over time, and to do this, they must be flexible and open, qualities that were, coincidentally, present in Olmsted and Vaux's design.[42]

Which brings us back, once more, to Harbor View Lawn. To be certain, Brooklyn's residents will make the lawn their own. They will read picture books to their children on it. They will become friends or lovers on it. They will argue over it. They will dance to their own music on early autumn evenings. They will make it subjectively meaningful and useful in ways that are unanticipated by its design. But beyond this, their ability to adapt the space to their needs seem likely to be limited, both by the rigid material design of the park and the private structure of the regulatory body that maintains it. Any future physical or regulatory changes to BBP will not be in the purview of a government agency, nor will they require that the changes be brought before local community boards, as is required of development that will affect the land use in the city. The future of Harbor View Lawn lies in the hands of an organization that will be funded by the residents of the luxury apartment towers that loom over it. In light of this, the lawn's ability to adapt to the evolving needs of its future public remains unclear.[43]

For Olmsted and Vaux, the social value of a lawn relied on its ability to spontaneously create a public on its own terms—to bring together the diverse peoples of the modern city in a peaceful and egalitarian setting. The architects recognized that social boundaries are reinforced by the urban built

FIGURE 1.6. The Pierhouse looms behind the flexible spaces of Pier 1. This luxury apartment building, situated inside the park, boasts some of Brooklyn's most expensive real estate, and funds the park's operating costs. It is unclear what will happen when the interests of its residents conflict with the public uses of the park, which seems inevitable. Central Park has provided a home for some New Yorkers, and a political protest site for others. When the public makes similar uses of Brooklyn Bridge Park, how will the park's resident benefactors respond?

environment. For this reason, manmade elements were famously concealed throughout Central and Prospect Parks. Even the walking paths were sunk below the surface of the lawn, so as not to compromise the perception of unbroken green space. The forests and meadows favored by Olmsted and Vaux exhibited a lack of specificity with regard to the class-bound or culturally inflected activities that dominated the urban landscape beyond the park's borders.[44] In light of this, the crucial material characteristic of a lawn was that it is free of manmade elements and architectural structures that would serve only to reinforce the social, cultural, and economic separations of the city. But the design did not just negate social division—according to Olmsted, it affirmed something else. A lawn accommodated the desire of city residents to gather and interact, and to enjoy a natural landscape, while denying the social divisions and hierarchies of urban society.

There is an undeniable disjunction between this social agenda and the politics behind Brooklyn Bridge Park. The design of BBP represents an exquisite compromise between a variety of competing demands, but it also reflects a concession that even the most aspirational of urban environments cannot be insulated from the socioeconomic inequality in the city at large. It merges public good with private amenity in a way that directly contradicts Olmsted and Vaux's democratic aspirations, inviting social class directly into the heart of ostensibly public space. Immediately behind Harbor View Lawn is the Pierhouse, a luxury condominium building whose opulence is almost unparalleled in Brooklyn's real estate. The material facts of the lawn—its location and orientation, its stubborn resistance to ball playing, picnicking, and large organized gatherings—make it an attractive and calm centerpiece for this building's multimillion-dollar vista. Like every object, the lawn reflects tradeoffs. Like every object, it is political. Even this nonobject, the most innocuous of things, suggests a program of use that reflects a set of social concerns, political agendas, and economic interests. Luckily, in this case, the task confronting the public is a pleasant one. Relax and enjoy the view. But when we are sitting, appreciating the majestic waterfront, we will not merely be consuming the scenery, we will be part of the scenery. Ornaments on a very expensive lawn.

2

The Folding Chair

FIGURE 2.1. The folding chair.

The folding chair sits by itself on the sunlit side of Diversity Plaza, a newly created public space in Jackson Heights. It has a flat backrest and seat, supported by an X-frame. The design has been around for centuries. It seems to have migrated, like spaghetti and the fork, from Asia to Western Europe, and subsequently to the United States.[1] The folding chair is an undeniably modest public object, built for durability rather than comfort or style. And yet it appears unapologetic. Its cheerful blue paint is scratched and chipped, but still bright, and its slender legs splay almost jauntily. It has something to offer. Like a park bench, or a tenement stoop, the chair promises nothing less than the quintessential urban recreation—sitting and watching the world go by. And in this plaza, such clichés are warranted. Jackson Heights is a famously multiethnic neighborhood in a city renowned for its diversity. Immigrants from South Asia, Central America, South America, and Europe populate the surrounding area and move through this bustling public space. On any given day, the plaza holds multitudes.

But an empty chair sitting alone in a public plaza also conveys something more complex and uncertain. An absence rather than a presence. A potentiality rather than an observable fact. Who, exactly, will choose to sit in the blue folding chair? An off-duty nurse, eating a sandwich after a long shift at a nearby clinic? A college student, studying for her midterm exams during spring break? Or perhaps a heroin addict, dozing in the afternoon sun after scoring in one of the vacant lots on the other side of Broadway? The folding chair does not discriminate. It extends its welcome to everyone. It invites the unknown. To some, this characteristic of public space is threatening. An ambitious program run by the city government has created new pedestrian plazas by closing roads and placing similar chairs on patches of repurposed asphalt across the city. In practically every neighborhood where they have appeared, they have been controversial.

But for now, the folding chair is oblivious to these debates. It greets everyone with measured trust. Lightweight and portable, the chair empowers the people who use it, inviting them to reconfigure the space as they see fit.[2] In this respect, the chair exemplifies the idea that urban design should be flexible and adaptable to a variety of user needs. The city is a demanding place, full of environments that ask much of New Yorkers—competence, awareness, tolerance, endurance. The folding chair, on the other hand, demands almost nothing. It offers a uniquely unpresuming affordance—a place to do many things, or nothing at all.

On a quiet Tuesday in mid-July 2016, I inconspicuously watched the blue folding chair for a total of seven hours, logging a day in its life in my field notes.[3] The chair made its way around the plaza throughout the late morning and early afternoon, as one user after another picked it up and moved it, placing it beside other chairs, or pulling it up to one of the matching blue tables. As the sun dipped behind a nearby building, the entire plaza was cast in shade. Imperceptibly, the user population changed, and the configuration of the chairs changed with it. Earlier in the day, men dominated the plaza. They lined up the folding chairs along the plaza's shady southern edge, alone or in small groups, smoking and chatting, sometimes animated in conversation, but mostly just passing the time. As the afternoon progressed, women and children appeared, and the ragged lines of chairs migrated toward the center, gradually giving way to more complex shapes: triangles, squares, and loose circles, reflecting the changing geometry of social interaction in the plaza. The chairs were moved, rotated, folded and carried, pulled and pushed into a limitless variety of spatial arrangements. The diversity of the plaza's users was complemented by the flexibility of its form.

Throughout the afternoon, even the chair's social function evolved. It became a table, and briefly held a cup of tea. Then it became a footrest for a Tibetan American teenager, who communed with friends over bubble tea and soccer highlights on a cell phone. For a few minutes, it became a backstop for an impromptu session of batting practice, catching a rubber ball thrown past a boy who lashed the air with his plastic bat, only rarely connecting. From 5:10 p.m. to 5:27 p.m., the chair was actually occupied by two people at once—a young South Asian woman and a small child, who perched in her lap and greedily enjoyed a snack from a ziplock bag, while intently watching the grown-ups around her.

Finally, as the light began to fade on the multicultural tapestry of northern Queens, an unhoused man whom I had heard about, who goes simply by the name Jesse, veered toward the chair while careening erratically across the plaza. He casually picked up the chair and inspected it, as if it were his first-ever encounter with this kind of object. For a brief moment, he talked to the chair quietly and almost conspiratorially, glancing around as if to see who might be listening in. Then, abruptly, he spun and launched it with both hands, smashing it against the cement wall of a nearby bank building. The chair lay on its side, its trust betrayed, until just after eight, when a plaza custodian picked up the chair and chained it against the wall, ready to serve again the following day.

I watched the folding chairs of Diversity Plaza on many other occasions, on different days of the week, and during different seasons. And all of this, even the physical abuse, turned out to be typical. "Yep, they throw the tables and chairs," an official associated with the plaza later told me, with a wry chuckle. "That's an everyday thing at Diversity." In one corner of the plaza, its unofficial "Mayor" typically holds court. He is a unhoused man known as Angel, a Colombian immigrant in his late fifties, who takes it upon himself to police the social and physical disorder in the plaza. On a worn tablet with a cracked screen, Angel keeps a photographic log of vandalism and disorder. He posts small cardboard signs on the planters and tables, admonishing would-be litterbugs. When I described what I had seen the day before, he had something to say. "That Jesse is a fucking son of a bitch, you know that? Pardon my language, but I'm being honest. He treats the poor chairs very badly, and they don't do anything to him."

Over the last fifteen years or so, the New York City Department of Transportation (NYC DOT) has created more than sixty new public plazas in locations across the city, in an ambitious attempt to make the city more livable, comfortable, sustainable, and safe. In neighborhood after neighborhood, the agency proposed a similar material intervention: replacing a dangerous or underutilized section of roadway with café tables and folding chairs. Like a natural experiment in urban planning, the program injected the same set of material objects into a diverse set of urban contexts. Local reactions to this experiment shed light on the unique set of aspirations, conflicts, and anxieties that prevail in each location. They point to the roles of local culture and power in shaping collective responses to new public objects. And they suggest the formidable obstacles facing city officials in their attempts to remake the social fabric of a city like New York—an urban mosaic of neighborhoods, each one irreducibly and intensely unique. In this chapter, we visit seven of these locations in order to see what happened next, exploring a range of surprising and unpredictable outcomes when a city agency decided to offer New Yorkers a place to sit.

Open Space for All

The process that led to the folding chair began in 2006. In a pilot project, the NYC DOT shut down an underutilized section of Willoughby Avenue in downtown Brooklyn and converted the space into a plaza, complete with café seating and potted plants. The next year, under the leadership of newly appointed commissioner Janette Sadik-Khan, the NYC DOT created another similar space in Brooklyn's DUMBO neighborhood, painting a green triangular plaza onto a patch of pavement previously occupied by a short section of road and a parking lot. These experiments were viewed by Mayor Michael Bloomberg as successful, and when his administration released a strategic plan for the city later in 2007, it promised the creation of many more public plazas. The NYC DOT's Plaza Program was born, an initiative tasked with creating similar public spaces across the city.

The plaza project was in keeping with Bloomberg's emphasis on environmental sustainability and quality of life. The administration's PlaNYC signaled the administration's embrace of the sociological tenets of new urbanism, and suggested that every neighborhood in New York City should have a public plaza and that every resident should live within a ten-minute walk of open public space.[4] The NYC DOT was the ideal administrative actor to carry through on this promise for a simple reason. It literally owns the streets. The agency controls thousands of acres of asphalt, including redundant side streets, underutilized concrete traffic islands, and roughly four million parking spaces.[5] At many intersections in the city, a few granite blocks and a coat of paint were the only modifications needed for the NYC DOT to repurpose an underused piece of urban real estate and create a public plaza virtually out of thin air. Backed by the entrepreneurial ethos of the city's billionaire mayor, Sadik-Khan pushed the initiative forward.

As straightforward as this process may sound, the plaza project was an ambitious undertaking—one that would attempt to succeed where several prior city initiatives had failed. The desire to improve the quality and quantity of public space in the city had inspired the city's first zoning code in 1916. Later, it prompted parks commissioner Robert Moses to embark on a massive expansion of public parkland during his twenty-five-year tenure. But neither of these efforts added public space where it was arguably needed most, in the most densely developed areas of the city.

In 1961, the city adopted a new zoning code that sought to answer this need by providing incentives for developers to create new public plazas on private land. The measure was intended to create public space where buildable vertical space was a highly valuable commodity. Developers who added a public plaza at street level would be rewarded with a density "bonus"— an increase in how high they could legally build. The "bonus plazas" that resulted from the new law would be "privately owned public spaces": open to the public, but designed, managed, and maintained by a private landlord.[6] In purely quantitative terms, the new law was successful. Hundreds of new public plazas were constructed in the 1960s and 1970s amid a growing forest of skyscrapers in Midtown and Lower Manhattan, where developers were eager to take advantage of the height bonus in order to maximize their vertical real estate.

But if the idea was to create vibrant, attractive, well-used public spaces, then the law failed. In the late 1960s and early 1970s, sociologist William H. Whyte rigorously documented the social life of these plazas, while working for the New York City Planning Commission.[7] He found that many of the plazas were unpopular and underutilized, and showed that poor design and indifferent management were to blame. Physical barriers often separated the plazas from the street, hiding them from view or making them difficult to access. And the material elements that attract pedestrians to plazas—sunlight, greenery, comfortable seating, and so on—were typically missing. As a result, the plazas were stark and inhospitable places that failed to attract the human activity vital to any lively, safe, and appealing public space.

As Whyte acknowledged, the sterility of these spaces was partly by design. The bonus plaza program coincided with an era of increasing social inequality in New York City. During this period, public behavior was politicized and subjected to increasing social control throughout the city, as middle-class and affluent Manhattan residents displayed growing anxiety at sharing space with low-income or unhoused residents. In this climate, high-rise developers and property owners saw little to gain in building a vibrant, inclusive public plaza. Maintaining a well-used public space requires ongoing investments of time and money—it was easier and less expensive to create an intentionally dull or hostile space than to address the physical and social disorder that might ensue if a space were actually used. In some cases, developers created public spaces that were "prickly," in the words of geographer Steven Flusty, using brass spikes or ribs to discourage sitting. In other cases they made bonus plazas "slippery"—obscuring their entrances or hiding them from the street.[8] These design elements did not just discourage passersby from stopping in the plazas; they had the added benefit of deterring undesirables who rely more heavily on public space—panhandlers, buskers, the unhoused, and so on—groups who are marginalized and stigmatized in the social and legal orders of the city. In contrast, Whyte argued for a more inclusive and humane approach to urban design that embraces a diversity of uses and types of user. Whyte's key insight was that the vitality of urban spaces is what makes them orderly and safe.

The NYC DOT's plaza project was heavily influenced by Whyte's work, and was conceived as a response to the failure of the plaza bonus program. By creating pedestrian plazas across the city, agency officials hoped to make New York's neighborhoods safer and healthier, but they also harbored sociological aspirations, envisioning the plazas as spaces for New Yorkers to sit for a moment, suspend the frantic pace of their lives, and connect with the people around them. According to urban sociologists and the new urbanist school of planning and urban design that draws on their work, an inviting pedestrian plaza provides the material preconditions for informal urbanism to thrive.[9] When city planners create flexible public spaces in which people are mostly free to do as they wish, they demonstrate faith in the informal social order of the city. Conversely, by reducing or regulating public space, they acknowledge that unconstrained human behavior contains risks. Viewed in this light, the humble blue folding chair in Diversity Plaza represents a deceptively grand proposition. It is an expression of trust in urban society itself.

At the head of the newly created Public Space Unit within the NYC DOT was Andy Wiley-Schwartz, an unabashed admirer of Whyte, who had previously worked for the Project for Public Spaces, the organization that grew out of Whyte's efforts. In 2007, Wiley-Schwartz assembled a team and began developing a plan to create public plazas across the five boroughs. Early on, he made an important choice concerning the administration of the program, deciding that it would be decentralized and partly privatized in its funding and management. Proposals for new plazas would typically originate not within the NYC DOT, but with a partner organization from a given community, usually a local merchants' association or a Business Improvement District (BID). If the NYC DOT agreed that a plaza might enhance pedestrian safety or improve traffic flow, then a temporary plaza would be created. Typically, the area of the plaza would be resurfaced to distinguish it from the surrounding roadway and sidewalk. Concrete separators and planters would then be deposited, along with a set of distinctive folding chairs and tables, painted in a bright primary color. In the case of each new plaza, this temporary phase was meant to establish "proof of concept": to test the effect of the plaza on traffic patterns and, perhaps more importantly, its popularity within the community. If this temporary space were deemed successful, the NYC DOT would assist in the design and construction of a community-based plan for a permanent plaza at the site. But throughout the plaza's life, maintenance would be funded and organized by the local community partner, generally the same organization that proposed the plaza in the first place.

According to Wiley-Schwartz, this model was controversial when he first proposed it, as it took the funding and management of the plazas out of the city's hands. In defense of the decentralized plan, however, Wiley-Schwartz claims that it is crucial to the program's success, ensuring that a local stakeholder would be heavily invested in the stewardship of each new public space.

It's a buy-in, like, "we're going to make this an authentic expression of our neighborhood and our community." That's the key outcome that you want. You can go and plop down very similar playground equipment in playgrounds across the city, but you can't program a public space from one neighborhood to the next in the same way. It has to be right for each neighborhood, and the government isn't going to be able to do that.[10]

Wiley-Schwartz was convinced that if a government agency were charged with the design and maintenance of the plazas, the result would be a "race to the bottom" that would replicate the failures of the bonus plaza program, resulting in "the lowest common denominator of management and maintenance . . . useless triangles and planted areas that nobody can do anything in, because they're easier to take care of."[11] Under his leadership, the plaza program took off, initiating more than 30 temporary plazas in its first two years, and expanding to include more than 170 plazas over the next decade. The program's hallmark beige asphalt and brightly colored patio furniture quickly became a routine sight across the city.

The Commercial Commons

One of the first plazas created under the initiative was also one of the most controversial. In late May 2009, Janette Sadik-Khan and her team walked across Broadway at Times Square and placed a series of orange barrels on the roadbed, closing the road to traffic. In doing so, they created several large pedestrian areas in the heart of Midtown. Since the early twentieth century, the iconic bow-tie-shaped intersection had been a thoroughfare for both automobiles and pedestrians. Times Square was the frenzied, cacophonous "crossroads of the world," where congested lanes of car traffic were flanked by narrow sidewalks choked with tourists, commuters, street vendors, street performers, buskers, panhandlers, and so forth. In a matter of minutes, the NYC DOT had effectively reprogrammed the city's most famous public space, upending the rules that had governed it for more than a century.

Reducing Midtown congestion and increasing pedestrian safety were the initial rationales for closing the roads, but Sadik-Khan saw something larger at stake. On the streets and in the subway, urgency and social disengagement are the norm. The new pedestrian plazas were meant to serve as the antithesis or antidote for these congested transportation spaces. User surveys conducted by the agency had shown New York City to be a "city without seats"—a metropolis with ample public space, but very little seating, where foot-weary pedestrians were forced to make do with fire hydrants, stoops, planters, and the like.[12] The effect, according to Sadik-Khan, was not just physical inconvenience but a denial of community as an organizing principle for urban space. In opening a similar plaza in Brooklyn the year before, she had framed the initiative as "a celebration, not of our ability to move, but of our ability to stop, to take a moment, to chat with our neighbors and to be part of our communities."[13] Public spaces with generous amounts of seating were a necessary counterweight to the dynamism of the city, encouraging people to pause and interact with one another.

Ironically, just hours before the street closure was slated to occur, the new Times Square still lacked seating options of any kind. The patio-furniture order was not due to arrive until August. In a last-ditch effort, Tom Tompkins, director of the Times Square Alliance, the organization that had sponsored the plazas, placed a call to a neighborhood hardware store in Brooklyn, securing several hundred aluminum and rubber lawn chairs in bright primary colors, for a little more than $10 each.[14] For months, taxi drivers and other opponents of the plan had focused their ire on its proposed traffic patterns, predicting crippling congestion in Midtown. But once the plazas were in place, controversy immediately shifted to the seating.[15] The lawn chairs themselves were derided for their "tacky," "cheesy" visual aesthetic, more reminiscent of suburban backyards and crowded beaches than a cosmopolitan urban center, in the eyes of some observers.[16]

These complaints were quickly subsumed within a larger concern for how this new seating changed the social meaning of the space. The *New York Post* was particularly ruthless in its descriptions of the new pedestrian-friendly Times Square. A mere week after the creation of the plaza, a pair of columnists targeted the litter created by the throngs of visitors drawn to the plazas:

> The Crossroads of the World looks more like a city dump these days, thanks to those new pedestrian plazas. The cheapo tables and chairs set up in the pedestrian-only sections of Times Square have become a magnet for nightcrawler slobs who carelessly toss hot-dog wrappers, empty soda bottles and McDonald's bags on the street.[17]

There was an ironic undercurrent to such criticism. The project's discontents saw in the new Times Square a tawdriness reminiscent of the bad old days of Midtown, when peep shows, pornographic theaters, and street hustles of every conceivable variety defined the street life of the area. A columnist from the *Post* later made the parallel explicit:

> IT TOOK 25 years to save Times Square from its dark age, and it took City Hall just three months to turn it into a squatters' camp. Despite all of yesterday's ribbon-cutting hoopla, complete with a confetti-firing cannon, the Crossroads of the World looks almost exactly like what it's been all summer—a five-block-long sea of dazed, low-rent tourists glued like chewing-gum wads to the cheapest seats in town. . . . The disconnected,

awkward plazas that chopped up Times Square and gutted its energy are unworthy of a prison yard. . . . [They] are an affront to Times Square's historic central role in the life of the city, and to the power and glory of its landmarks.[18]

By closing Times Square to traffic and ceding it to pedestrians, in other words, the city had somehow diminished the grandeur of its most hallowed public space. According to critics, in place of the seediness and crime of the 1970s and 1980s, the city's planners had inadvertently encouraged new forms of social disorder, less severe but still unpleasant—throngs of loitering, littering tourists who gathered within the new pedestrian plazas, agog at the sensory spectacle of the square.

But the worst controversies were still to come. In the months following the street closures, performers in costumes began showing up in the new pedestrian plazas, soliciting tips in exchange for photographs. In 2009, the *Daily News* reported that a man dressed as a wildly popular Sesame Street character was routinely harassing tourists who refused to tip, dubbing the man "evil Elmo."[19] In the following years, similar accusations proliferated, provoking sustained outrage from the New York tabloids. A male performer dressed as Super Mario allegedly groped a female passerby, while another, dressed as Cookie Monster, was charged with child endangerment after shoving a toddler whose mother could not pay for a photograph.[20] According to Tompkins, of the Times Square Alliance, some costumed performers held on to tourists' children, refusing to return them to their parents until paid a tip for a photograph.[21] A performer dressed as Spiderman was charged with assaulting the mother of two small children after a disagreement over a tip.[22] Another Spiderman was arrested three times for various offenses, including throwing folding chairs into a crowd of tourists.[23] It is difficult to say how common such incidents actually were, but from the perspective of the plazas' reputation, the frequency with which they occurred was irrelevant: the steady drumbeat of negative coverage had its own effect on public perception, painting the new Times Square as not simply a lowbrow mecca of crass commercialism but also a potentially menacing place.[24]

In 2013, the costumed characters were joined by a new type of performer—topless women known as "desnudas" who posed for photos with plaza visitors, typically covered only by a swimsuit bottom and some body paint. The desnudas were permitted under New York City law, which allows public nudity above the waist, but they opened a new front in the war for Times Square's reputation, and reminded some longtime New Yorkers

FIGURE 2.2. A strip club without walls. The appearance of "desnudas" in Times Square had the ironic effect of creating open-air burlesque shows in a district previously known for its strip clubs and triple-X theaters. Here, a group of unaccompanied men, in the foreground, lounge in the NYC DOT's patio furniture and take in the show.

of the seedy Midtown of old. Several visits to Times Square in spring and summer of 2015 revealed a form of informal urbanism that supported such comparisons: throngs of single men sitting nonchalantly in the plazas' folding chairs, eyes glued to groups of desnudas soliciting tips. While strip clubs had long been exiled from Midtown, a combination of newly created public space and topless street performers had come together, providing a sort of free, open-air burlesque show. In 2015, the city's media registered an increase in "aggressive panhandling" by the desnudas as well, prompting a public reaction from Mayor Bill de Blasio and NYPD commissioner William Bratton. Both officials lamented that their hands were tied. Public performance for tips on public streets or sidewalks was a protected activity under the First Amendment. Only when the performers broke a law could they be ticketed or arrested.[25]

Throughout these controversies, critics in the media drew a straight line from the newly created pedestrian spaces to the controversial street performers who congregated within them. Prior to the street closings, the logic went, disorderly commercial activity had been constrained by the crushing congestion on the sidewalks, which kept foot traffic moving and prevented sustained interaction between street performers and passersby.

The folding chairs in the square invited disorder by permitting tourists and other pedestrians to stay put, where they became an audience for crass and exploitative forms of entertainment. A *New York Times* reporter observed that the pedestrian plazas provided "more room for the people in costumes to operate", and likened the new Times Square to a petri dish, where an Elmo or two had seeded a "culture" of problematic solicitation.[26] The *New York Post* was more blunt:

> It's obvious what draws Cookie Monster & Co.—the Bloomberg pedestrian mall, or rather the tourists who infest it, wandering lost on their way to American Girl or FAO Schwarz. The whole plaza is an intrusion on the square. . . . It's not even really a draw for out-of-towners, just a vacuum they're pulled into—an invitation to spend more time looking at the jumbotrons rather than heading off somewhere to enrich the more legal parts of the economy.[27]

In a separate editorial, the paper referred to the new Broadway as the "Great Blight Way," and rhetorically asked, "Is this better? Once a haven for hookers and junkies, Times Square is now overrun by swarms of tourists, peddlers and street performers."[28] By closing parts of Times Square to traffic, Bloomberg and Sadik-Khan had succeeded in fostering social interaction in the heart of Midtown. But they had not foreseen the potential for the social and economic context of Times Square, a mecca of tourism and unconstrained commercialism, to determine the nature of many of these interactions. The social contact between strangers in the plazas was increasingly viewed as problematic.

By summer 2015, the city's newly appointed mayor appeared to have become convinced that the plazas themselves were to blame for quality-of-life complaints pertaining to people in costumes and desnudas. NYPD commissioner William Bratton declared his desire to "dig the whole damn thing up," and Mayor de Blasio publicly floated a plan to remove the pedestrian plazas and reopen Broadway to automobile traffic.[29] Six years after the orange barrels were dragged across Broadway, Sadik-Khan's largest, boldest effort to remedy the problems of a "city without seats" was imperiled, brought to the brink of reversal by the aggressive solicitation of tips by a small army of costumed characters and topless women.

In 2016, the NYC DOT decided that the plazas it had created were too open and too unprogrammed, ceding too much freedom to their users. The agency's leadership became convinced that new rules were necessary to balance the openness, flexibility, and public accessibility of the plazas with firmer mechanisms of social control. However, the agency had come up against a legal roadblock in its attempts to regulate the spaces it had created. Desnudas and costumed characters, could not be regulated on public sidewalks unless they broke an existing law, and the ordinances governing these spaces allowed for a wide range of activity, including Constitutionally protected forms of expression. The NYC DOT began to lobby the City Council for a piece of legislation that would define public plazas and codify a set of distinct rules that would apply to these spaces. In spring 2016 a set of rules was passed, and they went into effect in June of that year.

In Times Square, the rules distinguished "designated activity areas" from "pedestrian flow areas," assigning distinct spaces within Times Square to street performance and panhandling, while reserving other spaces for pedestrian movement. In all plazas, "disorderly behavior" of any sort was prohibited, including acts that would disturb the "peace, comfort, or repose of a reasonable person of normal sensitivities," a vague, catchall formulation meant to empower NYC DOT employees and police officers to regulate the plazas in the name of public nuisance control. The rules stipulate that one should not occupy more than one seat with oneself or one's belongings, clearly targeting the overnight use of the plazas by unhoused people. Smoking, bathing, littering, climbing, skateboarding, gambling, camping, and carrying signs larger than two foot by three foot were all similarly prohibited. At the same time, the rules sought to preserve the publicness of the plazas, specifying that any person may enter and use a pedestrian plaza at any time. In an interview, Emily Weidenhof, director of public space at NYC DOT, described these measures as an inevitable tradeoff between idealism and pragmatism that would allow the public to continue to enjoy "the most democratic spaces that we have."[30] The fundamental promise of flexible, public space—its openness to multiple interpretations and forms of expression—according to Weidenhof, had to be balanced with the regulation required to keep the plazas welcoming and orderly.

A young experiment in urban planning had progressed past childhood, into its troublesome teenage years.

Amor a Primera Vista

On a sunny afternoon in early October 2016, I sit on a bench on the northeastern end of Corona Plaza, in the neighborhood of Corona, Queens, and look around at an urban landscape that is calmly brimming with life. A Cumbia song quietly buzzes from a portable speaker held by a man sitting next to me, while dominos clack on a yellow aluminum table not far away. The intense sunlight bifurcates the plaza. Around me is a shaded area cluttered with folding tables and chairs, where practically every sittable surface is occupied. Beyond the shade lies an expanse of hot, beige concrete dotted with granite blocks and large planters, yellow marigolds punctuating the muted landscape. A boy of six or seven, approximately the age of my own son, rides a scooter in figure eights, making a tight loop around a table where several older kids sit, then carving a larger oval out in the asphalt expanse of the rectangular space, which runs the length of the block. The freedom offered by the plaza is evident in his movement, which no public sidewalk could have afforded. For him, this plaza is a playground. For his older sister, seated nearby, her brows knitted over a geometry textbook, it is a library. And for the men playing dominos, it is simply a place to socialize and pass the time, before or after work.

A yellow Sunday school truck sponsored by an evangelical church is parked in the center of the plaza. The truck is staffed by three enthusiastic White women with blond hair and egregiously flawed Spanish. They are trying to get thirty or so elementary-school-aged kids excited about the candy and breakfast cereal they are giving away. "Put your hands up!" one yells, "mucho rapido! Everybody say, 'I am Christian!'" The speaker leads the group in the Christian Pledge of Allegiance, directed toward a white flag with a red crucifix in the corner. I get up and wander away from the scene, finding a seat next to the four men playing dominoes. Along the edges of the space, street vendors are selling chicharróns, tacos, and "hot dogs estilo Mexico."

Less than a decade ago, the space where I was sitting was regarded by local officials as a problem to be solved, a congested parking lot full of dirty white box trucks, many of which remained stationary for hours and even days at a time. These were *las mudanzas*—the movers—people in the plaza spit the word out with mild contempt, or shake their heads wryly when mentioning them. For many years, this location has served as a meeting place for trucks that will transport furniture and other belongings around the city for a fee. The informal market operates much like the street-corner shape-ups where day laborers ply their construction or landscaping skills. "Word got out that if you needed something moved, you could go up to Corona Plaza, and hire somebody cheap," says Ricardi Calixte of the Queens Economic Development Corporation, one of several local organizations involved in the management of the plaza. Now, the mudanzas that were displaced from the plaza line up just beyond its perimeter along Roosevelt

FIGURE 2.3. Before the plaza. Archival footage taken by film producer Clarence Eckerson prior to the creation of Corona Plaza shows a man and a boy seated on a large tree stump, the only seating available. Like the "desire lines" cut by pedestrians through patches of grass, the photo demonstrated an implicit need, illustrating the potential value of a public place to sit.
Photo credit: Clarence Eckerson / Streetfilms.

Avenue, the box trucks surrounding the new public space, appearing almost resentful at their eviction.

In the old days, when the mudanzas still dominated this space, the sidewalk along Roosevelt Avenue was a gathering place for single working men, teenagers, and other people who found themselves with time to kill and no burning desire to be indoors. Census numbers reveal that Corona has had some of the highest rates of residential crowding in the city for several decades: outdoor public space has been a scarce and much-needed resource in the community for a long time.[31] The groups of men and teenagers who congregated on the block in the 2000s drew the attention of a city police force that was implementing a "broken windows" approach to policing public space. Starting in the early 2000s, the NYPD sharply escalated routine searches of individuals deemed suspicious. "It was one of the highest stop-and-frisk zones in the city," said Prerana Reddy, the director of public events at the nearby Queens Museum of Art, another organization that was instrumental in creating the plaza. "There was tension about young people. There was no place to stand and wait. People were getting loitering tickets, etcetera. There was tension about the moving trucks that were there all day long. So, what was there was problematic."[32] According to Reddy, flexible public space has a particular use value for single men, one of the largest demographic components of Corona. Just around the corner is a small park with a baseball diamond, and a playground lies several blocks away. But, as Reddy pointed out, these spaces are not welcoming to this constituency.

> Parks with playing fields and playgrounds, that's not a place where they can be, because they look like predators, right? Where do they get to hang out? After they've been working a 12-hour shift and before they go back to an overcrowded apartment where they might have 10 people in 2 bedrooms. People needed a public space that was not overly pro-grammed or overly fixed—that had enough openness to it.[33]

Given the social stigma attached to single men and teenagers congregating in public space, it is conceivable that the proposal to construct a public plaza at Corona station might have met with a lukewarm response from local stakeholders. But when the NYC DOT brought a plan before the local community board, the presentation received a standing ovation. According to NYC DOT officials involved in the project, a handful of dissenters—business and property owners concerned about the loss of parking spaces—were quickly won over by the project's local proponents. As soon as the plaza was created, parents flocked to the beige rectangle of pavement, giving their children free reign among its colorful tables, chairs, and flowerbeds. Informal communal childcare became commonplace in the plaza, as female caregivers entrusted their young wards to friends, while food shopping or visiting the medical clinic.[34]

According to Laura Hansen, director of the Neighborhood Plaza Partnership, a nonprofit that assists in plaza maintenance, the popularity of the plaza for families immediately shaped the character of the space. Hansen's crews were surprised to arrive at Corona Plaza and find it already clean, thanks to voluntary sanitation work and the informal policing of litterers on the part of the plaza's regular users. "Corona has a lot of families, and that changes the whole tenor of things. When you've got Mom's 'eyes on the street' it's a different thing, there's a different dynamic."[35] Four field visits to the space during warm weather showed that large numbers of men and teenagers continue to use the space, alongside elderly people, children, parents, and other caregivers. During a visit on a sweltering afternoon in July, I sat at the edge of the plaza along Roosevelt Avenue, closest to the mudanzas, chatting with several men who often rest there after concluding a job with one of the moving trucks. When I casually suggested that a cold beer would make the heat more tolerable, two of the men chuckled ruefully. One told me, with a soft Norteno lilt, "No, too many kids here. Too many babies. Too many women. They would yell at us if we did."

Approximately eight miles away, in the borough of Manhattan, another plaza offers a similar success story. La Plaza de Las Americas, in Washington Heights, is a trapezoidal space created by closing a block of 175th Street to traffic. Like Corona Plaza, La Plaza, as it is called for short, encountered little local opposition when initially proposed. It was one of the first plazas outside of Midtown or Downtown Manhattan to be transformed from a temporary space to a permanent one, and it now looks and feels official, with ornamental paving stones, a fountain, and a public restroom. The plaza hosts an outdoor market most days of the week, but it often seems to draw as many nonshoppers as shoppers—people attracted to the relaxed yet sociable environment.

At La Plaza, single male users described coming to sit in the fringes of the street market, a practice that predated the plaza, and engage in some relaxing people watching. "I come here every day after work," Frankie, a fifty-year-old cable repairman and a lifelong resident of Washington Heights, told me. "It relaxes me. Been doing it for years. I come to sit, watch the people." I asked him where he sat before the benches were installed. "On a milk crate," he replied with a smile. "I would just grab one of those crates right there and sit. . . . It was the same, but different. Less comfortable. You couldn't do this." Frankie leaned back on the bench, a smile on his face, and struck a blissfully recumbent pose, putting one leg up on an empty vegetable box in front of him. As in Corona, La Plaza formalized the informal social behaviors that were already taking place in the space. Frankie's milk crate was replaced by a bench, and in the process, he and the other longtime users of this patch of pavement— young people, single men, street vendors—gained a degree of legitimacy in their leisure. In this way, urban planning and design can perform a type of social alchemy, architecturally endorsing informal behaviors associated with marginalized users, and, in the process, changing the meanings of a space.

In explaining the popularity of these two plazas, new urbanists might point to the universal appeal of open space, and the perhaps surprisingly pro-social tendencies of harried urbanites, when provided a pleasant gathering space in the heart of the city. Interviews with plaza organizers and users, however, reveal that two factors—one symbolic and one functional—were actually vital to the success of these two spaces. When attempting to explain the favorable reception of a new idea, cultural sociologists point to something they refer to as "resonance"—the degree to which an idea fits into an existing cultural framework.[36] If a new concept or object is understandable to a given

FIGURE 2.4. A game of dominoes in Corona Plaza. One of the notable things about this public space is the demographic variety it contains and the versatility it offers. Multiple generations and genders in a wide variety of configurations frequent the plaza, and carve out their own meaningful spaces within its expanse. On this day, and many others, several tables of men playing dominoes brought a competitive masculinity to a shady section of the plaza, while teenagers and children played nearby.

population, given the preexisting stock of thoughts, beliefs, and experiences that they share in common, then it is more likely to be accepted or adopted.

Both neighborhoods have large populations of immigrants from Latin America, a factor that partially accounts for the plazas' immediate popularity. At Corona Plaza, Josefina and Antonio, an elderly Mexican couple, were sitting on folding chairs in front of the Walgreen's on an unseasonably cool afternoon in late August. The two have been living in Corona for twenty-nine years. When I asked if they viewed the plaza as successful, Antonio looked at me as if I were crazy. "Well, yes, see for yourself," he gestured broadly toward the plaza, which was full of school-aged children and adults engaged in a wide range of activities. When I asked why it was successful, he looked away in thought, frowning under his mustache, and said, in forceful Spanish, "The Hispanic community is very strong here, very strong. . . . There are many nationalities here, Ecuadorian, Colombian, Mexican, and they all like to be outside. They all like to be *together* outside." At this point Josefina interrupted in English, "It's in our culture. This plaza can maybe be an example for other parts of the city, where they don't like plazas."

At La Plaza de Las Americas, in Washington Heights, users had similar explanations for the success of the plaza. A Dominican man named Carlos, in his sixties, offered the following account (translated from Spanish):

> I am certain 100 percent that this is because of who lives here. People here, to them, this is very typical. In the Dominican Republic, in Mexico, in Costa Rica, in Argentina, in Chile, in Ecuador, in Colombia, the plaza is something typical. They know what to do here. They know how to act in this place. And they know that it has a value. Look at what you see happening here—this is the community. Yes or no?

This explanation was echoed by officials and representatives of the organizations that helped to create the two plazas. "They're coming from cultures where the town square is very much a central part of social and cultural life," said Reddy. "And that was missing in this place. And so the potential that this could be there and serve as that kind of space that was missing in their lives could relieve a lot of tension for them. It would be a public living room in a way."[37] Replacing a congested parking lot with a space similar to the *zocolos* and plazas of home offered a recognizable and natural solution to an existing problem for residents of Corona. The idea had "resonance," and this preempted any political friction that might have been created by the proposal.

But, as sociologists Tavory and McDonnell argue, cultural familiarity is probably not quite enough for a new idea to resonate—it has to be pragmatic, solving a problem for a group of people, for them to recognize it as valuable. So, a new object that on the one hand fits into the existing mental frameworks that a group of people possess and on the other hand addresses a pressing issue or concern—this object is likely to be well received.[38] A second factor that appears to help explain the success of the two plazas was functional rather than symbolic. Open, flexible space solved problems that exist in both neighborhood contexts, offering open, outdoor space that was desperately desired by the demographic subgroups—families with young children, teenagers, single men—who can be found in the plaza at any given time.

The plazas in Corona and Washington Heights fixed another sort of problem for the residents of those communities. They serve as informal town halls for communities in which immigration status often prevents full participation in civic life. In every field visit to Corona Plaza, saving two trips when rain kept the plaza largely empty, I saw employees or volunteers at the circular tables in the shade, presiding over stacks of leaflets advertising various social, medical, or legal services. Directly adjacent to the plaza is a medical clinic and a grocery store certified by the city's Women, Infants, and Children nutritional program, which offers free or discounted food, including fresh produce. City officials conveyed the significance of this, explaining that the plaza is used by local medical or social service providers to inform the population about flu screenings and shots, social and legal services, and other resources that they might not be aware of, or might be scared to pursue in more formal, institutional settings. "How can we create a safe space where people could access these things?" Prerana Reddy asked rhetorically. "The plaza gave us that space."[39]

Agoraphobia, or Fear of Public Space

In Brooklyn's Sheepshead Bay neighborhood, next to the eponymous subway station, an entire block of East Fifteenth Street is closed to motor vehicle traffic. Across the entrance to the block, slender bollards stand in a row like plastic soldiers, warding away the motorists cruising down Sheepshead Bay Road. The asphalt behind the bollards is painted beige, in keeping with the NYC DOT's color scheme for newly created public plazas, but the space itself is conspicuously empty. There are no places to sit here—no folding chairs or benches, café tables or potted plants, nor any other signs that this is a plaza. And, technically, it is not. After a series of serious traffic accidents at this location, one of them fatal, the NYC DOT closed the street in order to improve the safety of the adjacent intersection, offering to build a plaza in its place. In a presentation by the NYC DOT hosted by a local civic group, residents shouted down city officials and accused the government of a dictatorial abuse of power.[40] The community board echoed these sentiments and rejected the city's proposal. Now, the barren rectangle of asphalt speaks of a bitter standoff between local power structures and city agencies.

Along one side of this nonplaza is a visual artifact that sheds light on the community's opposition to open space. The eastern side of the block is bordered by a massive mural. This piece of public art was commissioned in the early 1990s by the Bay Improvement Group, a local neighborhood beautification association. The mural depicts an oddly anachronistic reimagining of a nearby intersection, in which historic streetcars share the road with modern automobiles. Flanking the large, divided roadway in the mural are more signs of wishful nostalgia. Postwar apartment buildings have been replaced by detached homes, and the nightclubs that now lie along the avenue's commercial strip have been supplanted by picturesque storefronts, their goods on display under striped awnings.

FIGURE 2.5. A plaza that isn't. In Sheepshead Bay, the NYC DOT exercised its authority to close the street, but no community-based organization stepped forward to maintain a plaza in the pedestrian area that the closure created. As a result, the space is uneasy and liminal, defying categorization. Most of the time it is empty, but when a train or bus arrives it becomes an active pedestrian corridor, before emptying out again within a matter of minutes.

The title of the mural, "Sheepshead Bay's Historic Future," is telling. It depicts an idealized future for the neighborhood, in which the past is selectively brought back to life. For many decades, Sheepshead Bay has been a diverse community with distinctly urban problems, such as traffic congestion and densely concentrated poverty. But in the mural, the neighborhood is re-envisioned as a homogeneous, quasi-suburban utopia—an exemplar of physical and social orderliness.[41] Even the time-honored urban practice of jaywalking has been expunged. At the center, a family crosses the massive, divided roadway in the crosswalk, passing neat rows of flowers that adorn the center median. The mural gestures toward a neighborhood identity preferred by community leaders at a time when crime rates and racial tension were running high throughout the city. Sheepshead Bay, the mural asserts, is a traditional, all-American neighborhood, not to be confused with the dense, diverse, and disorderly urban places found throughout much of Brooklyn and the city as a whole.

At the bottom left-hand corner of the mural is a representation of the man who was chiefly responsible for its creation. He looks out at the viewer, standing next to a young girl. This is Steve Barrison, the president of the Bay

FIGURE 2.6. Suburban Brooklyn. A mural running down one side of the closed block in Sheepshead Bay offers clues to the neighborhood's self-image, at least according to the civic association that commissioned the artwork. The painting depicts the neighborhood as a wholesome, orderly, quasi-suburban community steeped in history. A large parkway runs down the middle of the image and suggests that an automobile-focused lifestyle is central to the neighborhood's identity. As a prominent member of the community put it, "everybody drives to their mailbox."

Improvement Group. Barrison's moustache has grayed during the twenty-five years since the mural was painted, but he remains a fierce defender of the rights of two local constituencies—motorists and small business owners. He spearheaded the mural project as a way of reclaiming a space that was perceived as physically and socially disorderly, applying something like the broken windows theory. "It was this big ugly cement wall that was always covered with graffiti and had bums and derelicts hanging out," Barrison told a reporter for the *New York Times*. "Once we put the mural out, it changed everything."[42] In the recent fight over the closure of Fifteenth Street, Barrison has argued, along with other prominent residents, that a pedestrian-oriented public space would run contrary to the identity of the neighborhood. "This is not Manhattan. This is not Williamsburg. This is not Copenhagen," Barrison told me in an interview. "This is *suburban* Brooklyn. Everybody drives to their mailbox."[43]

When the NYC DOT suggested creating the pedestrian plaza on East Fifteenth Street, Barrison and other local stakeholders viewed the proposal with dark foreboding, and had little trouble envisioning a worst-case scenario in which social and physical disorder escalate as a result of the public space. "Is it going to become a garbage dumping ground? Is it going to become a place where the homeless are gathering and loitering?" asked Teresa Scavo, the chairperson of the local community board, when I asked her about the empty section of East Fifteenth Street. "And who's going to maintain this closed street? Who's going to go in and clean it? And what is the future of that street going to be?"[44] Rhetorical questions of this sort have frequently been raised in response to the NYC DOT's Neighborhood Plaza Program, and are not limited to Sheepshead Bay. At least one other plaza project in the city was abandoned altogether in response to such hostility on the part of community board leadership. In Astoria, Queens, the plaza was rejected after a community board meeting devolved into an acrimonious shouting match between a group of newcomers and a vocal majority of old-timers, who repeatedly raised the possibility that a plaza would attract "the bad element"—namely, alcoholics, "mental patients", and other undesirables.[45]

Another somewhat similar case lies just north of Sheepshead Bay, in the community of Midwood, home of one of the city's largest concentrations of Orthodox Jews, as well as one of Brooklyn's most diverse public high schools. Where Avenue M intersects with East Fifteenth Street, just one block away from Edward R. Murrow High School, is another nonplaza, in this case a cement triangle containing a small, fenced-in rose garden. A plaza was proposed here in 2015 by a local partner organization, the Midwood Development Corporation (MDC), and the NYC DOT hosted a visioning session at which residents were encouraged to create drawings expressing their aspirations for the space.

But the plan quickly fell apart amid fierce opposition from within the neighborhood. Representatives of the local Orthodox community speculated about the consequences of giving the high-school kids a place in which to gather. In an interview, Ephraim Neirenberg, a local businessman and member of the community board, summed up the concerns raised in local meetings:

> I'm not a very big fan of people just sitting there and hanging out. Right now the kids from Murrow go from school to the train and they leave. You give them a place to hang out, I don't know what will happen. I don't know if it will be good. I don't know if it will be bad. I just don't know.[46]

As in Sheepshead Bay, potentially problematic groups within the neighborhood were viewed as less threatening if they were kept on the move, forced to come and go, circulate within the neighborhood, and ultimately disperse.

Designating a space for them to "hang out," on the other hand, was a troubling and uncertain prospect.

But some residents who attended public meetings on the proposal were more specific in their fears. Herman Rothberg, a longtime resident of the neighborhood who was vocal in the debate over the proposal suggested that the plaza would lead to violence. When I spoke with him, he elaborated on this concern, citing a case in which a road construction project had deposited a series of concrete barriers along a street near the high school, inadvertently providing places for students to sit after school. "The kids would be sitting on them—30 or 40 kids—watching other kids fight. Maybe it's just play fights, but they use their fists a lot. If the kids don't sit, they don't congregate. If they have a place to sit, they don't just sit. They make trouble."[47] Rothberg was sympathetic to the high-school students but viewed a plaza near the subway station as a recipe for disorder. In his formulation of the risk involved, otherwise well-behaved groups of kids can devolve into violence when provided with a patch of cement and some folding chairs—material inducements to gather and loiter.

In public meetings, on a Facebook page, and in interviews, other opponents expressed similar fears, suggesting that a plaza with folding chairs would lead teenagers to congregate and behave poorly. A longtime resident worried that the teenagers would use the chairs as weapons. The plaza would be an "attractive nuisance," according to a local elected official who opposed the proposal.[48] During one of my visits to the site of the proposed plaza, a bodega owner described her objections to the plaza. "I like the high school kids. The kids after school—they already come here. If there were chairs, more would come here, and they wouldn't leave. They would cause trouble. Like it was their living room." Denying young people public places to sit was a way of reining in their behavior, channeling them into the private spaces of local shops and cafés, and ultimately encouraging them to disperse as quickly as possible on school days. In the face of this opposition, the MDC eventually rescinded its offer to sponsor a pedestrian plaza. Instead, the organization solicited funds from the city councilperson's office to install a small flowerbed surrounded by a wrought-iron fence, a space that improved the visual appeal of the location but that actually reduced the square footage available for users to physically occupy.

The rejections of the plazas in Sheepshead Bay, Astoria, Midwood, and a handful of other neighborhoods are revealing in terms of neighborhood collective identity. In every case, anxiety concerning the social consequences of public space was rooted in broader insecurities tied to ostensibly disorderly

FIGURE 2.7. A defensive planting. In Midwood, a proposed plaza project was abandoned, and this flowerbed was placed on a triangular concrete median instead, courtesy of the New York City Parks Department and city council member Chaim Deutsch. Although aesthetically pleasing, the flowerbed reduces the amount of space for pedestrians, providing an affordance that is diametrically opposed to that of a plaza.

groups within the community. The plaza proposed in each instance was interpreted as an arena of dubious social control, where teenagers or the unhoused would be given free rein, a prospect that objectors viewed as detrimental to the safety and stability of the surrounding area. In cases such as those described above, community members gave voice to a form of collective agoraphobia, or, literally, fear of public space.[49]

This sentiment has a long history in the United States. In the mid-1800s, as class relations deteriorated in American cities, middle-class and wealthy city dwellers came to fear interaction with poor and working-class urbanites, and sought to insulate themselves via spatial, legal, and technological means.[50] As part of this effort, public space was increasingly regulated. Previously innocuous forms of behavior, when enacted in public, were categorized as nuisances, and formally sanctioned. Occupying public space without a clear purpose became "loitering"; lacking a private domicile became "vagrancy."[51] The resulting legal framework labeled everyday reliance on public space as a form of social deviance. This, in turn, stigmatized the unhoused, panhandlers, street vendors, buskers, and other social groups who were dependent on public space for their survival. By the same token, the public realm itself was culturally contaminated, as an arena of uncontrolled contact with the "dangerous" classes.

To be clear, the association of urban public space with the presence of unhoused people, teenagers, and other groups labeled as deviant or problematic is not without a basis in empirical reality. Teenagers gather in public because they typically lack private spaces of their own, and because public spaces offer a freedom that they do not have when under the supervision of teachers, parents, or shopkeepers. Unhoused people gravitate to train stations, parks, plazas, and other public spaces for an equally obvious reason—they lack private spaces of their own and can be lawfully expelled from any private property owned by someone else. The legal designation of public space offers a degree of protection to these and other groups, endorsing their right to occupy parks, plazas, sidewalks, and so on, so long as they pose no "nuisance" or threat.

But it was not solely the prospect of public space that worried some residents and organizations in Sheepshead Bay, Midwood, and elsewhere in the city. It was the specific social programming of a public plaza that made it threatening—a space for sitting and remaining stationary amid the urban ebb and flow of people and things.[52] This was made clear by Theresa Scavo, in an interview with a local newspaper. "Right now, you go to the train station, and I will guarantee a minimum of three to four homeless people are there right at this moment. . . . Now you're giving them a place to live."[53] Creating a new plaza obviously does not increase the prevalence of homelessness, or unruly teenagers, or public drunkenness—these are, quite clearly, broader societal problems. But Scavo's comments reveal a fear of legitimizing and prolonging the presence of undesirables by giving them a place to sit. The solution to local social disorder, then, is to avoid making the public spaces in a neighborhood too comfortable—to keep everyone standing, walking, driving, or otherwise on the move.[54] In Sheepshead Bay and Midwood, local civic leaders sought to invert Sadik-Khan's aspirations for the city and create neighborhoods without seats. Give an unhoused person or a group of unruly teenagers a chair in which to sit, opponents argued, and they will make this place their home.

The Thomas Theorum

Times Square and its unique problems aside, in a handful of cases, creating a public plaza did attract a notable degree of social disorder, validating some of opponents' concerns. These cases are particularly interesting for what happened next. In two highly controversial plazas—one in Jackson Heights, Queens, the other in the Bedford-Stuyvesant neighborhood of Brooklyn— stakeholders responded to vandalism, harassment, and crime through what might be considered a reputational intervention. By rebranding the plazas, they tried to activate a self-fulfilling prophecy of sorts, in which perceptions that the spaces were vibrant and safe would make them so in reality. This version of the "Thomas theorem," the sociological hypothesis that "if men define situations as real, they are real in their consequences,"[55] is endorsed by new urbanists such as Jacobs and Whyte, who argue that spaces that are believed to be appealing, orderly, and safe will become more so over time, as social activity itself discourages disorder and encourages informal social control.

Diversity Plaza, the Jackson Heights plaza described at the beginning of this chapter, was born into controversy. In 2011, the NYC DOT closed the block to motor vehicle traffic in order to improve safety, without first securing the support of a local sponsor. The owners of storefront businesses along the block saw the street closing as a top–down and undemocratic process, and it caught them by surprise. In the months after the plaza was created, they watched the space become a haven for a group of unhoused men with substance-abuse problems, who had previously taken shelter in nearby parking lots, alleys, and sidewalks. Particularly during the mornings and early afternoons, these men were among the most frequent and consistent users of the space. Much of the time, they sat staring into space or dozed peacefully in the plaza's folding chairs, bothering no one. But interviews and direct observation in the plaza indicated that several of the men exerted an occasionally menacing presence within and around the plaza, throwing the tables and chairs, fighting, masturbating in public, and confronting other plaza users.

Other, less violent forms of disorder also plagued the plaza, some caused by poor planning, others by intentional misuse. The potted plants initially installed by the NYC DOT died within a week. When flowers were planted in their place, they were dug up and stolen, or sat upon and crushed. Several local businesses took to surreptitiously dumping their garbage in the plaza, in order to save the money and effort of contracting private waste disposal. In response to these issues, the NYPD fielded dozens of calls a day complaining about the condition of the space, some undoubtedly by residents and businesses that resented its very existence in the community. According to one of the plaza's advocates during this period, the NYPD became noticeably slower to respond after months of such complaints.

By spring of 2012, six months after the street closing, the physical and social condition of the plaza had deteriorated precipitously, and local opposition to the space had become a thorn in the side of the city officials who had endorsed the project. Late one evening, long after the street closing, I spoke with one of the project's discontents, a man in his midsixties who said he had been forced to close his newsstand because of the change in traffic patterns. He leaned against a lamppost, chain-smoking, barely able to contain his rage, and gestured scornfully toward the plaza, which was still humming with activity in spite of the late hour. "They make these decisions. They don't ask anyone. I used to sell hundreds of newspapers every morning. My business vanishes. And now look what you've got. Look at these assholes—drunks, drug users. Somebody is making money off this. But I lost everything." In the months after the street was closed to traffic, business owners mounted a public campaign against the plaza, threatening hunger strikes if the street were not reopened.

City officials disputed the charge that they had not done adequate outreach prior to the street closing. On paper, the space needed a pedestrian plaza. At one end of the block was a dangerous five-way intersection, and when they initially closed the street, NYC DOT planners had been primarily concerned with preventing traffic fatalities at this corner. According to Wiley-Schwartz of the NYC DOT's Public Space Unit, "the plaza was a straight safety play."[56] But the surrounding area also had many of the sociological ingredients necessary for a successful public space. The block had a constant flow of foot traffic, owing to the subway station in its center, and a vibrant mix of shops, cafés, and restaurants lined the street, drawing activity at various times of day—the classic traits of safe and lively public spaces.

The early problems of Diversity Plaza showed that these factors are not enough. For Laura Hansen, who heads the Neighborhood Plaza Partnership, a nonprofit that assists in the maintenance of the plazas, Diversity Plaza offered compelling evidence of the need for formal management and maintenance in creating effective public spaces: "Yes, you can have this beautiful design, but the minute you walk away, it starts to be used in all sorts of different ways, and the management of those uses is a day-in and day-out year-after-year commitment. And that's something I think is missing from the conversation."[57] Normally, under the formula devised by the NYC DOT, a partner organization would have handled this work. But the agency had alienated local merchants and underestimated the disorder that the plaza would attract. By summer 2012, the plaza that would later be named Diversity Plaza was a chaotic and, at times, menacing space that desperately needed a local sponsor, but that was unloved by the businesses and civic associations around it.

At this point, a pivotal sequence of events went into motion. Agha Saleh, a Pakistani man in his sixties and the co-owner of an internet café on the block, had initially been a vociferous critic of the plaza. However, as he tells it, he eventually resigned himself to the street closure and the new public space it created, deciding to help build support for the project among other business owners. Saleh started to meet with city officials to discuss a way to make the plaza work for the community, but the politics surrounding the project had become so toxic that Saleh held these negotiations in secret, far from Jackson Heights. Andrew Ronan, a NYC DOT official at the time, recalled meeting with Saleh in "cloak-and-dagger" fashion in a restaurant in Astoria, behind a partition that hid the participants from view. Eventually, Saleh won over several other business owners, created a nonprofit organization named SUKHI to manage the plaza, and signed a memorandum of understanding with the city staking out a role in the plaza's management.

The problem with Diversity Plaza was that although pedestrians moved through the space throughout the day, the combination of physical and social disorder kept many people away, preempting the day-to-day use that would make the plaza safer and more appealing. Saleh and Ronan saw the answer in the social identity of the neighborhood itself—an extraordinarily diverse community that is starved for public space. Jackson Heights has a Little Bangladesh, Little Pakistan, and Little India, each offering different varieties of South Asian food, music, clothing, jewelry, and culture. Himalayan restaurants serve *momo* (dumplings) and other regional specialties to the Nepali and Tibetan immigrants who live nearby. Elsewhere in the neighborhood, entire blocks are devoted to Colombian culture, while others are monopolized by "bailarina bars" where Mexican and Central American men buy dances for $2 per song. Still other blocks are dominated by the vibrant gay and lesbian nightlife that has long been a fixture of Jackson Heights. The plaza emerged as a space that served a purpose distinct from these demographically specific commercial corridors—a gathering place that is not symbolically dominated by any one social constituency, but rather offers a sort of crossroads, where the neighborhood's diversity is foregrounded and celebrated.

Ronan and Saleh seized upon this potential, coordinating their efforts with a group of local artists and residents who, though initially skeptical of the plaza's value, had formed in order to work toward its success, calling themselves Friends of Diversity Plaza. This local coalition made a conscious effort to rebrand the plaza as a public space where everyone is welcome, hosting public events that they hoped would draw hundreds of visitors to the

FIGURE 2.8. Diversity Plaza, on a fairly typical afternoon. On the far end of the plaza, a string of flags representing the nations of the world festoons the southern entrance to the plaza.
Photo credit: Jisun Reiner.

space. Each successful event, they reasoned, would help to counter the negative reputation of the space. Over the next several years, the plaza hosted a Christmas-tree lighting with musical accompaniment from a mariachi band, a concert by a Pakistani drum corps, a performance by a transgender Bengali dance troupe, and dozens of other unique cultural events. The plaza, in Ronan's words, "ratcheted up the sense of tolerance,"[58] capturing the plurality and hybridity that were already hallmarks of the neighborhood.

Perhaps just as consequential as these cultural events were civic occasions that brought together multiple constituencies working toward a common goal. Ronan succeeded in moving periodic meetings of the neighborhood's representative body into the plaza, where the typically insular and sparsely attended community board meetings could take place in the open, drawing hundreds of participants. During the 2012 presidential election, Saleh organized the public broadcast of one of the televised debates between candidates Barack Obama and Mitt Romney in the plaza. And at times of collective crisis or mourning, the plaza offered a place in which to seek information and emotional support. After a devastating earthquake hit Nepal in 2015, the plaza became a command center and a church for the many Nepali immigrants who live in the community, hosting eight days of vigils and coordinated relief efforts for the victims of the natural disaster.[59]

By 2016, the plaza had begun to receive broad recognition. Although it is rare for the city to rename a street after a concept rather than a person, in May 2016, Thirty-Seventh Street was officially renamed "Diversity Plaza" on the block that the plaza occupies. Two months later, *Time* magazine featured the plaza in a July 4th issue titled "240 Reasons to Celebrate America."[60] A two-page illustration attempts to capture the social milieu at the public space, down to the handwritten signs that Angel, the plaza's unhoused, self-appointed custodian, tapes to planters asking users not to sit on the flowers.

On the one hand, Ronan and Saleh's strategy worked. By rebranding the plaza and hosting frequent formal events and activities in the space, they had recast a problematic and controversial place as a unique cultural asset, changing the meanings attached to the plaza both inside and outside of the community. On the other hand, this transformation had come at an enormous cost in terms of time and effort. A small army of employees and volunteers works on behalf of the organizations that have partnered in support of Diversity Plaza to organize events, maintain the plaza, and suppress ongoing social disorder. Saleh eventually created a nonprofit organization to formally partner with the city and handle the work. "The challenges have been huge," he told me over the phone in late 2016. He continued:

> The problems will remain. . . . The plaza's partners are also the plaza's marshals. The public safety issues . . . the vagrants, the homelessness, the drunks—there are so many issues [that] are related to this plaza. Alone, SUKHI cannot eliminate every issue. But we can work together with other organizations for the development of this little block, because it holds the world.

For Saleh, programming and publicizing Diversity Plaza has been a necessary countermeasure to the social disorder that continues to plague the space. Far from the organic, naturally occurring social control espoused by Jane Jacobs and William H. Whyte, Diversity Plaza has required a concerted effort to build up and maintain the "eyes on the street" and devote formal maintenance to the space in order to make it safe, reasonably attractive, and viable. For this reason, Saleh argues, the history of the plaza should not be romanticized: "We are trying to communicate the best message to the rest of the world. But the inside story is also a heartbreaking story. There is a bright side to this, but there has also been a dark side, and to ignore the dark side would be an injustice."

Nearly six miles to the southwest of Diversity Plaza, in the Clinton Hill neighborhood of Brooklyn, lies a similarly conflicted public space. The controversies that have beset Diversity Plaza parallel those that have erupted around Putnam Plaza, a diminutive pedestrian area adjacent to Fulton Avenue, one of Brooklyn's main commercial corridors. The social and cultural context surrounding Putnam Plaza, however, is quite different. Walking down Fulton in either direction away from the plaza reveals a mix of new, high-end boutiques and coffee shops, as well as long-standing, independently owned businesses, like the Associated Supermarket, where a signed photograph of local hero Christopher Wallace (a.k.a. the rapper Biggie Smalls, or The Notorious B.I.G.) hangs proudly on the wall. The 1990s and early 2000s brought rapid gentrification to this historically Black neighborhood, sparking tension between longtime residents and the young White people moving into the community. When a six-year-old nonprofit organization called Fulton Avenue Businesses (FAB), itself somewhat controversial, sponsored the creation of Putnam Plaza, some locals saw a conspiracy between FAB and the NYC DOT to create a public amenity that would raise local property values and further gentrify the area.[61]

Among the most vocal objectors to the plaza was Schellie Hagen, a resident of the neighborhood and a fierce antigentrification activist. Hagen organized a petition opposing the plaza and filmed a series of short documentary films criticizing the project. Hagen is well connected in the neighborhood and built her case through dozens of interviews with residents and business owners who were skeptical of the plaza project, punctuating her cinematography with satirical flourishes. In one of her films, an interview is followed by a surrealist animated sequence in which the storefront restaurants, cafés, and bodegas adjacent to the plaza are demolished in a cloud of dust and smoke. A luxury high-rise emblazoned with the NYC DOT logo, surrounded by manicured landscaping, rises from the debris, symbolizing what Hagen viewed as an attempt to replace mom-and-pop businesses with high-end development for "the 1%." "The plaza will knock out those little stores," Hagen told me over the phone in July of 2016. "The BID promised it would boost business, but it's going to knock them out. Eventually, you'll have new development. That's what it's all about."

Even as Putnam Plaza came under fire as an implement of gentrification, some of the plaza's critics viewed it as a very different kind of threat. Grand

Avenue, which runs along one side of the triangle, has long been the site of a vigorous local drug trade.[62] The plaza itself was created on the site of a traffic island that, according to residents of the neighborhood, was often used as a site for drug deals. As in other cases across New York City, critics raised the prospect that the plaza would exacerbate existing social disorder by giving it a home. Like Agha Saleh and Andrew Ronan in the case of Diversity Plaza, the chief public advocate of Putnam Plaza sought to change the public perception of the space in order to change its reality. Before the street was even closed, Phillip Kellogg, director of the organization that sponsored the plaza, chose the site for a Christmas-tree giveaway:

> We decided to do it there because of the transformative power of changing the activity that is associated with the place. We had a two-day event planned. We gave away all the trees in two hours. You had this area that was notorious for all the wrong reasons, with a couple hundred people lined up around the corner waiting to take their tree home. It was a beautiful festive thing. It proved that the community would welcome something like a plaza. . . . It was only after that that we applied to the plaza program.[63]

After the street was closed and the NYC DOT placed tables and chairs at the site, however, neighbors complained that it was periodically taken over by people who were drinking or dealing drugs, and remained desolate and uninviting at other times. In response, Kellogg has devoted the majority of his organization's programming budget to organizing a series of events at the plaza, trying, like Ronan and Saleh, to change both its public image and its uses:

> The plaza is not waving a magic wand—it doesn't make that stuff go away. We continue to deal with it. Putnam needs the energy that programming brings. . . . Drug dealers don't like to be there when there's 250 kids singing along with a children's performer. . . . You drive foot traffic to the area and you've got more eyes on the street. It tells the drug dealers that they don't own it anymore.

Nevertheless, in 2015, when Kellogg's organization, FAB, unveiled a final design for the plaza's construction, the physical form of the space reflected its troubled recent history. A shade tree at the center of the plaza was removed, Kellogg explained, because it blocked sightlines through the plaza. The amount of lighting in the plaza was increased dramatically, for the same reasons. And the new benches installed in the plaza would not be placed "where people might want to hang out—we're putting them where they're more exposed and visible." Through a combination of physical and social programming, in other words, Kellogg hoped to redefine the space in a way that made it look and feel safer, thus converting perception to reality.

Inkblot Urbanism

In neighborhood after neighborhood, the Plaza Program produced interesting sociological side effects. Many of the people I spoke to about the program were quick to emphasize the importance of the local social and economic context to the success of any given plaza. The urban sociologists who inspired the program celebrate the resilience of informal urbanism— the ability of the city's people to bring order to the public realm, if given the space to do so. The experience of the Plaza Program suggests that the reality is somewhat messier.

The seven cases I investigated in detail reflected a broader variety in the Plaza Program across the city, which was strongly shaped by socioeconomic variations across neighborhoods. In affluent Manhattan communities, the local partners who took on management and maintenance of the newly created spaces were typically BIDs funded by local property owners, who (not coincidentally) might stand to profit from the creation of a vibrant public space. Flush with financial resources and well staffed, these organizations were easily capable of keeping the plazas clean and orderly. In the less well-to-do neighborhoods, on the other hand, the community organizations charged with day-to-day maintenance lacked the capacity to clean and monitor the new plazas. This gap in resources was exacerbated by the prevalence of poverty and homelessness within the neighborhoods where some plazas were created. A new plaza on 125th street in Harlem was filled with mattresses and shopping carts within a week of being opened, and the benches of another new plaza, near Penn Station, instantaneously became a refuge for the unhoused people who take shelter in and around the transit hub. The spatial inequality that exists between neighborhoods was reflected in the street-level reality of the newly created plazas.

The cases discussed here, however, suggest that the socioeconomic variability of New York City neighborhoods does not tell the whole story. A set of essentially similar proposals to convert underutilized parking lots and traffic lanes into public seating areas elicited a wide variety of qualitatively distinct responses. In each neighborhood, the prospect of creating a new public space created a miniature drama that played out on a local stage, against a backdrop of community board meetings, neighborhood blog posts and newspaper articles, and street-corner conversation and debate. In these discussions, the same basic objects—folding chairs, café tables, and planters—were cast in a wildly different light depending on the neighborhood and the speaker in question. It can be argued that this interpretive flexibility is due to the nature of the objects themselves. A public plaza presents a range of behavioral options, and this openness encourages dystopian as well as aspirational thinking. As noted at the start of this chapter, an empty folding chair invites the unknown.

But the range of local reactions to this ambiguity provides insight into how we collectively respond to any new public object. In each neighborhood where a plaza was proposed, it served as a sort of inkblot test, revealing the unique social tensions and aspirations within that neighborhood, which in turn reflect the surrounding community's cultural outlook and social structure. New public objects, by offering novel affordances, prompt a form of collective introspection—they lead members of a community to think about and articulate a conception of self in the process of developing a response. When a new object, place, or space appears in our neighborhood, it says to us, *this is for you*, offering a challenge of sorts. Reacting to this assertion requires answering a set of implicit or explicit questions: *Do we want this? Do we need this?* And, by extension: *Who are we?* In a place like New York, neighborhoods' answers to these questions reflect the full diversity of the city's urban mosaic, variations in demographics, local history and culture, and different trajectories of social and economic change.

In the case of Corona and Washington Heights, the appearance of a flexible public space revealed these neighborhoods' underlying capacity for social cohesion and generalized trust, bringing even historically marginalized groups—male laborers, teenagers, undocumented immigrants—into a spatial manifestation of community. In Sheepshead Bay and Midwood, public seating areas were viewed as threats to local social order. A pedestrian plaza in the heart of these neighborhoods would deprive local stakeholders of their ability to control the movements of unhoused residents or teenage high-school students and, in doing so, remove an important tool with which to police the social boundaries within. In the cases of Jackson Heights and Clinton Hill, the image that emerged from the Rorschach test applied by the Neighborhood Plaza Program was more complicated—in these communities, simmering social disorder and resentment coincide with a desire to celebrate diversity and cultural vitality.

These examples remind us that the material world is irreducibly local. The very process of perception, comprehension, and interaction through which we make sense of new objects is inflected with social meanings that belong to a specific place and time. In the case of the folding chair, collective reactions were freighted with conceptions of community and collective identity, as well as long-standing traditions of ambivalence concerning people who linger or "loiter," remaining rooted in place amid the ceaseless movement of the city. A large body of research has shown how new technologies are socially "constructed," but this chapter shows that this process extends to very old technologies as well, when they appear within a defined social space. In a metal folding chair on a beige patch of pavement, New Yorkers perceived their collective hopes and anxieties reflected back. For some, what they saw was comforting, reminiscent of a former home in another country, or a future in which the neighborhood itself could become more of a home. Others, when envisioning a space for people to gather and sit in the heart of their neighborhood, did not like what they saw. Flexible public space is an expression of trust in urban society. But not all communities trust themselves.

PART II

Disruption

3

The Traffic Divider

FIGURE 3.1. The traffic divider.

Between the westbound and eastbound lanes of New Jersey's Route 30, locally referred to as "White Horse Pike," sits an unadorned traffic divider made of dirty white concrete. Linked to a countless number of identical dividers, it forms a short, stout wall that stretches as far as the eye can see in either direction, unbroken by crosswalks or intersections. No famous architect or designer is responsible for this wall. It owes its existence to a faceless bureaucracy—the New Jersey Department of Transportation (NJDOT). Nor does the wall have a sophisticated aesthetic or ideological agenda. The social program of the wall is straightforward and obvious. Named after the state where it was invented and, coincidentally, where it is currently deployed, the task of this "Jersey barrier" is to insert a waist-high buffer of concrete between two lanes of traffic, preventing head-on collisions.[1] Rigidly steadfast in its work, the wall is a brutal, utilitarian complement to the sleek machinery of modern travel. Its job is to protect us from ourselves. The divider acts on a symbolic as well as a material level to control motorists' behavior. Like a painted double yellow line, it tells us to stay in our lanes, but the wall backs up this message with coercive physical mass. Crossing a double yellow could result in a traffic ticket and a fine, if a police officer is on hand. The wall promises far worse, and enforces its own directives.

To the extent that it is successful in its task, the wall is not particularly interesting. As a basic, functional component of transportation infrastructure, it epitomizes the type of object that is probably safe for us to ignore. Sociologists are often vexed by the relationship between structure and agency, but not in the case of the wall. When it does what it is supposed to do, it is all structure, and seemingly has no agency at all. By channeling drivers safely toward their destinations, the wall simply guides social processes wherever they will go.

The intended beneficiaries of this object are the motorists on White Horse Pike. However, according to my fieldnotes from a warm, early summer evening in 2010, this particular wall has a different type of "user," if the term is appropriate in this case:

> A Latino man in his late 40s named Junior is sitting on the wall. Headed home from his job bussing tables at a nearby restaurant, he perches on the narrow crown of the wall, one foot dangling on the eastbound side of the road, the other remaining in the westbound side. As I watch from the relative safety of the highway's shoulder, Junior pauses for a moment, straddling the barrier as if on horseback, while waiting for a break in the stream of traffic between us. A gap appears between a sedan and a minivan, and he sees his opportunity. Sliding his right leg over the top of the wall, he jogs nonchalantly across the traffic lanes, ignoring a short burst from the horn of the oncoming minivan. "See?" he says when he arrives, slightly out of breath. "Not so hard."

At the point where Junior crossed the wall, two budget motels lie immediately on one side of the road, and a discount store, an automotive supply chain, and a restaurant are on the other. Similar businesses line both sides of the roadway, to the east and west. If one waits long enough on a summer evening such as this one—forty-five minutes to an hour, judging from my notes—one will see a pedestrian, individually or as part of a group, cross the road and climb over the wall, as Junior did, to get from one of these businesses to another, or to cross to a bus stop.

For these pedestrians, the primary significance of the wall is neither straightforward nor obvious. The motor-vehicle traffic is impressive both in its velocity and in its volume. The posted speed limit is forty miles per hour, but many motor vehicles are traveling faster than this—in some cases, judging from the roar of their engines and the rapidity with which they pass into the distance, much faster. Although rush hour is over, impatient motorists continue to speed toward home or other destinations, thirty or forty feet separating one vehicle from the next. Crossing the road under these conditions is not merely inconvenient but fraught with danger. For pedestrians, the primary relevance of the divider is that it complicates an already difficult and perilous task. It represents a bulky cement hurdle at the halfway point of what has to be a well-timed crossing of perhaps a hundred feet of asphalt, spanning six lanes of traffic. The wall requires that the pedestrian slow his or her pace in the center of the road, at the precise position of greatest risk, where several feet of precious space separate one's body from the hulks of metal hurtling past on either side. For a person who needs to cross the road on foot, the wall is the opposite of functional. It is stubbornly obstructionist. Its agency sits in plain view, amid the blur of passing cars.

The difficulty posed by the wall, however, is entirely accidental. The height and weight of the Jersey barrier and its physical contours are intended not to complicate road crossings but to reduce the damage caused to a vehicle upon impact. In this sense, its role as pedestrian obstacle does not reflect intentional design so much as a sort of error in translation. When a person is forced to climb the wall, a programmatic conflict exists in this encounter between human and object—an incompatibility between the object's intended function and the needs of a user. This kind of conflict is actually the opposite of an affordance. For pedestrian users of this space, the wall does not suggest or accommodate a behavioral option. It complicates and frustrates a course of action that is, or at least might be, inevitable. Given all of this, it is it almost surprising that the divider was *not* created out of overt hostility toward Junior, and the many other people forced to navigate this place on foot. But instead of any personal animus, it conveys mute, unyielding indifference—an indication that one is in the wrong place.

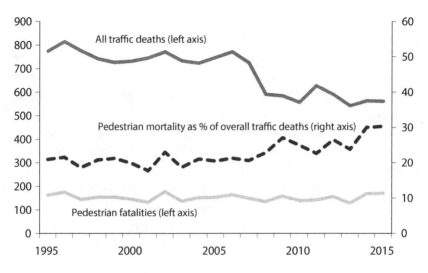

FIGURE 3.2. New Jersey traffic deaths, 1995–2015.
Source data from the Fatal Accident Reporting System (FARS).

What brought me to this nondescript location in 2010, as well as other similar sites in southern and central New Jersey, were indications that an unsettlingly large number of people were similarly out of place on the state's suburban roadways. In the year before, 158 pedestrians were fatally struck by automobiles in New Jersey—one of the highest annual death tolls since the mid-1990s. To be clear, the figure did not signal that pedestrian deaths were trending upward in the state. Instead, it showed that they were stubbornly refusing to drop. Traffic fatalities overall had been on the decline across the country for decades, propelled by improvements in automotive safety features, increased seat-belt use, and reduced drunk driving. In New Jersey, pedestrian risk was bucking this trend. For the first time since the early 1990s, when reliable traffic fatality statistics began to be collected, more than one of every four people killed in traffic accidents was on foot when struck by a motor vehicle. This proportion continued to rise in the ensuing years: by 2015, it was approaching one in three.

The story of pedestrian risk in New Jersey's suburbs is, like all of the narratives in this book, a story of troublesome objects. But unlike the objects and places discussed in the previous two chapters, which create trouble simply by being new and ambiguous, the objects in this section of the book create trouble by disrupting human needs and desires. In the sprawling suburbs of the United States, a history of uncontrolled development has produced public spaces that, increasingly, conflict with the needs of many of the people who move through these spaces. The affordances of this built environment reflect a strong set of expectations about human behavior—assumptions that are embedded in asphalt, concrete, and steel. In recent decades, they have been violated more and more often, with dire consequences for low-income inhabitants of suburban built space. The accidental public spaces of the sprawling suburbs—overlooked and uncategorized areas in the margins of an environment built for the automobile—have become places not just of inconvenience for people who cannot afford a motor vehicle, but of injury and death.

In the chapter that follows I tell this story, drawing on archival records to reconstruct the social and material conditions that led to fatal encounters between people and things on New Jersey's suburban streets. However, to explain the state's stubbornly high pedestrian risk in recent years, it turned out, I had only to look around me, at the landscape of the White Horse Pike. New Jersey has many such places, where the built environment is hostile to pedestrian use. And it has a growing population of people who, like Junior, are forced by financial necessity to traverse these landscapes on foot. To understand how things came to be this way, it is necessary to look backward and outward, to the period following World War II, when a wave of suburban expansion led to the proliferation of places like this. And to grasp how things might be resolved, we have to look forward, to the range of options available when objects and humans come into observable conflict.

Accidental Public Space

White Horse Pike is a roughly linear conglomeration of asphalt, cement, and steel, that cuts a fifty-five-mile southeasterly path through the forest and marshland of Camden and Atlantic counties. The road is flanked for much of its length by retail businesses, isolated or clustered in strip malls, along with the occasional residential development. This landscape has many functions, which are jammed together and juxtaposed along the sides of the road and then advertised to passing motorists. Comprising many moving and nonmoving objects, each with its own story to tell, the White Horse Pike was produced collectively and gradually, through a sort of unplanned accretion of material elements. The road is not a masterwork of urban planning so much as it is an accident of history. But White Horse Pike and its surroundings are no less consequential—no less "political"—simply because they were unintended.[2] A look back at the history of suburban development helps to explain how this problematic place came to be.

The White Horse Pike was built in the mid-nineteenth century, during an age when toll roads were extended deep into rural areas by private authorities.[3] Like many such turnpikes, the road served as a conduit connecting a metropolis to a popular resort area, linking the city of Philadelphia with the casinos and beaches of Atlantic City. The White Horse Pike's first travelers were borne by horse-drawn carriages rather than by buses and cars, but later the road lent itself to the automobile. Graded, smooth, and direct, it was ideal for high-speed travel by private motor vehicle. What was once a two-day carriage ride to Atlantic City now became a two-hour drive. A summer vacation at the beach became a weekend trip. Western Atlantic County drew within commuting distance from Philadelphia or Camden, New Jersey, a thriving industrial city in the early 1900s. In the 1910s and 1920s, as automobile ownership grew, the White Horse Pike, along with a newly built sister road, Black Horse Pike, opened a vast expanse of southern New Jersey farmland and forest to residential development.[4] In this way, the roads created their own geographic and social context—a sprawling landscape of satellite communities, motels, and roadside stands, all predicated on the private motor vehicle.

The Great Depression and World War II slowed suburban development in Atlantic County, but in the late 1940s real-estate developers funneled resources into the area, aided by a massive federal investment in the nation's expanding suburbs. As in other parts of the country, newly built suburban communities in southern New Jersey were promoted through the association of the automobile with homeownership. Buying a motor vehicle and a home in the suburbs went hand in hand, part of a middle-class lifestyle that emphasized independence and convenience. Advertisers successfully linked this lifestyle with a broader array of cultural themes, including patriotism, upward mobility, and domesticity.[5] But in spite of the public resonance of the expanding suburbs, private home builders, rather than home buyers or government agencies, charted the course of the resulting development. Developers sought out the most inexpensive land in order to maximize profit, a logic that led to a proliferation of haphazard development outside of urban centers, or, more colloquially, suburban sprawl.[6] Seeded by federal subsidies and the availability of cheap forest and farmland, residential communities sprouted up along the White Horse and Black Horse Pikes, like cultures in a petri dish.

In the early 1950s, the federal government made another policy change that shaped the material landscape of White Horse Pike and similar roads across the country. Developers were offered a federal tax incentive to build roadside commercial buildings. They responded by constructing restaurants and retail structures on inexpensive plots of land, that were often far from residential communities, in order to maximize their return on the tax benefit. New businesses cropped up along arterial roads such as the turnpikes, rather than in nearby town centers with restrictive zoning codes and dwindling pedestrian activity.[7] In the 1950s and 1960s, the Garden State Parkway and Atlantic City Expressway opened, making the White Horse and Black Horse Pikes redundant in their role as high-speed conduits to the Jersey shore. Consequently, the character of the two roads became even more commercial in nature.

This embedded an odd paradox in the landscape of the two roads. They were material spaces designed to accommodate high-speed, linear movement over long distances. But they would now also perform the commercial and civic functions traditionally served by dense, downtown areas. The White Horse and Black Horse Pikes retained physical reminders of their status as expressways, even as they were repurposed as commercial corridors. These four-lane roads, with typical speed limits of forty-five to fifty-five miles per hour, were now lined with hotels, restaurants, and retail businesses. In a functional contradiction that no rational urban planner would have chosen, a space to drive at high speed would be crammed together with places to shop, work, and live.

Many decades later, the legacies of this process are contradictory and accidental public spaces. In places like the White Horse and Black Horse Pikes, the twin behavioral imperatives that powered the postwar economy—driving and consumption—are reflected in a sort of fun-house mirror, exaggerated and merged in a nonsensical manner.[8] Motorists travelling at high speed are required to decelerate rapidly and turn into congested parking lots and onto side roads. Roadside signs compete for the attention of these drivers, inviting them to make a spontaneous stop for coffee, or attempting to convince them, within a fraction of a second, that they need a lobster dinner, a fountain for their front yard, a home equity loan, a new mattress.

Meanwhile, the landscape contains outdoor public spaces that were never conceived as such by their creators. Anemic and unplanned, these public spaces occupy the margins and interstices of this landscape—the edges of parking lots, the verges and fringes along the road, nameless and purposeless chunks of land necessitated by the geometry of the turnpikes. Crosswalks are infrequent and sidewalks almost nonexistent. But this strange landscape is practically the only place in the vicinity to shop, to work, and, for many, to live. A physical environment singularly hostile to pedestrians contains stores, restaurants, and hotels that might theoretically generate a substantial amount of foot traffic. All that is needed for this landscape to pose a serious public health problem is a population forced to navigate this landscape on foot.

Places vs. People

In recent decades, the pedestrians have arrived. America's suburbs are increasingly home to people who lack the financial resources to own and maintain a private motor vehicle. A trend of economic decline is affecting suburban communities across the country, introducing changes in the way suburban spaces are used. Initially, postwar suburbia enjoyed upward mobility and sustained affluence, but in the 1980s suburban demographics began to change. Per capita income leveled off, and pockets of suburban poverty proliferated. Since 2000, this process has extended from "inner-ring" suburbs in large metropolitan areas to a wider range of suburban communities.[9]

By 2010, when Junior and I crossed the White Horse Pike together, demographers at prominent think tanks and academic research institutions were sounding the alarm. America was witnessing the "suburbanization of poverty."[10] In fact, the majority of America's poor now live in the nation's suburbs. Ironically, suburban poverty is increasing in precisely those communities that were built in the 1950s and 1960s to offer a desirable middle-class lifestyle to postwar suburban home buyers. While planners and private developers have reconfigured gentrifying urban neighborhoods to make them more inviting to a white-collar workforce, postwar suburbs have become increasingly hard places to live.[11] In 2010, Atlantic County's poverty rate ticked upward sharply and was approaching 14 percent. Suburban spaces like the White Horse Pike were on the leading edge of a national trend.

In January 2010, as a flurry of newspaper headlines brought New Jersey's pedestrian fatality "epidemic" into the public eye, I drove south from my home in New York City. I was headed toward an area of the state that had been identified as an epicenter for pedestrian risk by the Tri-State Transportation Campaign, a prominent regional advocacy group. After passing through Staten Island via the Verrazano Bridge and the Outerbridge Crossing, I drove about ninety miles south on the Garden State Parkway, watching the dirt on the sides of the road turn to sand as the highway edged closer to the Jersey Shore. I turned off of the parkway at exit 36, and abruptly found myself on the Black Horse Pike, where I swerved to avoid three teenage boys:

The boys, two wearing backpacks, had darted across the road from the side of a highway overpass that hid them from view. I pulled off the road into a parking lot and looked around me, a bit shaken up. On one side of the road were a community food bank, a soup kitchen, and a trailer park. On the other side were an automobile dealer and a gas station.

I had come to Atlantic County to gain a ground-level view of the state's pedestrian risk problem, and it had taken me less than five minutes to get right to the heart of the matter.

In the years that followed, to achieve a more detailed understanding of the conditions that led to fatal crashes in Atlantic County, I immersed myself in a morbid form of detective work, attempting a variation on what sociologist Eric Klinenberg refers to as "social autopsy."[12] I gathered as much data as I could from a variety of sources on every pedestrian death that occurred over a nine-year period (2005–13) in the county.[13] I developed short narrative accounts of each of these seventy-eight fatalities, including a description of the immediate location of the incident, biographical information on the victim, and an account of his or her activity at the time that the incident occurred. My working hypothesis was that the localized combination of poverty and automobile-centered planning was likely to explain high pedestrian mortality rates in suburban Atlantic County. Residents or workers who were not able to afford motor vehicles would be most likely to traverse this hostile landscape on foot, putting them in harm's way. The many deaths on local roads in recent years, I surmised, were caused by programmatic conflict—an incompatibility between the resources and needs of low-income suburban residents and the material affordances of the built environment.

Public-health research, however, provided a variety of alternate explanations that help to explain high pedestrian fatality rates across the country. Demographic factors, such as age,[14] and race or ethnicity,[15] are linked with elevated pedestrian risk. But the evidence I had compiled did not support these factors in the case of Atlantic County.[16] Alcohol use is to blame in many fatal traffic incidents, and inebriation on the part of drivers or pedestrians also seemed important to consider, in light of Atlantic City's casinos and nightlife.[17] Again, the data did not point strongly in this direction.[18] Instead, my records of pedestrian deaths suggested a spatial and material account of risk—an explanation rooted in problematic objects and places.[19] The vast majority of Atlantic County's deceased pedestrians were killed while walking in the road's shoulder, or while attempting to cross,[20] in areas with high

FIGURE 3.3. Quotidian violence. Along the sides of White Horse and Black Horse Pikes, mixed in with improvised pedestrian spaces, are constant reminders that motor vehicles frequently stray from the road without notice. Bent metal, broken glass, and skid marks are commonplace. More than 60 percent of Atlantic County's fatal incidents occurred in areas where the speed limit was 45 mph or above. This aligns with the insight from accident research that the likelihood of a pedestrian dying increases substantially at higher motor-vehicle speeds.
This image previously appeared in an article published in *City & Community*, June 1, 2018, © American Sociological Association, available online: https://doi.org/10.1111/cico.12302.

speed limits.[21] Areas directly adjacent to shopping centers and bus stops emerged as focal points of violence.[22] Fully half of the crashes occurred along two major roads, the Black Horse Pike and the White Horse Pike. Fatal incidents were arrayed along these two arteries, clustering in locations where they crossed through high-poverty census tracts. The material configuration of place, this empirical exercise suggested, was a key to the geography of pedestrian deaths. The Black Horse and White Horse Pikes accommodated retail and commercial businesses, but they offered no physical accommodation to the pedestrians who relied on these establishments for work or habitation. People frequently died here, not principally because of their demography or their lifestyle, but because the place itself, like the wall discussed at the start of this chapter, was brutally indifferent to their needs.

I then investigated the socioeconomic status of the people who had been killed in Atlantic County over the nine-year period. Although no income data were available on victims, medical examiner's reports, newspaper articles, and obituaries mentioned occupation in many of the cases. Heavily represented were service workers. Construction worker was the most common occupational category among male victims. The occupations of the female victims were also largely service-sector jobs: casino workers, waitresses, department-store cashiers, nursing students, and a post-office clerk. In general, my data painted a consistent picture of the pedestrians as working poor residents employed in low-wage occupations—jobs that provided enough income to sustain a residential arrangement in private suburban housing, but not enough to afford a private automobile. The short narratives that I compiled revealed how the material and social dimensions of place come together to pose a lethal risk to everyday users of the Black Horse and White Horse Pikes. Public objects and public spaces are implicated in these accounts, as are the economic resources and the practical needs of the people involved. The following two stories are illustrative.

During a two-month period in late 2005 and early 2006, two pedestrians were killed in the same short stretch of the Black Horse Pike—a location where four other fatal accidents had occurred between 1998 and 2005.[23] The Black Horse Pike in this location consists of four lanes separated by a wide cement and dirt median. A dimly lit bus stop sits on the eastbound side of the road, which leads to Atlantic City. Directly across the street is the Pleasantville Shopping Center, a medium-sized shopping mall containing a Kmart, a Family Dollar discount store, a Dunkin' Donuts, and the Asia Supermarket, a large grocery store specializing in Chinese food items. At 7:30 p.m. on a Saturday in late fall of 2005, Emily Spencer, a forty-eight-year-old cashier at the Kmart, got off work. Spencer lived approximately ten miles away, in Galloway Township. By crossing the Black Horse Pike and waiting at the public bus stop across from the shopping center, Spencer could catch a public bus into Pleasantville, where she could connect to another bus to the neighborhood where she lived. Leaving work on the early winter night, Spencer was wearing dark clothes as she attempted to cross the westbound lanes to get to the bus stop. The driver of a sports utility vehicle with New York plates did not see Spencer and knocked her a hundred feet down the road where, according to police reports, she was hit by at least two other vehicles. She was pronounced dead at the scene.

At 6:45 p.m. on a Tuesday evening approximately forty days later, Juan Rodriguez, a construction worker by occupation, was crossing the same stretch of road after having dinner at a Mexican restaurant. Rodriguez, forty-two, had immigrated to the United States from Mexico, obtained citizenship, and moved to Atlantic City with his wife. The location of the accident suggests that Rodriguez, like Spencer, was trying to get to the Atlantic City–bound bus stop. A sixty-two-year-old male driver from nearby Egg Harbor Township had just passed a green light when Rodriguez attempted to cross the road. The automobile knocked Rodriguez forward and then swerved to avoid striking him a second time, but according to the police report he was likely to have died upon the initial impact.

As these narratives suggest, Spencer and Rodriguez appear to have had little in common, sharing nothing apart from their reliance on a public bus stop on the side of the Black Horse Pike. The closest crosswalks to the bus stop are several hundred yards in either direction. The speed limit is forty-five miles per hour in this stretch of roadway. Street lamps are infrequent here, the periphery dark at night. Spencer and Rodriguez inhabited a landscape that was largely blind and deaf to their needs, calibrated for someone else. The asphalt expanse, the concrete median, the dusty fringe where there might have been a sidewalk, the yawning intersection where there might have been a crosswalk—these objects embed behavioral assumptions related to socioeconomic class in the durable material fabric of place. The affordances of this space negate the very possibility of life here without a car. They assume users to be behind the wheel, rather than crossing on foot or walking in the margins. Spencer and Rodriguez violated this assumption, along with seventy-six other people over an eight-year span, and for this they paid a terrible cost.

Life in the Margins

Between 2010 and 2013, I visited Atlantic County eleven times, driving its roads, walking its streets, and interviewing the county's workers and residents. These visits revealed people who, by necessity, moved through an environment of tangible physical risk. Navigating this landscape on foot required a combination of improvisation and sacrifice. On a humid evening in July 2010, I observed an elderly man carrying a large shopping bag down the shoulder of the Black Horse Pike. He was sweating through a white windbreaker that he was wearing, in spite of the heat, to avoid being hit during his twice-daily trip to the bus stop, a twenty-minute walk from his house. His niece had been struck by a sports utility vehicle the year before, and had spent nearly a month in the hospital recovering from a severe concussion.

Elsewhere, I found signs of attempts to adapt the built environment to pedestrian needs. At a spot between two distant intersections, someone had cut an irregular opening in a fence with pliers, permitting me (along with a construction worker walking home from work) to step through the hole and cross from a shopping area on one side of the road to a bus stop on the other. In the grassy margins adjacent to the shoulder of the White Horse Pike, pedestrians had worn a dusty path, creating a sidewalk where neither private developers nor state traffic engineering standards had regarded one as necessary. At several of the bare-bones bus stops on Black Horse Pike, riders had flipped grocery carts on their sides and left them in the dirt to serve as improvised benches.

In general, however, the landscape was immune to improvised safety measures and resistant to modification. In many areas along White Horse Pike, pedestrians were denied even the areas along the sides of the road by natural or manmade obstructions. In these areas, they occupied the asphalt shoulders of the highway, walking among pieces of shredded tire rubber and pieces of broken safety glass and plastic taillight, remnants of the quotidian violence that accompanies high-speed automobile traffic. A field visit to White Horse Pike in the early twilight of a winter afternoon revealed a team of four hotel cleaners in uniforms, two of them apparently elderly women, climbing a cement barrier and hurrying across four windswept lanes of high-speed traffic to move from one place of part-time employment, a budget motel, to another, an auto dealership. While formal and informal transportation systems—specifically, several public bus lines as well as informal ride-sharing arrangements—permit residents without automobiles to travel safely through many areas of Atlantic County, the built space of these roadways greets pedestrians with near complete inflexibility, forcing users to sacrifice ease of movement, or physical safety, or both.

My field visits revealed an important insight that I could not have come by through detached statistical or spatial analysis. Importantly, this landscape does not just impose risk on its pedestrian users, it offers constant reminders of their subordination within the system of social categories (consumer/service worker, driver/pedestrian) around which the environment is organized. In this case, marginalization is literal as well as metaphorical, material as well as social. Occupying the shoulder of a highway is dangerous, but it also communicates, in no uncertain terms, where one stands in a social

FIGURE 3.4. Fear lines. White Horse Pike is lined with dusty footpaths that run through grassy margins and fringes, highlighting the need for sidewalks that do not exist. Urban planners refer to these signs of an unmet pedestrian need as "desire lines," but the term does not seem appropriate in this place. The worn-out tracks in the soil convey an effort by pedestrians to put space between themselves and the high-speed traffic of the highway, and say more about a concern for personal safety than aspiration. The footpath in figure 3.4 was obstructed by a thicket of roadside signs just behind the camera's position, forcing pedestrians out into the unprotected shoulder of the highway.

FIGURE 3.4. (*continued*)

hierarchy that is produced and reflected by the material configuration of the place. A passage from my notes describing a June 2015 field visit illustrates this dimension of life in the margins of a high-speed arterial road:

> I stood on a patch of dirt on the side of Black Horse Pike that serves as a bus stop. There was no seating available, so my companions, an unemployed bartender and a cook at a nearby fast food restaurant, were sitting on the ground when heavy gray rain clouds rolled in. The bartender was on her way to her grandmother's house for dinner, and had left her home, a mere 21 miles away, more than two hours earlier. After walking a mile and a half and taking two buses, she still had another 30-minute bus ride ahead.
>
> As large raindrops began to fall in the dust and a peal of thunder suggested worse to come, I retreated several hundred feet away to the overhanging roof of a gas station, along with the six or seven other people at the bus stop. A few minutes later, the sky opened up, and sheets of cold rain kept us pinned under the overhang when the bus arrived. Already 16 minutes late, the bus cruised by the bus stop at what appeared to be at least 30 or 40 miles per hour, as there was nobody there to hail the bus. Two of the people waiting alongside me were brave enough to chase after the bus and received nothing in return but drenched clothing, while

a disabled military veteran standing next to me spit a series of color-ful invective into the rain. The next bus would not come for nearly 40 minutes. A series of apparently unrelated inconveniences—the lack of shelter, the speed of traffic on the pike, the infrequency of service—had conspired against us, revealing that these inconveniences were, in fact, related after all.

This experience, and many others, showed me that beneath the discrete moments of risk captured in mortality statistics, there exists an entire world of inconvenience and humiliation for the pedestrian users of this space. Historically, spatial relationships within a given place have been used to concretize and signify social hierarchies: the upstairs/downstairs logic of the Victorian manor, or the front/back logic of Jim Crow laws in the American South. On White Horse and Black Horse Pikes, a similar relationship holds between central and marginal spaces. To motorists, Atlantic County offers reasonably direct routes through space and the ability to choose one's own schedule. From unemployed bartenders and other people reliant on the area's anemic public bus system, the landscape demands a haphazard, rec-tilinear slog, interrupted by gaps in the bus schedule and long walks on the sides of highways, all while surrounded by the road dust and noise generated by more-affluent users of the space. The pedestrian deaths I investigated were only empirical traces of more subtle indignities imposed by program-matic conflict on the low-income users of the pikes on an everyday basis.

In another field visit in late spring of 2015, I spent an entire day walking Black Horse Pike, travelling seven miles down its length, utilizing the worn pathways on the side of the road, as I had seen others do during my field visits. Travelling on foot through this landscape, the danger of being struck by a motor vehicle is impossible to ignore. But I also found that it induced another, unanticipated sensation—a sense of cognitive disorientation produced by bodily proximity to a deafening stream of high-speed traffic. This sensory experience is compounded by a lack of spaces and objects that visibly shelter pedestrians or, alternatively, that imbue the surrounding environment with a comforting kind of meaning, telling them where to stand or walk.

Late in the day, as I stood in the glass-strewn shoulder of Black Horse Pike with a retired casino worker, waiting for the bus back to my hotel, the entire environment seemed to vibrate with programmatic conflict. In the center of the road was a traffic divider like the one described at the beginning of this chapter, and it occurred to me that it was far from alone—its message was

FIGURE 3.5. Life in the margins. Many of the fatal crashes along White Horse and Black Horse Pikes occurred at or near bus stops. The man pictured here was on his way home after working a shift as a security guard, a job that involved being on foot for hours at a time. The bus stop offered no seating aside from an overturned shopping cart that appeared to have been left there for that purpose.

reinforced by objects on all sides that clashed with our psychological and physiological needs. Endless parking lots were punctuated by enormous signs. Every break in the curb was a space of enhanced danger, where at any moment an automobile might make a frenzied escape from the highway. The scale was wrong, as was the speed at which objects moved. There were no sidewalks or striped crosswalks. No white figures or flashing red hands to signal right of way. The environment was incoherent and menacing.[24] A dangerous foreign land.

How Things Change

Anthropologist Susan Leigh Star observed that material infrastructure becomes visible when it breaks.[25] The same can be said for moments when human needs arise that are poorly served by the objects around us. According to philosopher Martin Heidegger, things become "conspicuous" not just when they fail to serve their intended purpose but when we need to do things that are not suited to the material objects that are at hand.[26] In the remainder of this chapter, I look at how local and state officials attempted to address the problem of pedestrian risk once it became visible and, in political terms, unavoidable. Although policy and planning are not the principal subjects of this book, they bear heavily on the interactions between people, places, and things that are its main preoccupation, by (re)programming the built environment and shaping the affordances it offers to human users.

When pedestrian deaths rose in New Jersey in the late 2000s, the attention of state and local officials turned to the places where pedestrians had lost their lives. It is typical for the media to treat car crashes as idiosyncratic—tragic moments of human or technical error. But in this case, the frequency with which pedestrians were dying led journalists to view fatal crashes as a public health epidemic.[27] Just three years earlier, New Jersey's governor, John Corzine, had announced a major pedestrian safety initiative, allocating $74 million for the re-engineering of state roadways, increased enforcement of traffic safety laws, and pedestrian education. Corzine's administration was embarrassed by the mounting evidence that this initiative had failed to produce results, and in late 2009 the administration went on the defensive, issuing press releases pointing to the improvements that had been made under the program. Meanwhile, local and regional pedestrian advocacy groups called for additional measures to protect nonmotorists in the state.[28]

This public attention to the issue of pedestrian risk forced troublesome public objects into the consciousness of public officials, who were tasked with resolving fatal collisions between motor vehicles and pedestrians. State and local officials responded by taking a variety of actions at different scales, from the municipality to the state. Their responses to programmatic conflict reveal the underlying politics of apparently pragmatic decisions regarding transportation infrastructure. Officials had to choose between reinforcing or altering the prevailing affordances in places of high pedestrian risk. The tools at their disposal were material, symbolic, and regulatory.[29] These choices were far from straightforward. In fact, they were loaded with social consequence. Like the concrete divider at the start of this chapter, responses to programmatic conflict are made political by their social context. Pragmatic and utilitarian considerations mask the hidden sociological work that new objects, signs, and laws do—their uneven implications in an unequal social world. The key to moving beyond dry policy or planning discussions, and understanding these implications, is bringing users and places into view, and exposing the role of material objects in shaping their lives.

MATERIAL FIXES: FENCES AND OVERPASSES

Perhaps the most obvious reaction to conflict between people and things is the material fix. By changing the physical landscape, officials can engage in social control, curtailing an unexpected pattern of user behavior. Alternately, they can physically adapt space to accommodate users' changing needs, programming space to reflect new affordances. A pair of material interventions pursued by New Jersey state officials illustrate these approaches, which have very different political implications.

One solution undertaken by the New Jersey Department of Transportation (NJDOT) on roads across the state was the installation of median fences—chain link barriers inserted between the central lanes of a roadway. On Black Horse Pike, between a residential development and a shopping mall, a six-foot median fence was erected along the center of a grassy median—a strip of land separating the road's eastbound and westbound lanes. Unlike other material fixes for pedestrian safety problems, median fences can be erected relatively cheaply, and on short notice. The NJDOT guidelines allow for their installation on state roads such as White Horse or Black Horse Pikes without public input, but warns that they are not an optimal solution and should be installed only where illegal pedestrian crossings are "an ongoing patterned problem," rather than sporadic in occurrence.

Elsewhere in the state, a law enforcement officer explained the logic manifest in the median fences to a local newspaper reporter: "If people go by the rules and the laws of the road, right now our roads are very safe for pedestrians."[30] By asserting the need to obey the institutional programming of the space—the "laws of the road"—in order to resolve programmatic conflict, the officials offered a discursive translation of the logic that is materially manifest in the fence itself, which prevents fatal accidents by physically preventing pedestrians from crossing. The fence, in other words, materially reinforces the dominant program of the space, reasserting the priority that high-speed automobile traffic holds over pedestrian use. The Jersey barrier we visited at the start of this chapter is functionally indifferent to pedestrians, but the fence is not. Its job is to convert the median into an intentional symbolic and physical deterrent.[31]

In Denville, New Jersey, where Route 46 intersects with Savage Road and Franklin Road, a very different approach was adopted by state transportation officials. The setting bears a passing resemblance to that described above. Route 46 is a six-lane divided highway with no shoulder. A Burger King and a Charlie Brown's Steakhouse are situated along one side of the

FIGURE 3.6. A symbolic and material fix. In this location on Black Horse Pike, a bus stop is situated on the westbound side, across the highway from a large shopping center. An intersection with a crosswalk is perhaps a hundred yards away. The sign reinforces the message that is conveyed (and physically enforced) by the fence. Together, these objects encourage pedestrians to trade convenience for safety, while preserving the priority that drivers hold in the programming of this place.

road. Unlike the site on Route 1, this spot on Route 46 has an intersection, with a stoplight, designated pedestrian signals, and a striped crosswalk. But the sheer size of the highway and the speed of traffic nevertheless makes crossing dangerous, as pedestrians are required to cross nearly eighty feet of pavement in a relatively short time. Setting aside the physical similarities, the surrounding area offers a sharp socioeconomic contrast to the trailer parks and budget motels along stretches of Black Horse and White Horse Pikes. On one side of Route 46 is Indian Lake, an upper-middle-class community composed of 1,200 large suburban homes clustered around a private lakefront club requiring membership. On the opposite side of Route 46 is a large and well-maintained public park.

In 2009, after a sustained lobbying campaign by the Indian Lake community, the NJDOT unveiled a $3.3 million pedestrian overpass that would cross Route 46 at the intersection with Savage Road. Again, the target audience for this modification was unambiguous: residents of Indian Lake seeking to cross to the playing fields and walking paths of the public park. But the process, in contrast to the construction of the median fences on Black Horse Pike, was prolonged and intentionally democratic, including public meetings at the Denville Municipal Building where community members were invited to offer input on the design.[32] In the discourse of public officials, the overpass was presented as evidence of a broader governmental commitment to walking and bicycling. Governor Jon Corzine, in a press release, explained the logic manifest in the overpass—the logic of program adaptation: "The Route 46 pedestrian bridge reflects the State of New Jersey's dedication to improving pedestrian safety. . . . [It] will encourage residents to walk rather than drive."[33] Not only would the overpass accommodate existing pedestrians, it would create more of them.

As two quite different material responses to pedestrian risk, the fence and the overpass speak of power and inequality. The degree of involvement that pedestrians enjoyed in the process that led to the two objects was quite different. But more importantly for the present discussion, the objects *themselves* empower and disempower. By constructing the median fence in Monmouth Junction where Route 1 passes through low-income communities, the state transferred the costs of alleviating conflict entirely to these pedestrians. Pedestrian users were made safer by this intervention, but their marginalization within the symbolic and the functional terms of the space was only reasserted by the material fix that was employed. The fence reinforces a physical program (*this space is for driving, not for walking*), thus prioritizing the needs of one category of user over those of another. In doing so, it perpetuates a local power imbalance that is rooted in social inequality, working on a material as well as a symbolic level.

In contrast, the Savage Road overpass does not reinforce the apparent behavioral rules of the space—it changes them. By constructing the overpass, state officials replaced a dangerously inadequate crosswalk with a massive, permanent structure, whose only purpose is to accommodate pedestrian users and to insulate them from the high-speed automobile traffic below. The overpass adapts the program of the immediate area, redefining the intersection as a space conducive to travel by foot. Both objects respond to a similar need, but the responses differ in the capacities that they assign to the two classes of users. In their material form, they enact a politics, selectively empowering or disempowering users who differ, between the two sites, in both their socioeconomic status and their representation in the political process behind the two pieces of public infrastructure.

As a means of guiding or regulating user behavior, material fixes like the fence or the overpass have several clear benefits—they are durable and, in the case of the fence, physically coercive. But they are also limited by their physicality. The NJDOT design manual describes a median fence as a temporary fix, noting that it prevents "90% of pedestrian crossings" but should nevertheless be used "as a last resort."[34] The pedestrian overpass, with its cumbersome stairs and wheelchair ramps, can easily be ignored by a group of teenagers in a hurry. Even more importantly, the physicality of material fixes anchors them in space and thus constrains their jurisdiction. The median fence and the crosswalk stand to affect the behavior of *only* a proximate population of users. In a region where space tends to be sharply segregated by class, this is an important point. By responding to localized political pressure and adopting different material fixes in different places, state officials changed the built environment in ways that reflected and reproduced the deepening spatial inequalities of the contemporary suburbs.

SYMBOLIC FIXES: SIGNS AND SYMBOLS

A second option when trying to resolve conflicts between people and things is the symbolic fix. Symbolic solutions act on a discursive, communicative level, and are therefore more useful in reinforcing existing programs than in fostering new ones. In this regard, they are particularly well suited to respond to a weakness in material fixes—insufficient or incomplete awareness concerning how an object is to be used. They are usually applied in conjunction with material and/or institutional fixes, acting to clarify the program embedded in a material object ("Emergency Exit") or to specify a legally endorsed pattern of behavior ("No Loitering"). In these cases, they act as a stopgap in cases where the built environment is deemed insufficiently legible by the people or institutions who are responding to programmatic conflict.

In the case of pedestrian risk in New Jersey, officials applied symbolic fixes both in order to underline the old rules and to advertise the new ones. A case in point is a sign posted on the new median fence on the Black Horse Pike, discussed above. "Use Crosswalk," the sign says, pointing pedestrians toward a distant intersection (see figure 3.6). The symbolic fix here simply makes the program explicit, reinforcing the message already sent by the fence. In similar fashion, state agencies made small, yellow traffic cones emblazoned with stop signs available to municipalities across the state to place within pedestrian crosswalks. In Linden, New Jersey, state funding was provided for a more substantial form of signage—a movable, five-foot tall, wedge-shaped object that could be erected in front of any crosswalk, advising motorists to use caution. The object could then be relocated to other crosswalks, in order to ensure that its message would reach a broad population of drivers.

INSTITUTIONAL FIXES: REGULATION AND ENFORCEMENT

Material fixes and symbolic fixes are limited by their materiality. However, as outlined in the introductory chapter, there are alternate methods of programming built space that have very different properties. Institutional fixes, for example—changes in the formal rules that govern how space is to be used—are less constrained by physical space than are material responses to programmatic conflict. Their jurisdiction—the spatial extent of their behavioral impact—is defined by socially constructed political or legal boundaries, rather than the size of a material object or its position within Euclidean space. This makes institutional fixes potentially easier and less expensive to apply across large and diverse territories.

In 2009 and the years that followed, municipal police departments in Atlantic County towns such as Ventnor and Pleasantville experimented with a new state-funded program intended to strengthen the enforcement of an existing traffic law. In doing so, they highlighted the principal advantage of using regulatory means to restore harmony between people and things. The law in question was an uncontroversial state law requiring that motorists "yield" to pedestrians in crosswalks. In an attempt to increase compliance with this law, police officers disguised as civilians walked the streets, giving tickets to motorists who failed to yield when they crossed the road.[35] The enforcement regime was applied aggressively at high-traffic-volume intersections in order to maximize its effect on driver psychology—at one "pedestrian decoy" checkpoint near Black Horse Pike in Ventnor, police officers wrote fifty-five tickets in two and a half hours.[36]

The advantage of this mode of enforcement lay in its ability to adjust human behavior across a variety of material contexts. As a method of social control, the "pedestrian decoy" program encouraged drivers to internalize their own compliance—to police themselves. A local newspaper headline neatly summarized the implications of the enforcement regime for drivers, warning, "That Longport Pedestrian May Be a Cop."[37] If the strategy proved effective, it would convert all local pedestrians into potential law enforcement officers, producing a panoptic form of self-discipline that would follow drivers wherever they went within the municipality.[38] To be clear, other, more conventional forms of institutional reinforcement were also pursued, such as simply raising the traffic fines for violating existing laws. But the pedestrian decoy program highlights, in particularly clear terms, the logic behind *any* form of institutional reinforcement. By changing the risk calculation in users' minds, officials were attempting a consistent change in behavior across a defined legal jurisdiction, thus alleviating programmatic conflict at a potentially lower cost than that of material redesign.

An alternative to increased enforcement of existing laws is to alter the rules altogether, pursuing institutional adaptation as opposed to reinforcement. In 2010, under pressure to lower pedestrian risk across the state, New Jersey's government changed state traffic law for the first time in more than fifty years.[39] Where previously drivers were required to yield to pedestrians in crosswalks, the new law, referred to as "Casey's Law" by state officials, required that drivers come to a full stop. The political impetus for the change centered upon a symbolic victim. A twenty-one-year-old female pedestrian named Casey Feldman, the daughter of a prominent Philadelphia attorney, was killed in a crosswalk in Ocean City, New Jersey, in July 2009. Feldman's death, coinciding with the aforementioned statewide increase in pedestrian deaths, prompted extensive media coverage and a political campaign mounted by the victim's family. In March 2010, the legislation was announced in a public ceremony in which members of Feldman's family appeared alongside state transportation officials.[40]

By enacting the law, the state sought a specific change in the formal rules and the engrained behaviors governing intersections across the state. The apparent political motivation for the law centered upon the high-profile death of a young, White, middle-class woman, but the behavioral changes sought by the law stood to empower pedestrians throughout New Jersey. Low-income residents, like those in Atlantic County, whose reliance on foot travel is a function of economic necessity, would be protected alongside middle-class teenagers. Unlike the physical fixes of the median fence and the crosswalk, a new state law or local ordinance empowers or disempowers through changes in the legal context that guides the use of material objects and built spaces. This context is reflected and embodied by the cognitive and ethical awareness and, eventually, hopefully, by the engrained habitual behavior of individual human actors, rather than the design of material objects. Once embedded in behavior, institutional fixes may be more easily scaled across areas that differ socioeconomically, racially, and ethnically, as well as materially.[41] But what institutional fixes gain in scalability they lose in coercive ability. A median fence may be vulnerable to a strong set of pliers, but it takes only a moment of cynicism or uncertainty to puncture a traffic law.

Back to the Wall

More than four years after conducting a first round of fieldwork in Atlantic County, I drove south on the Garden State Parkway for what I thought might be the last time, to check up on the wall, and to see for myself whether the responses outlined above had made a meaningful difference in the material, institutional, and symbolic programming of White Horse and Black Horse Pikes. I had every reason to be hopeful. In 2013, the pedestrian fatality rate in Atlantic County had dipped to a twenty-year low, as only three pedestrians were killed on the county's roads. I suspected that Casey's Law, increased enforcement, and an array of state-funded improvements to the pedestrian infrastructure had something to do with this.

But I was to be disappointed. During my visits to Atlantic County in 2014 and 2015, I found the same conditions that I had observed in 2010. The bus stops that I had visited years earlier seemed, if anything, even more neglected, uncomfortable, and unsafe, their grocery-cart benches rusting away in the dirt. My interviews with pedestrians evinced the same mixture of indignity and physical endangerment that had been expressed to me years earlier. I met a physically disabled woman who walks with a cane through a thickly wooded area in order to avoid navigating a dangerous intersection on Black Horse Pike. She told me she does this at least six times every week, occasionally tripping over exposed roots or stumbling over the brushy, uneven terrain. I spoke with a burly dishwasher who told me, sheepishly, in Dominican-accented Spanish, that at night he takes refuge among the trees on the edge of those same woods while waiting for the bus, and has done so ever since he saw a pickup truck jump the curb at night and partially destroy a speed limit sign. I rode the bus with a worker at a fast-food restaurant who had arrived in the area from Chicago a year earlier and, after growing tired of living without an automobile in Atlantic County, was now trying to raise enough money to move back. "Have you been to Chicago?" he asked. "Things aren't easy there, but getting around is not one of your problems. I don't understand why people live down here. To me [he gestured out the window at the passing landscape of White Horse Pike] this is another country." My impressions were soon corroborated by a new round of statistics. Early the following year, the fatality figures for 2014 were released. Pedestrian fatalities had once again spiked across the state. In Atlantic County alone, eleven pedestrians had been killed.

When pedestrian risk drew media attention in 2009 and 2010 in New Jersey, it seemed that a range of actors—nonprofit pedestrian advocacy groups, local police officials, state transportation officials, and so on—had come together and recognized the problematic nature of places like the White Horse Pike. Unfortunately, their efforts had not been enough. At fault were all the weaknesses of the various possible fixes for programmatic conflict: the particularistic nature of material responses and the easily ignored nature of new laws. Pedestrian safety funding had been used to build five thousand feet of new sidewalks along areas of the Black Horse Pike, but the sections were discontinuous and sporadic, leaving miles of roadway where pedestrians were forced to walk in the shoulder. The pedestrian decoy program and Casey's Law had failed to produce meaningful changes in areas that lacked crosswalks to begin with. Elevated traffic fines and stepped-up enforcement had not succeeded in changing the behavior of drivers or pedestrians on the pikes. A concerted effort by local and state agencies, in other words, had failed to make a dent in pedestrian risk along two of the most notoriously dangerous roads in the state. What had gone wrong?

The answer is deceptively simple. The built environment of White Horse Pike and Black Horse Pike, like many other similar places across the United States, took many decades and many hundreds of millions of dollars to produce. In sheer physical terms, the pikes represent thousands of tons of asphalt, concrete, aluminum, plastic, paint, and steel. Their hard surfaces were intended to be durable and resist easy modification. But, just as importantly, the configuration of commercial and residential spaces around the road, as I argue above, echoes and reinforces its emphasis on high-speed motor-vehicle traffic. The density of the entire region is a reflection of this program, and density is far more difficult to alter than the width of lanes or the angle of an intersection. If the pedestrian risk incurred by this environment is now receiving some of the attention it deserves, the continuing toll taken by the White Horse and Black Horse Pikes in human lives, *in spite of this attention*, points to the stubborn durability, or, following social scientist Anique Hommels, the "obduracy" of this program, once it has become the basis of an entire social and economic ecosystem.[42] One measure of the enormous social and political consequence of suburban sprawl will be the money and sustained effort necessary to *undo* the damage it continues to cause in places that look, more or less, like this.

When a dirty cement wall meant to protect motor vehicles from one another becomes an obstacle to a person seeking to cross the road on foot, the behavioral assumptions behind the wall—its omissions and inclusions—become obvious. The material fact of White Horse Pike, readily observable at all times, becomes a sociological fact when someone can be seen walking along its shoulder. The program of the entire landscape emerges into view, as it did for me on the summer evening in 2010 when I crossed White Horse Pike with Junior. As suburban poverty becomes increasingly widespread and entrenched, landscapes similar to that of suburban Atlantic County are poised to be sites of programmatic conflict on a larger scale. Policy makers and planners are increasingly going to be confronted with a complex socio-material problem: how to balance the needs of low-income residents with inflexibly middle-class space.

The case of New Jersey suggests that this planning dilemma can be distilled to several essential questions: Should the programming of built space be reinforced or adapted? Should the rules be underscored, or should they be changed? And, crucially, how will responses to programmatic conflict bear upon the existing users of that space? When a stout cement wall and six lanes of traffic separate low-income suburbanites from where they need to go, should we up the ante with a seven-foot fence? Or should we tear down the wall and start over, reworking the built landscape of places like the White Horse and Black Horse Pikes to be more inclusive, but also more flexible and open to change? In the future, the suburban landscapes that surround us will have to accommodate not just the car-driving middle class of the mid-twentieth century or the working poor of the early twenty-first, but whoever comes next.

4

The Subway Door

FIGURE 4.1. The subway door.

The subway door opens smoothly and recedes into its pocket with a soft mechanical hum. At around 3 p.m. on a school day, many of New York City's subway trains abruptly fill up with teenagers, and this sparsely populated Brooklyn-bound F train proves to be one of them. Nine kids spill through the doorway, shattering the sleepy silence with noisy recaps of the day's events, while the doors sit open for maybe ten or fifteen seconds. The recorded voice of Charlie Pellet, a longtime news anchor for *Bloomberg News,* can just barely be heard behind the din. "Stand clear of the closing doors, please," Mr. Pellet asks, as he does thousands of times a day throughout the system, whether anyone is listening or not.

A boy who looks to be fourteen or fifteen years old, curly black hair protruding from under his maroon hoodie, jogs across the platform to the open door of the train. He stands in the doorway of the car and looks back at the turnstiles. A chime sounds, and a yellow indicator light above the door flashes. Inside a housing at the top of the door, an actuator converts electricity into forty-five pounds of horizontal force. Powerful magnets pull the doors from their pockets on either side of the opening. The boy is ready for the doors when they come at him. He wedges his left foot against one door and places both palms against the edge of the other, bracing himself with his legs and countering the door's force with the musculature of his wiry frame. He looks as if he has done this before.

The doors jolt backward, recoiling as if offended, and then come at him again, showing the conductor's frustration at the delay.[1] The boy pivots sideways, turning his back to the interior of the train, and wedges his right foot and elbow against the door. Now a voice crackles over the public address system, presumably the conductor. He doesn't sound angry, just weary, and matter-of-fact. "Do not block the doors, so this train can leave the station." The boy holds his ground, still staring toward the turnstile, waiting for a presumable travel companion to appear at any moment.

This situation, like so many situations in the social life of the city, is more complex than it seems. The boy is not just holding a subway door, another public object that becomes visible when it conflicts with human needs or desires. He is obstructing a wide array of objective social and material forces, many of which are unseen from his vantage point. First, and most obviously, a large number of people are waiting on him. We, the other passengers on the train, would like the doors to close. The conductor and the train operator also want the doors to close, as well as still other employees of the Metropolitan Transportation Authority (MTA)—men and women who sit at consoles in the windowless, subterranean chambers that are paradoxically known as "towers," monitoring the flow of train traffic through the system.

Even less obviously, the material components of the subway, in their own way, would like the doors to close. Foremost among these is the actuator, a four-foot-long assembly of circuits and magnets that is still toiling away inside a panel above the boy's head. Holding the doors in this way prevents them from gaining momentum and forces the actuator's linear motor to strain uselessly against the obstruction. Over time, repeated door holding will shorten the lifespan of the actuator, leading it to burn out, possibly while in service. (There are really very few good times for this to happen.) Along with the actuator, the motor that propels the train down the tracks wants the doors to close. Due to an "interlocking" incorporated on the city's subway trains following a string of frightening incidents in the 1980s, the electric motor cannot power the train forward until it senses that all of its doors are shut. In the meantime, the motor waits, channeling power to the lights and ventilation system.

Other, harder-to-define things are waiting for the boy to stop holding the doors. Our train's delay will postpone the train behind it, and this train will postpone its successor. In this way, even an isolated disruption can cause cascading, systemic delays that force compromises in other locations, at other times.[2] Lunch breaks and maintenance regimens may be curtailed; tracks may not be inspected as carefully; money may be wasted on overtime. These apparently unrelated contingencies are linked through the system's time-table, which is neither a human nor an inanimate object, but an abstraction. Other, similarly symbolic objects—capital budgets, reliability indicators, reputations—have a stake in what is happening in this particular car, and impose an invisible pressure on the system from afar.

A variety of objective things, in other words—material systems, collective desires, and bureaucratic constructs—all of which together compose the subway system, are embodied by the door at this particular moment. Like the door, or, more to the point, *through* the door, we are placed at odds with the behavior of an individual passenger, who is motivated by what appears to be an entirely subjective concern. Who is he waiting for? I wonder. What kind of social bond has invisibly inserted itself between the closing doors, bringing thousands of people and millions of dollars of machinery to an unexpected halt?

At this point, an interesting thing happens. Passengers who were dutifully avoiding eye contact begin to look at one another. The young woman next to me rolls her eyes in a public show of frustration. A rider who appears to be in his twenties glances up from his mobile phone to mutter, "Come *on*, man," loud enough to be audible to those around him. One of the kids who just boarded the train turns away from his conversation to say, with frustra-tion, "Stop holding the door, [bro]! Let these nice people get where they're going." This gets the other kids laughing, but he seems to be at least partly serious, as he continues to look expectantly at the boy holding the door. By alluding to the "nice people" on the train, he makes explicit the social mathematics of the situation: many of us are waiting on one. He could have said, "Let *me* get where I'm going," but he didn't.

In my subway car, something that I will call *normative infrastructure* is grinding into motion, and is exerting a qualitatively different type of pressure on the boy than the edge of the door, seeking to succeed where the material object is failing. The boy looks over his shoulder at the other passengers, looks back at the turnstile, and abruptly steps out of the train onto the platform. The doors close. He turns and gazes expressionlessly through the graffiti-proof window as the train begins to move away. Strangers inside the train trade furtive looks signaling relief. A woman shakes her head, as does one of the boy's friends, marking the closure of the episode. The boy in the sweatshirt was briefly a member of our transient collectivity. He set himself against the door, and, in doing so, he set himself against us. We gently punished him, and he reluctantly gave in. This allowed us—the actuator, the engine, the conductor, the passengers, the timetable—to get on with things.

What, exactly, happened here? A public object made trouble, or, more accurately, a person made trouble by denying a public object's function. This brought things, and people, to a standstill. If the subway is indeed a place (there is no consensus on this, by the way), then it is a place defined by anonymity and transience, with an overarching, collective purpose— movement.[3] The boy, a stranger to most in the train, denied this movement, until it became socially uncomfortable. How do we make sense of this discomfort? What does it tell us about the relationship between people and things in the places of the city?

In the preceding chapter, we looked at a different sort of disruption, a conflict between people and things, and pondered the political question of how such conflicts are to be resolved through material, symbolic, or legal/ regulatory means. In this chapter, we continue to examine troublesome encounters between people and the material objects that compose public space. But in this case, we focus on the role of social action and interaction in creating conflict, and social norms as a means of resolving it. These social norms are specific to a certain kind of place, which is simultaneously a unique public space, a specific material environment, and a vital urban infrastructure: the subway.

Normative Infrastructure

Say "infrastructure" to most people and they think of massive, durable structures and vast networks of inanimate objects. A highway system is infrastructure. An electrical grid is infrastructure. Reluctantly, some people might think to include the humans who maintain and operate these systems—construction crews, toll collectors, and civil engineers, for example. But the situation described above suggests an even more inclusive understanding of this term. The force that ultimately propelled the train down the tracks did not originate in the network of people and things that constitute formal infrastructure: it resided in the culture and the ongoing social awareness of the subway's users. It was, as symbolic interactionists would say, an "emergent" phenomenon, a form of psychological pressure that grew out of the collective social dynamics of the situation.[4] It drew strength and coherence from shared understandings that passed through the air during the moments when the boy was holding the door. This force weighed more heavily upon the situation as time went on, ultimately succeeding where others had failed. Infrastructure is not just below the streets and behind the walls—it is in our heads, and works through our bodies.

A code of behavior has developed among New York City subway riders. But unlike the social "etiquettes" that apply in other settings—for example, around the dinner table—the norms in question are functionally related to a material infrastructure.[5] In modern urban settings, similar norms are at work everywhere, all the time, helping formal infrastructures to do their jobs. When a driver flashes the headlights to signal that another driver should go first, or a person shuffles to the right to allow several additional passengers to enter an elevator, he or she has contributed to normative infrastructure, perhaps without even thinking about it. It is commonplace to suggest that we rely on material objects and technologies to get where we're going, and to do what we do. It is also obviously true that objects rely on predictable human action to work as they are supposed to: the car cannot move, or the elevator ascend, until a key is inserted, a button pushed. But less obviously, things also depend heavily on patterned social behavior. To work as intended, they need us to act predictably, consistently, and even, as I will argue, ethically *toward one another*.

The New York subway offers a particularly interesting setting in which to examine informal social norms, because it contains surprisingly little in the way of formal social control. Although the subway has rules, there are no stoplights governing passengers' movements through the system, or licensing procedures that certify subway riders as knowledgeable and competent. The most common human agents of social control in the subway, conductors and operators, are typically absent or invisible, unlike bus drivers or traffic cops, and rarely intervene in passenger behavior.[6] In the subway, normative infrastructure takes on a crucial role, doing much of the work that codified and enforced rules and regulations do in other kinds of settings.

At the open doorway of the subway train, etiquette gains urgency. With a bit of imagination, the New York subway can be envisioned as a massive circulatory system. The system pumps away around the clock, moving people and things between the city's core and its far-flung extremities on an ongoing basis. But unlike our own complex network of blood vessels, which relies on a single, powerful muscle, the subway system has thousands of beating hearts. The pace of the system is set by a rhythmic pulse of arrivals and departures at subway platforms located at 472 different stations across the city. When the system is on schedule, subway doors open and close with the regularity of a metronome, enveloping passengers in one location, discharging them in the next. But if passengers take too long to exit or board the train, the amount of time a train spends lingering at the platform creeps upward. When this "dwell time" exceeds forty-five seconds, the system slows down and runs off schedule, developing the equivalent of arteriosclerosis.[7]

At the time this chapter is being drafted, cascading delays of this sort are happening with unprecedented frequency in the New York subway. The system is experiencing a crisis, and it has much to do with how subway riders behave. In recent years, a steady increase in ridership has led to severely crowded conditions on the subway's trains and platforms and a noticeable deterioration in passenger behavior. Between early 2012 and late 2015, the frequency of weekday delays more than doubled across the system. According to the MTA's own data, delays specifically caused by "overcrowding" quadrupled during this time. To be clear, overcrowding causes delays by placing passengers' bodies between the doors at the time when the train would need to leave to stay on schedule. Passengers crowd into the opening of the train, and force the conductor to keep the doors open, in many cases holding or blocking the doors while boarding. By early 2015, the regular occurrence of cascading subway delays had become a source of embarrassment and frustration for city officials.[8] Meanwhile, other more troubling indicators of social and psychological duress in the subway have steadily ticked upward, tracking the crowdedness of the system. MTA records show that delays caused by "unruly" and "sick" passengers have increased, as have incidents of physical assault. These trends suggest that a broader decline in social order may be taking place within the subway.

In the pages that follow, I describe the normative infrastructure of the subway and explain how and why it fails. I draw on archival sources, official statistics, a quantitative study conducted over several months in late 2015, and three months of almost daily participant observation in the New York subway during roughly that same period.[9] Based on this evidence, I argue that the way we think about material infrastructure and similar technologies is incomplete. Social theory suggests that objects and their users adapt to each other over time, approaching an equilibrium state in which material artifacts and technologies become unproblematic and disappear into the background of social life. But rather than accommodating each other, as we might expect, the subway and its human users have always been locked in an uneasy, often dysfunctional embrace. As a technical system, the subway often fails the people. And as the users of this system, the people often fail the subway.

Domestication and Discipline

Where does normative infrastructure come from? Social theorists offer a plausible set of answers. Technologies do not fall from the heavens in Promethean fashion. They are human creations, and as such, are "socially constructed" by designers and engineers who are embedded in specific ideologies and social structures.[10] To a degree, new objects and infrastructures anticipate human needs and desires, but they do so imperfectly. Inevitably, they provoke novel controversies and dilemmas, but over time we "domesticate" them, a process that involves smoothing their rough edges and figuring out how to incorporate them into social structures and routines in a way that causes minimal disturbance. An important part of this process requires making new technologies less disruptive through iterative redesign and modification.[11] This process of domestication is evident in the early years of the New York City subway system. When the subway first opened, progressive reformers worried that subterranean transit would be disorienting and claustrophobic, expressing doubts that, as a contemporary commentator put it, passengers could be convinced to "go into a hole in the ground and ride."[12] To compensate, the subway's builders went out of their way to make stations bright and elegant. The first ticket booths to grace New York City Subway stations were stately, wood-paneled podiums staffed by ticket agents. But widespread fare beating quickly forced the system's administrators to adopt the more utilitarian turnstile in its stead. Through a recursive, back-and-forth process, the new transportation technology was domesticated and refined, adapted to human psychology and social behavior.

But we do not simply fine-tune new material technologies to suit our needs. Following Michel Foucault, a new type of object can be said to "discipline" its users, requiring that they develop and internalize social norms and bodily practices that did not exist before its invention.[13] Like the domestication of new technologies, the disciplining process is gradual, cultural, and demographic. Every new important innovation results in a new cohort of people who know how to use it. The adoption of the home telephone required that users learn a new set of rules concerning when it was polite to call. The invention of the typewriter, like many workplace technologies, created an entirely new marketable skill. And the popularization of the automobile required that drivers be habituated to local traffic codes, to avoid mayhem on urban roads.[14] By the same token, as Stefan Hoehne observes, the subway required that every New Yorker learn to be "a passenger"—a person who has internalized a code of behavior appropriate to riding the subway.[15]

What kind of discipline does the subway require? Normative infrastructure is compensatory with regard to material infrastructure—it grows in and around the blind spots in certain objects and technologies, addressing the areas of ambiguity or inadequacy that are left behind after material design and formal regulation have had their say. In the case of the subway, these norms fall in two categories: the first category responds to the scarcity of time and space often encountered in the subway; the second responds to the harshness of the built environment of the subway.[16]

Perhaps the most fundamental behavioral norms involved in riding the subway are those that promote the physical coordination of subway riders in a crowded, chaotic, and labyrinthine environment. Space and time are often restricted, and the scarcity of these resources leads to collective-action problems at the system's various points of entry. Alleviating these problems quickly and smoothly requires that passengers synchronize their collective behavior with a sense of spatial economy and urgency:

5:46 p.m.: Weekday in late January. Canal Street Station: A steady stream of passengers is exiting the 6 train and making its way toward the turnstiles. At the bank of turnstiles, the stream separates into rivulets that flow quickly and methodically through the turnstile gates, one passenger at a time. A smaller, incoming stream of passengers is making its way through one of the turnstile openings. Outgoing passengers have ceded this opening to the incoming riders. At this point, with the train still in the station, a young white woman in business clothes breaks away from the back of the incoming line, during a brief interruption in one of the outgoing streams, and heads toward an empty turnstile. An outgoing passenger, a middle-aged black man in a blazer, simultaneously moves forward on the outgoing side, ready to exit. There is a brief pause on both sides at this point, as the mutual visibility of the two people produces a moment of concentrated ambiguity, and then the outgoing passenger steps aside, or more accurately, angles himself toward the adjacent turnstile on his right, merging with the flow toward that opening. Meanwhile, the incoming passenger, without acknowledgement, pushes through, with a newly formed line of incoming passengers behind her. The train's doors close before she can reach them, and she throws up her hands in frustration and glowers back, not at the passenger who blocked her—he has vanished into the crowd—but at the turnstiles.

The female passenger's annoyance in this case resulted from a complicated set of rules that applies to the subway's turnstiles. The openings are typically distributed to incoming and outgoing flows in accordance with the size of those flows, but when a train is in the station, outgoing passengers will often cede an opening to incoming passengers in order to improve their chance of making the train. A set of rules that responds to spatial scarcity, in other words, is momentarily suspended in order to acknowledge the priority of temporal scarcity.

The material environment of the subway produces an almost uninterrupted series of such ethically charged microsituations, in which the system requires that passengers act in concert for the greater good. The good news is that the solutions to these collective-action problems are typically uncontroversial and merely require recognizing the behavior appropriate to a particular object or space and applying these rules on the fly. Just as the velvet rope or the ticket booth alludes to a social practice known as "queuing" or "waiting in line," the arrival of the subway train invokes a process of moving toward a door and then shuffling to one side to make way for those who are exiting the train. On stairways, an informal expectation holds that people will stay to their right; on escalators, the same rule holds, but only for those who choose to stand rather than walk; once inside a crowded train, passengers are expected to move in as far as they can, to make room for more. The pole is to be held with one hand, not hugged or leaned on. Bags and backpacks go on the floor, not on the adjacent seat. Similar "coordination games" prevail throughout the system, whenever and wherever space and time are made scarce by the material technology of the subway.[17]

Subway riders share a stake in the overall speed and reliability of service, so the ethics of these norms can be viewed through a utilitarian lens. Small individual sacrifices are warranted by a higher collective payoff. Everyone will get where they are going faster if each person is willing to accept a small delay or two along the way. Behaviors of this sort do not have to be deliberate or rational. They can be habitual, motivated by automatic cognition rather than conscious thought. But a legitimizing logic runs through the background while riding the subway at all times. The implicit reference point for this ethical rationale is what the formal infrastructure requires to function effectively. In this sense, the subway relies upon what might be called *systemic justice*: a given course of behavior is correct because the system requires it; and if everybody follows the rules, the system will produce benefits for all.[18]

But the mechanism that distributes these benefits is opaque and raises troubling questions for subway riders. Does it *really* matter if I run down the left side of the stairwell to make a departing train? How much is the train *actually* going to be delayed if I hold the doors for a friend? Transit officials may know the answers to these questions, but subway riders do not. They lack the information necessary to comprehend the indirect, systemic consequences of their individual decisions.[19] Because of this, subway etiquette means following a set of rules that one assumes will produce a more just outcome when distributed across the system.[20] Normative infrastructure, in other words, relies on both ingrained habits and a willingness to engage in small leaps of faith—a trust that the system will eventually reward the conscientious passenger.

Coordination is not the only type of norm that passengers are expected to internalize. A second type of behavior that has evolved in and through the subway's harsh material spaces is altruistic in nature and represents a tacit acknowledgement that the built environment of the subway is unequal in its consequences. The subway's many staircases for example, are indifferent to the needs of solo caregivers for young children, buskers, and other workers whose jobs require that they transport bulky items, as well as elderly or physically frail commuters:

1:30 p.m.: Wednesday afternoon in early December, Cortelyou Road Station. A heavyset woman with thick, black curly hair, in her late 50s or early 60s is slowly making her way down the stairs. She holds a cane in her left hand, and a blue rolling suitcase in her right, which prevents her from holding the handrail. Her strategy is to crabwalk sideways down the stairs, one stair at a time, planting the cane on each step before stepping down, all while leaning sideways to stabilize her body as much as possible on the handrail and counterbalance the weight of the suitcase. It looks like she may have put some thought into this strategy, but it still seems precarious. The bulk of the luggage is the biggest problem, as it keeps bumping the side of her leg on the way down. I ask if I can help and she smiles, a gold plated incisor glinting at me, and hands me the bag. I'm surprised by how light it feels to me. I carry it to the bottom of the stairs and walk back up to help her down, but without the bag, she tells me she's okay. "There's an elevator at the other station," she says. I ask her if she has to carry the bag a lot. "Every day," she says. "But there's generally somebody who is here to help me, even if I have to wait for him. And if not, I just go slow."

As this example suggests, the inequitable impact of the subway's built environment is implicitly acknowledged by the normative infrastructure of the subway, and has produced a compensatory set of norms. These behaviors are readily on display at rush hour throughout the system, as fellow passengers help to carry a stroller or shopping cart, hold the door for a frail or slow-moving passenger, or offer a seat to an elderly or pregnant passenger. Normative infrastructure incorporates not just systemic justice but the exercise of a quotidian form of altruistic *social justice*—a set of social norms that has developed in and around the material elements of the subway system that are most uneven in their human consequences.

As these examples illustrate, subway riders internalize a set of social norms when they ride the subway—they are disciplined by the technology to engage in behaviors that are helpful to the efficiency and accessibility of the New York City Subway as a mass-transit system. This social accommodation is accompanied by the adaptation or "domestication" of the material technology itself, and this theoretically might result in a stable condition in which material objects become socially unproblematic. Through this recursive process, an infrastructure and its users move toward equilibrium: things and their users reach a compromise. Eventually, a technology that initially appeared foreign or controversial is naturalized and disappears into the background of social life. Its controversial qualities are "black boxed," reemerging into light of day only when the technology malfunctions or is encountered for the first time by an unfamiliar user.[21] According to an abundance of social theory, this is how it is supposed to go. But this is not at all what has happened in the case of the New York City Subway.

Feral Technology

The New York City Subway has never been fully domesticated. It remains inhospitable in ways that conflict with its users' desires for safety, predictability, and flexibility. The system's resistance to domestication is rooted in two overarching constraints that have checked the efforts of policy makers, transit officials, and advocates to make the system more "user-friendly" over the last century.

The first of these constraints is material in nature. Much of the subway system was built in the late nineteenth and early twentieth centuries, and relied upon the primitive construction technologies of the day. The subway's engineers had to devise ways of building over and under densely built-up streetscapes and dauntingly uneven geological formations.[22] They made free use of stairwells, escalators, and connecting passageways. As a result, making your way to the platform from the street often meant navigating long, dimly lit pedestrian tunnels and steep flights of stairs.[23] The necessity of inserting subway stations into the existing urban landscape also insured that no two stations in the system would be laid out in an identical fashion. Many elevated stations are roughly similar, but every underground station has its quirks: long, narrow platforms; blind turns and strange angles; stanchions that obstruct the conductors' view of the passengers, or passengers' view of one another. As artist George Tooker conveyed in a 1950 eponymous painting of the subway, the system is an alienating maze, whose labyrinthine corridors can invoke a vague sense of social danger.

Although early subway cars featured padded seats and other material concessions in order to attract passengers away from viable transportation alternatives such as streetcars and elevated trains, the transit agencies that managed the subway quickly adopted a utilitarian approach to architecture and design that prioritized economy and efficiency over comfort and elegance. Passengers were required to wedge themselves into hard plastic or wooden bucket seats that have periodically drawn complaints for anatomical assumptions that are far from universal.[24] Even the devices that granted access to stations could be brutal and forbidding. Now-decommissioned turnstiles known colloquially as "iron maidens" required passing through a narrow, enclosed compartment made of thick iron bars. Equally formidable

FIGURE 4.2. Feral technology. A vestigial "roto-gate" high-exit turnstile at City Hall station. These brutal-looking devices were once ubiquitous throughout the system at unmonitored access points, where a waist-high turnstile could be jumped with impunity. The entrances and exits of subway platforms, like the doors on the train, are locations where the material infrastructure becomes more direct and precise in its control of human bodies. Two systemic priorities are at play in these locations: preventing "fare beating," and moving passengers quickly and efficiently into and out of the system. In pursuit of these objectives, sacrifices in physical and/or psychological comfort are often required.

"high exit" turnstiles feature a seven-foot-tall set of interwoven metal teeth and are still in use, in spite of the fact that they are demonstrably unsafe and required a wholesale exemption from the city's safety standards.

The stark and uncompromising nature of the subway's built environment alone, however, did not prevent a process of domestication. The system's rough edges might have been smoothed, if not for a second type of constraint, which was political in nature. Throughout the life of the subway, attempts to improve the system and, at times, even to insure its basic maintenance have fallen victim to chronic fiscal deficits and delays that stem from the political economy in which the infrastructure is situated. This perennial inability to address the system's inadequacies goes beyond the run-of-the-mill inefficiency that can be found within almost any large bureaucracy and speaks of a particular brand of political inertia. Politicians and transit officials alike have sought throughout the subway's history to avoid fare hikes and service interruptions, the mere discussion of which has often been enough to elicit public outrage.[25] In the tradeoff between adequate present levels of service and improved future service, near-term considerations have generally prevailed, producing a system that often seems to be on the brink of physical and organizational catastrophe.[26]

The combined effect of material and political constraints on the domestication of the subway has been to preserve the conditions that require a strong and active normative infrastructure. Scarcities of time and space in the subway, for example, have been exacerbated by an official reluctance to fund needed upgrades and suspend service in order to expand the system and keep up with increased ridership. The most significant expansion plan, a proposed line running down Second Avenue in Manhattan, was in the works for almost a century but was repeatedly deferred owing to a lack of funding. Other improvements—for example, computerized signal systems—would stand to drastically increase the capacity of the existing track network, but would require extensive service interruptions to install. As a result, the system has grown very little in size since World War II, and relies upon antiquated signal circuits and other electrical and mechanical components that date to the 1930s or earlier, inhibiting both the capacity and reliability of service.[27]

These constraints have imposed on the subway a technological and material rigidity that prevents the system from easily accommodating fluctuations in ridership. Between World War I and World War II, crowding on its trains reached such extremes that women's associations decried the conditions as indecent.[28] The 1960s and 1970s saw a decline in ridership, but in recent decades, fed by a population boom and a robust urban economy, the subway is again straining to serve a user population that exceeds its realistic capacity, particularly given the antiquated technology upon which the system depends. As a result, passengers now routinely confront shortages of space on platforms and inside trains, while unprecedented delays lead to a greater urgency among the ridership.

By the same token, the political economy of the subway has perpetu-
ated the physical intolerance and cruelty of its built environment. In 1990,
the Americans with Disabilities Act (ADA) required that new and existing
public facilities provide access to the disabled, but the physical spaces of the
subway remain prohibitively unwelcoming to these passengers. Twenty-
five years after the passage of the legislation, fewer than a quarter of New
York City's subway stations are equipped with elevators. And the difficulties
involved in navigating the system are not limited to passengers who meet
the ADA's definition of disability. Given the agonizingly slow pace at which
the system is approaching full ADA compliance, altruistic norms will remain
crucial to the functioning of the subway system as a public service.

In contrast to what we normally expect from a technology, the subway
remains untamed and wild more than a century after it first opened its doors
to New Yorkers. A combination of material and political constraints have kept
the system from modernizing, expanding, and becoming more accessible in
order to meet the needs and desires of its human users. As a result, the system
refuses to recede into the background—it offers constant reminders of its
unpredictability, its frailty, and its punishing materiality, exposing its users to
ambiguous and mazelike spaces, indeterminate delays, physically and socially
uncomfortable levels of crowding, and long walks up or down steep concrete
stairwells. This leaves much to the riders of the subway, perpetuating exactly
the environmental conditions—scarcity of time and space, harsh physical
contexts—that are addressed by the normative infrastructure. As a technology,
the subway has offered little to its riders. And it has demanded much in return.

The Discipline of the Door

On the other side of the relationship between objects and their users are
riders, who are expected to internalize the discipline of the subway, following rules that allow the free and expeditious movement of trains and
people through the system. How might a technology discipline its users?
One mechanism is through the surfaces, signs, and edges that come into
physical contact with their bodies. Throughout the history of the subway, its
managers have repeatedly tried to modify the way subway riders behave at
the train doors through technological means. Their attempts, largely unsuc-
cessful, reveal an important insight. Wherever material infrastructure relies
upon normative infrastructure, concessions must be made to human subjectivity and morality. Users force their concerns and their consciousness
onto objects, demanding compromise at every turn.

Even though the stakes are high at the doors, efficiency has to strike a balance with humanity. A satirical YouTube film that appeared on the internet at the height of the subway's overcrowding issues in late 2015 ironically captures this tradeoff. The video simulates a local television news story based on a fictional plan by the MTA to line each subway door with thousands of tiny titanium blades. After a gruesome sequence reminiscent of a low-budget horror movie, a straight-faced technocrat appears on camera to admit that, yes, injuries have spiked dramatically, "but the trains run on time."[29] Although unapologetically campy, the film correctly identifies the practical and ethical dilemma facing the MTA. The most efficient design would be the least humane—the most merciless in its approach to disciplining human users.

The history of subway door design can be seen as a manifestation of the often-zero-sum relationship between efficiency and respect for norms of public decency. A ruthless effectiveness would result in greater reliability, but some leeway has to be provided for the physical safety and psychological comfort of passengers. Initially, each set of subway doors was manually controlled by a conductor, who could directly enforce the system's temporal requirements by closing the gate and ringing a bell to signal the train's departure. Every door was closed by an electro-pneumatic mechanism that used compressed air to activate a lever, closing and opening the door. In its design, the mechanism recognized that passengers would occasionally block doors or push them open, its pneumatic tubes incorporating a release valve that reduced the pressure exerted on the door when forced.[30]

In the 1920s, new subway cars incorporated a system, multi-unit door control, that allowed one conductor to open and close all doors on the train, while peering down the platform from a strategic perch between cars. In response to passengers' fears that automatic doors would cause injury, they were equipped with sensitive edges that would detect an obstruction and prompt the doors to automatically retract. The design of the doors was intended to reassure, but passengers still needed some convincing: in order to illustrate the sensitivity of their edges, a subway official reportedly inserted his own nose between a set of closing doors.[31]

At about this time, however, subway ridership experienced its first boom, resulting in crowded platforms and choked doorways. Riders took advantage of the technological concession that the transit agency had granted them, intentionally prying doors open after they had closed by wedging a hand or a foot into the door to activate the sensitive edges. This tactic became the basis of a spontaneous but socially organized form of subversion among subway riders. A contemporary *New York Times* article documents the transit agency's concern over an outbreak of door "rushing," and describes cases in which an unaffiliated group of passengers would storm the doors of a departing train, pry them open, and hold them for others to tumble through, risking injury to the passengers inside.[32]

The sensitive-edge design clearly offered too much leeway to riders, allowing them to exert their individual wills over the collective good. In the 1930s, the transit agency replaced them with new doors that were lighter and equipped flexible edges in order to prevent injury when they closed on a human body. The new doors embodied distrust: they could not be pried open, and were notched at the bottom in order to allow a passenger to withdraw his or her foot after a vain attempt to stop the doors from closing.[33] Just after World War II, in response to a continued epidemic of door prying, the transit agency decided to remove the sensitive edges altogether, reassigning ultimate control over the doors to the conductor. Simultaneously, the mechanical system at the conductor's disposal was made more unyielding. Pneumatic door closing mechanisms were replaced by electric motors featuring a "worm gear" that made the doors impossible to push open.[34]

This attempt to empower the conductor, however, produced an inverse problem, rendering the door mechanism unduly harsh and potentially lethal. If the conductor failed to notice a late-arriving passenger stuck between the doors, the remaining stopgaps consisted of a "push-back" mechanism incorporated into each door's motor and a circuit that extinguished a light in the conductor's booth, an alert that the doors had failed to close all the way. The push-back function was intended to prevent passengers from intentionally prying the doors open, while allowing them to free themselves if unintentionally pinned. Wedging a hand between the doors would no longer cause them to spring open: the doors could be forced, but only if they were already separated by a three-inch gap. If a door closed on a narrow part of a passenger's body or clothing, and the conductor failed to notice, an indicator light in the conductor's booth would signal the problem.

But this system could malfunction. In cases when it did, a passenger could be trapped in the doors or, worse, pinned and dragged by the train. In the mid-1980s, several passengers were killed in this fashion. A report by the MTA documented 121 known instances in 1986 in which the doors had remained open on moving trains and 56 "drag incidents" in the following year.[35] A task force created by the agency studied the problem and recommended a door redesign, but transit officials were reluctant to rework the doors and again give passengers the upper hand.[36] In the 2000s, sensitive edges were again installed in new cars in order to comply with the ADA, but older cars remained the workhorses of the fleet for many years, greeting recalcitrant passengers with hard rubber, and the clunking and whirring of the hidden worm drive within the subway's wall—an unyielding manifestation of the system's distrust of its human users.

In this brief history of a somewhat esoteric topic—the design and redesign of the subway door—we see the story of a technology that is perpetually at odds with its users. Repeatedly, subway doors have been made more responsive and sensitive to passengers' desires, only to later abandon these changes in favor of a more inflexible approach. The trains could run on time, but they would have to become technological monsters to do so, acting against notions of decency and basic public safety. The values that the system holds dear—punctuality, reliability, efficiency—are inevitably opposed to another set of human values, as well as the subjective needs and desires of individual users. Instead of a two-way process in which technology is steadily brought into line with social norms and expectations, the relationship between the subway doors and their users has been a mutually antagonistic stalemate.

Counting On Courtesy

In the attempt to discipline a recalcitrant user population, technology is not the only frontier. Throughout the history of the subway, its administrators have also repeatedly attempted a more nuanced form of behavioral engineering. Through public education campaigns, New York City's transit agencies have tried to activate the system of etiquette that guides passenger behavior at the subway doors, through public education campaigns. While their first efforts relied upon unadorned appeals to systemic imperatives, their messaging evolved over time, later seeking to rationalize subway etiquette through the free use of affective language and social signifiers tied to class and gender. The posters, signs, and symbols they have used reveal an attempt to humanize and personalize the dry abstractions of systemic justice, drawing on rationalizations linked with social justice, collective identity, and conventional morality.[37]

During the 1920s, as ridership on the system escalated, a series of advertisements appeared in Interborough Rapid Transit Company subway cars, each one laid out to resemble a fictional broadsheet newspaper, the *Subway Sun*. The posters asked passengers to observe various rules of subway etiquette that stood to increase the capacity or efficiency of the system.

Initially, the advertisements were spare and formal, and resembled a series of signs already posted inside subway cars that sternly advised passengers to refrain from smoking or spitting. An advertisement in 1927, for example, addressed passengers in black, bold-faced text, its only embellishment an imitation newspaper masthead:

> **Loading delays make train delays.** You can help greatly to speed up service if you will avoid crowding around doorways whenever this is possible and if you will always wait for people to get off before getting on.

Below this text, the transit authority signed the announcement in terse capitals, announcing its authorship. The poster starkly conveys the central rationale of systemic justice: let other passengers exit and help "speed up service."

From this point on, the advertisements quickly evolved in format and in tone, becoming less formal and seeking to personalize both the subject and the object of suggestions regarding passenger etiquette. In this way, they reframed passenger etiquette not simply as efficient behavior from the standpoint of the system but as a moral obligation to fellow riders. The new advertisements featured strongly normative language, depicting the victims of transgressions as polite and respectable, while their perpetrators appear as uncouth boors. In 1928, an illustrative example was modeled after an editorial response to a reader's inquiry:

FOR COMFORT AND CONVENIENCE

One of our patrons writes:
"What better can you do in the Subway Sun than to call emphatic attention, by illustration or otherwise, to the obnoxious custom practiced by both males and females of sitting with legs crossed and extending into the aisle to the great inconvenience and annoyance of other passengers."

We Suggest Also That You Don't Crowd Car Doorways or Hold Doors Open. Such Things Only Slow Up Service.

Whether the concerned "patron" was fictional or real, attributing the suggestion to an individual passenger served to personalize the advertisement's claim on the behavior of passengers, giving the request a different kind of authority than that of a faceless transit agency. Similarly, the advertisement rationalizes its request by referring to the impression made upon fellow passengers: obnoxiousness, inconvenience, and annoyance are the primary costs of violating norms of courtesy. At the same time, the advertisement is not wholeheartedly committed to this rhetorical approach. It concludes by again invoking systemic imperatives, suggesting that riders avoid behaviors that "slow up service."

Subway Sun advertisements later abandoned even this kind of language, further personalizing and moralizing subway etiquette. For roughly two decades, starting in 1947, the transit agency ran a series of *Subway Sun* ads that featured the work of a popular cartoonist named Amelia Opdyke Jones, or "Oppy." The ads went further in tying social class to improper subway etiquette, depicting a recurrent heavyset character with a porcine nose who was labeled in accordance with the behavioral program he was violating at any given moment, alternately appearing as the "door boor," the "door blocker," the "space hog," and so on. The victims of his rudeness were typically female—a young woman being pushed onto the tracks by the door boor in his hurry to get down the platform, or an elderly woman hitting him with a bag, while a caption reads, "Hit him again, lady! We don't like door blockers either."[38] Even when the advertisements seek to encourage coordinated collective behavior, rather than discourage individual transgression, they make appeals to immediate ethical principles rather than abstract systemic imperatives. "Have a heart for others, please load in line," an advertisement reads, depicting two scenes, side by side: one in which loading and unloading passengers clash in the open doorway of a subway car, resulting in a tangle of limbs and cries of pain; and another, framed within a heart-shaped motif, in which passengers smile at their compatriots as they unload and load the car in orderly, single-file lines.[39]

In the early 1950s, Oppy's *Subway Sun* advertisements were joined by audible etiquette advice offered by television actors and other well-known celebrities and broadcast via public address system in the busiest stations. Just as the visual ads humanized and moralized appropriate passenger behavior, the recorded announcements pursued a similar strategy:

> Attention all high school students. I know you feel good about getting out of class, but remember the men and women who are riding in that subway with you are people like your own fathers and mothers. Be respectful to them. Don't shove or horseplay in the coaches.[40]

In the early 1960s, the agency turned to a still different tactic for adding normative meaning to its passenger behavior campaigns. A talking kitten known as Etti-Cat appeared on posters inside subway cars, offering a combination of stories and advice. "I'm flabbergasted!" Etti-Cat says, in the first of these posters. "All I did was to give a seat to a little white haired lady

FIGURE 4.3. Posters designed in the 1950s by Amelia "Oppy" Opdyke Jones translated the functional requirements of the subway system into a colorful moral universe populated by chivalric altruists on one hand, and boorish rule breakers on the other.
Images: Amelia Opdyke Jones, New York City Transit Authority, "The Subway Sun, Vol. XVII, No. 3: *Have a Heart for Others—Please Load in Line*," 1950, XX.2018.4.8, Car Card Collection; "The Subway Sun, Vol. XVIII, No. 5: *Be a Knight for a Day!*," 1958, XX.2010.606.22, Subway Sun Collection, and "The Subway Sun, Vol. XXIII, No. 12: *Hit Him Again Lady!*," 1956, XX.2010.606.27, Subway Sun Collection; all at the New York Transit Museum. With permission of New York Transit Museum.

and they pinned a medal on me!"[41] By this time, the problems caused by excess ridership—those of the door boor and the space hog—were becoming increasingly irrelevant, and as the system entered the lean years of the 1970s, passenger etiquette faded from the chief concerns of the transit agency, which was now forced to contend with escalating crime, severely deteriorating equipment, and serious safety concerns. In a sign of the times, the second Etti-Cat poster discouraged vandalism rather than inappropriate crowd behavior.

By the 1990s, however, both the city and its transit system were experiencing a renaissance, and sustained economic growth led to a resumed increase in ridership. On packed platforms and in crowded rush-hour trains, chaotic passenger behavior again led to severely delayed service, as it had in the boom times of the 1920s, 1930s, and 1940s. To compensate for a lack of investment and expansion of the physical infrastructure, the MTA sought again to influence the normative infrastructure of the subway. This time, the agency pursued a comprehensive campaign entitled *Step Aside, Speed Your Ride*, which was modeled after a successful behavior modification initiative adopted in the Hong Kong underground. Conductors were instructed to close the doors and leave the station promptly after a forty-five-second dwell time, regardless of whether passengers were still attempting to board the train. Clocks mounted on the platforms visibly counted down the time until the doors would close. Thirty "etiquette officers" in florescent vests were stationed on platforms and entry stairwells in order to encourage passengers to move in an orderly fashion. Bright orange boxes were painted on platforms around the places where doors would open, showing people where to stand. Meanwhile, recorded messages on the platforms wished passengers a good morning and asked them to stand to the left or right of the boxes, further reinforcing the comprehensive symbolic and institutional reprogramming of the space.[42] These measures failed, and in 1998 the MTA turned to penalization and enforcement, making door holding a misdemeanor carrying a fine of up to $100—a measure of last resort. But this penalty was an empty threat: without additional MTA or police officers patrolling the platforms, it remained safe for passengers to hold the doors with impunity.

In the 2010s, as ridership continued to rise, the problems caused by crowding and passenger misconduct again reached crisis levels for the MTA. Simultaneously, the transit agency rolled out a new initiative reminiscent of the *Subway Sun* posters of the 1940s and 1950s. The *Courtesy Counts* campaign produced a series of illustrated etiquette advisories, each one encouraging or discouraging a specific pattern of behavior. In field observations conducted between 2015 and 2018, scores of these advertisements were visible throughout the system, typically in the interior of subway cars. Instead of the "door boor," or the "litter bug," the posters featured a series of green or red stick figures. To a degree, these representations of normative behavior are depersonalized, permitting us to freely fill in the faces of courtesy or rudeness with our imaginations. But they retain gender and class signifiers, showing the stick figures in attire. "Keep The Doors Clear So Others Can Board," one reads, depicting a gray male figure struggling through a crowd of red door blockers in business clothes. "Bottom Line: Blocking doors blocks traffic and slows service for everyone." Another poster targeted a breach of etiquette that was gendered by its very name, "manspreading"—a presumptively masculine practice that involves sprawling one's legs to the left and right. "Dude, Stop the Spread," the poster reads. "It's a Space Issue."

Although the design of subway doors and the rhetorical strategies of etiquette campaigns have evolved over time, their objective has remained the same—to make the system more efficient and more reliable by disciplining its users. Through a combination of material and symbolic intervention, subway administrators have sought both to control passenger behavior in and around the subway doors and to modify the way passengers think about this behavior. In order to do so, they have drawn upon systems of justification that depart from the underlying ethical principles that legitimize normative infrastructure.

For example, ad campaigns characterize breaches of normative infrastructure as directly injurious to other passengers, or associate these
breaches with social class or gender, invoking forms of etiquette more
commonly used to draw symbolic boundaries between classes of people,
rather than to ease the function of infrastructure. In essence, these campaigns draw on well-worn systems of everyday public morality that govern
behavior between strangers, and put these moral frameworks to work on
behalf of cold infrastructural benchmarks. The messages are transformed:
"Help speed service," gives way to "Be respectful," "Have a heart," or "Don't
be rude." Instead of simply emphasizing the detached systemic justice of
behaviors that improve reliability and service "for all," they resort to jus-
tifications that, from the standpoint of the passenger, are immediate, personal, and social. The objectives of the measures summarized above is to
convince subway riders to internalize the norms required by the formal
infrastructure, at which point, pushback mechanisms and public advertisements might become unnecessary.[43]

But this goal has never been achieved. Passenger behavior has proven
resistant to the MTA's repeated efforts to instill discipline through a variety of technological, rhetorical, and legal strategies. Journalists and transit
officials have offered a colorful explanation for the unique intransigence
of New York subway riders. In this essentialist account, New Yorkers are
regarded as stereotypically pushy and self-interested, culturally resistant
to the discipline the subway requires. In response to the 1990s *Step Aside,
Speed Your Ride* campaign, a *New York Times* columnist remarked that the
MTA was not merely involved in "crowd control . . . [W]hat the authority
is really up to is much more revolutionary: trying to teach manners to New
Yorkers."[44] The behavior of subway riders is based on "chaos and mercenary
striving," another writer for the *Times* noted. "Telling New Yorkers they
can't jockey for position is tantamount to telling Angelenos that they can't
wear sweatpants. It goes against their nature."[45] One newspaper editor, making a similar argument about New York rider culture, dismissed the entire
strategy as hopelessly idealistic:

> The top executives of the Transit Authority are periodically seized with
> the notion they are running the London Underground or some other
> orderly urban transportation system. Their latest idea is to speed the
> loading of subway trains by asking New Yorkers to develop a more refined
> sense of subway etiquette.

This is akin to dreaming that midtown traffic can be untangled, double parking can be eliminated and taxi horns silenced. New York is a boisterous place and its subway system is never going to be a model of decorum. . . .

Recent budget cuts have hurt service. Trains run less frequently and move more slowly, sometimes creating maddening delays and passenger congestion. Partly to compensate for the slower service, the Transit Authority now wants to move passengers off and on trains more quickly. Good luck. . . .

The Transit Authority is also under the misconception it can speed things along by ordering conductors to wait no more than 45 seconds at a station before closing the doors. Since when have conductors controlled when subway doors are sealed? The last time I looked, that was determined by the feet, arms and knapsacks of riders holding the doors open for fellow New Yorkers dashing to catch the train.[46]

While transit officials have voiced optimism about their etiquette campaigns, they too have often endorsed the notion that New Yorkers were exceptional in their pushiness and contempt for authority.[47] "You don't see this on any other transit system anywhere in the world," remarked a transit authority spokesman. "But we do have an in-your-face culture here in New York City."[48] These explanations attribute the stubborn indiscipline of New York City Subway riders to a stereotyped version of the city's social identity. Poor subway etiquette is less a New York problem than a "New Yawk" problem, a regional character flaw, akin to talking too loud, or honking as soon as the traffic light turns green. Rhetorically, this explanation turns the ethical logic of official etiquette campaigns against the city, suggesting that New York is a city of door boors and space hogs: if loading in line is an act of personal morality and ethical regard for one's fellow passengers, then a collective failure to do so suggests endemic rudeness.

The Subway and Its Discontents

My fieldwork in the subway supported a different explanation. In 2015 and early 2016, crowded and unpredictable conditions in the subway were rapidly becoming the norm. Delays were becoming more frequent and more prolonged, prompting growing concern among the city's transit advocates and journalists. *Gothamist,* a popular blog devoted to city politics and culture, initiated a series of sardonic reports chronicling particularly awful

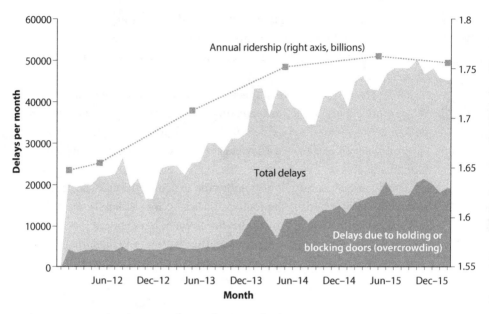

FIGURE 4.4. Delays due to crowding on the New York subway, 2012–16.

commutes.[49] By early 2017, deteriorating conditions in the subway had become politically toxic, and Mayor Bill de Blasio and Governor Andrew Cuomo traded barbs in city newspapers over responsibility for the growing crisis.[50]

During this period, I undertook an extended series of observations in the subway, focusing on the local conditions that precipitated moments of passenger misbehavior or poor etiquette. This research suggested that breakdowns in normative infrastructure are not rooted in the city's collective culture so much as they are prompted by specific environmental conditions that are common in its subway system, that become pervasive when the system is crowded and service is delayed. Tight spaces, collective urgency, and a lack of formal social control are the conditions that make normative infrastructure necessary in the first place and that prompted the system of social etiquette one finds in the subway. But when scarcity and ambiguity escalate beyond a given threshold, the normative infrastructure breaks down, precisely when it is needed most. Under these exceptional conditions, riders abandon their largely unconscious allegiances to the abstract principles of systemic justice, and run colder or hotter in their social cognition: some become calculating and strategic; others become frustrated, angry, upset.

When platforms and the trains become crowded, rule following can deteriorate for reasons that are selfishly rational. Against the norm of letting others exit before entering a subway car, passengers are more likely to push their way onto a train, creating chaos at the doors and producing bottlenecks that extend dwell time. In 2015 and 2016, with several colleagues in the Sociology and Urban Policy and Planning departments at Hunter College, I sent a team of trained graduate and undergraduate students into the subway to systematically observe the conditions under which passengers violate the turn-taking norm at the subway's doors. They found that the probability of rule breaking was positively correlated with crowding: the more people there are in a subway car when it arrives at the platform, the more likely passengers on the platform will push on board before everyone has a chance to leave. This tendency was most pronounced during the morning and afternoon rush, times of great collective urgency. A scarcity of space raises the possibility of not making it on board the train, and a scarcity of time—anxiousness to arrive at work or at home—raises the stakes involved in this prospect. This jolts riders out of their habitual obeisance to the subway's norms, and leads some to act selfishly, choosing tangible personal advantage over abstract collective benefit. Interestingly, pushing on board peaks when the subway car is approaching full capacity but has not quite reached this point—in other words, when breaking the rules is most likely to make a difference in getting on board.

Under a condition of urgency and uncertainty created by system delays, the spatial idiosyncrasy of the system acts to further encourage selfishly strategic behavior. The system's mazelike qualities frustrate riders' ability to apply spatial knowledge acquired at one station to another. As a result, the subway favors arcane, place-specific knowledge. In order to avoid the many choke points in the system, for example, many passengers will "prewalk," taking a position in a subway car that reduces the distance to their objective.[51] Rather than reducing congestion, however, this approach can simply displace congestion to the interior of an already-crowded subway car:

8:15 p.m.: Monday evening, March 2016, 6 Train. At 59th Street, in order to connect to the N, Q, and R trains in either direction from the downtown 6, passengers have to walk down a single set of stairs to a small landing, then down one of two sets of stairs to the platform. Much of the time, the initial set of stairs proves too narrow for the stream of passengers— the first passengers to arrive are able to make their way down to the platform quickly, but behind them, a large fan-shaped crowd quickly forms as passengers shuffle forward, waiting for their turn at the stairs. At rush hour it is typical for passengers to run across the platform toward the stairs in order to avoid being stuck in the bottleneck, or to weave frantically between slower moving passengers, hoping to beat others to the stairs and avoid the delay. I'm on the downtown 6 train approaching 59th Street, and a woman near the door has been behaving strangely. At every stop, she turns sideways in the door, making space (but not much space) for passengers moving in and out of the train. Blocking the door in this way is a clear breach of etiquette, and two passengers entering the train at 77th street are visibly put off, one scowling and the other shaking her head after pushing past the woman into the car. At 59th Street station, the door blocking woman's strategy becomes clear. As the train eases to a stop, she turns toward the door to exit, just as seven or eight passengers inside the car also ready themselves to leave. I realize that the door is almost perfectly lined up to minimize the distance to the stairwell down to the N, Q, and R. The door-blocking woman has been guarding an optimal position by the door for at least five stops that I have noticed in order to be first out the door and first to the stairs. The doors open, and she is off and running.

Under historically normal conditions in the subway, space and time are often constrained. Subway etiquette arises in response to these constraints, filling the gaps in the formal infrastructure of the subway by coordinating and regulating passenger behavior. But when space and time are too scarce, and conditions too ambiguous, this mode of habitual, coordinated, unselfish action can give way to other behavioral logics that do not serve the system well. Rather than a culture of endemic rudeness, New Yorker subway riders exhibit something more schizophrenic and complicated: a set of behavioral norms that break down in response to the very conditions they help to alleviate. In the cases discussed above, passengers become strategic and self-serving in ways that compromise the common good.

In other cases, passengers demonstrated a very different reaction to the temporal and spatial scarcity of the subway, becoming visibly frustrated, or, in the technical term used by ethnographer Jack Katz to describe road rage, "pissed off."[52] Crowding generates delays, and these delays make time scarce and also uncertain, creating a temporal ambiguity that produces a palpable anxiety among passengers. A precise timetable theoretically governs the arrivals and departures of a given train, but the rider's experience of time on the subway tends to be impressionistic. Elapsed time is measured against a baseline that we derive from experience, indicating how frequently trains should arrive, and how fast they should move at any given time of day. In an era of chronic delays, these expectations are routinely contradicted, heightening awareness of the passage of time and producing an ambiguity that provokes psychological stress:

9:11a.m.: Monday, late February, 2016. Newkirk Avenue Station. The B train is delayed. The express side of the platform is thick with passengers, while the Q train just left a few minutes ago, leaving the local side of the platform clear. I've been waiting for 12 minutes for the B train at a time of day when it should be arriving every 3–4 minutes. As the crowding on the platform intensifies, several passengers begin periodically walking to the yellow-painted edge of the platform and looking down the tracks. Eventually, they colonize this area completely, their bodies angled toward the direction from which the train will eventually come. Looking down the platform in the direction of Coney Island, from around the midpoint of the platform, I count eight passengers standing at its very edge. Their positions are forcing other passengers, those particularly intent on seeing as far down the tracks as they can, to lean out over the tracks and crane their necks.

I notice a short man in an orange windbreaker who is standing several feet inside the yellow paint, but making frequent trips into the danger zone. Again and again, at rapid intervals, he paces out to the edge and leans out over the tracks, lifting his left leg to place his upper body almost at a 45 degree angle. He goes and looks again. And again. Every 20–30 seconds or so. The waiting—the indeterminacy of the train's arrival—is visibly more than he can bear. I was already running late for an appointment and have now lost hope of being on time, but this concern has moved into the background. A nervous energy fills the air, fueled by our collective anxiousness and expectancy. Subjective emotional states are absorbed and subsumed within a collective hum of frustration and anticipation. It is us against the train. Us against the absence of a train.

To point out the obvious, passengers do not speed the arrival of the train by craning their necks or leaning dangerously over the track bed to look for it. This behavior, though perhaps understandable, is not rational. It speaks of a basic conflict between the broken rhythms of delayed train service and an aversion to ambiguity that is hardwired within human psychology. Our anxiousness to get on the train, when combined with the uncertainty concerning when it will arrive, creates psychological discomfort that we attempt

FIGURE 4.5. Expectancy. A passenger leans out over the tracks to look for the next scheduled express train at Newkirk Station. The anxiety of subway riders became palpable in 2015 and 2016, as service delays added unpredictability to the stress caused by crowding on trains and platforms.

to resolve by peering down the tracks. We know that will not make the train arrive sooner, but we also understand that seeing the train on its way will ease our discomfort.

On subway platforms, as in any crowd situation, collective emotional states are intensified by the behavior of individual actors, like the man in the windbreaker described above. New York City Subway riders are famous for their stoicism, and this reserve can be seen as an adaptation to crowded, anonymous conditions. But irregularities in the spatial and temporal environment of the subway can serve to puncture the impassive veneer that is the norm. The subjective psychological experience of impatience and frustration, when externalized on a crowded platform or in a packed train, can effervesce into a form of emotional energy, spontaneously generating small collectivities who are opposed to the system itself, which is now revealed as unruly and undependable:[53]

12:40 a.m., Saturday, early December. Canal Street Station. The platform is narrow at this stop, leaving not much space between the tracks and a wall running the length of the platform. It is cold and damp. I just arrived on the platform, but can tell that the Brooklyn-bound train is extremely late. Riders crowd the platform in ragged lines—many with their backs to the wall, others standing directly in front of them. There is just enough space between this waiting crowd and the tracks for passengers to walk along the yellow caution strip, although this brings them within inches of the platform's edge.

Periodically, a man down the platform is shouting, "Where's the fucking train?" After he does this two or three times, at seemingly regular intervals, I start walking in the direction of the voice, hoping to catch a glimpse of him. I hear it again, and I realize I am close to its source, within maybe 30 or 40 feet, but there are so many people on the platform that I can't pinpoint it. Finally, he shouts as I pass next to him, and I am able to identify the shouter. He is a tall, white man in his twenties, standing with his back against the wall. He has slightly shaggy brown hair and is dressed in a nondescript, casual fashion, except for some conspicuously high-tech blue running shoes. I am surprised to find that he does not appear visibly anxious in the slightest. He is not peering down the platform into the darkness of the tunnel, as others are, but is instead staring blankly into the space directly in front him, his gaze perpendicular to the tracks.

"Where's the fucking train?" he shouts, for the fifth or sixth time. I settle into the crowd near him, and realize that, rather than seeming alarmed by his shouting, others nearby are trying to engage him in an affirmative way. A middle-aged woman directly in front of me looks toward him when he shouts again and nods enthusiastically as if in support of his line of inquiry. A younger man to my right echoes him quietly. "Where's the fucking train?" he says, after the next shout. "Where is it?"

Such situations (and such people) are rare, but they reveal an implicit social dynamic that may not be uncommon, particularly in times of chronic uncertainty. The ethical logic that justifies subway etiquette relies upon a conflation of the subway system, a massive sociomaterial construct, with the common good. Moments of dysfunction, unreliability, or discomfort in the formal infrastructure of the subway break this bond, placing groups of passengers or individual passengers at odds with the system.

In other cases, I witnessed passengers directing their anger and frustration with delays not at the system but at one another. It is easy to think of these cases as random and personality driven, but they often coincide with service disruptions or crowding, and seem to arise from the unique interpersonal and physical conditions that these problems cause. Viewed through the lens of normative infrastructure, such episodes reveal themselves as violent breaches of norms of coordination and compromise that bind together riders in a sort of transient community.[54]

In 2015 and 2016, as ridership and delays mounted rapidly, the MTA observed an increase in unwell and "unruly" passengers on the system, including an escalation in the number of physical altercations. On nine occasions during my participant observation, I observed disputes between passengers that were related to crowded or ambiguous conditions.

6:10 p.m., Wednesday in February, 2016. West 4th Street Station. The train is crowded, but not quite a sardine can. Lots of passengers getting on and off at each stop. A heavyset Black guy and a Latino guy of medium build, both apparently in their 20s, collide when simultaneously attempting to pass through the doors. The Latino guy is knocked sideways as he exits, while the Black guy continues into the car and sits in a newly vacated seat, seemingly oblivious. A moment passes as more people enter the train and take positions in the car. Just as the doors are closing, the Latino guy appears again, holding one door with both hands. "Hey" he says. "Hey!" Eventually the larger man looks up. "You should learn to say excuse me," the Latino guy says. "Huh?" the Black guy responds. "You should learn to say excuse me," the Latino guy repeats, angrily. "Okay," the other guy answers slowly and with pronounced indifference, looking back at a comic

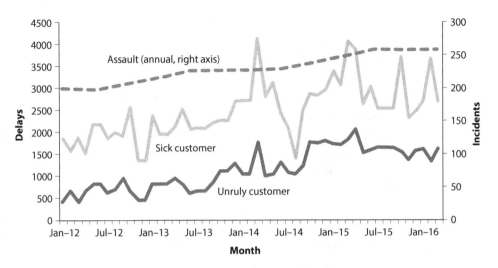

FIGURE 4.6. Assaults and delays due to unruly and sick customers on the New York subway, 2012–16.

book he has pulled out of his bag. "No, not okay," the Latino guy says, still blocking the door. There is a long pause as the two men stare at each other. "How about this?" the Black guy says, now seething with rage. "Fuck you, okay? Not today. Not today motherfucker." At this point, many other passengers are observing the interaction, but seem to become almost instantaneously tired of the drama. "Let it go Papa" says a Latina woman who looks to be in her late 50s or 60s, seated to my left. She is addressing the Latino guy in the door, and it occurs to me that I don't know if she means to let the door go or to let the quarrel go. The quarrel is stopping the door. "Next time be more polite!" the Latino guy says. Several people—I don't see who—now audibly grumble or sigh to my left and right. The Latino guy nods emphatically, as if to indicate he's made his point, and lets the door close. The Black guy proceeds to chuckle and mutter under his breath for the next few minutes as the subway moves toward the next station.

I observed many minor verbal confrontations of this sort during my fieldwork. The reaction of the aggrieved party in this exchange is telling—the initial physical contact was, as far as I could tell, neither man's fault, but what he ultimately wanted was a show of politeness and contrition that would provide closure. A restoration of etiquette. This was typical. Subway riders' disputes focused narrowly on physical breaches of the social norms of the subway. On a downtown C train, a short White man in a camouflage army baseball cap who I took to be a tourist failed to move far enough into the car for a tall Black woman. The woman berated him, "Get in the train, slow-poke!" Anger briefly flashed across his face, but he then held up his hands in apology and shuffled sidewise toward his female companion and three children I assumed were his kids. The quaintly chiding insult, "slowpoke," appeared to disarm him, in spite of his humiliation. Within moments, he and his accuser had moved on, the man enjoying his ride with his family, the woman bobbing her head to music on her headphones. On another occasion during my research, on an extremely crowded, moving B train during the morning commute, two men came to blows over accusations that one had shoved the other as the train bounced and shimmied down the tracks. Several onlookers pulled the larger man back, while the other slipped and sprawled on the floor under our feet. "He fucking pushed me!" he yelled up at us.

Temporal ambiguity on the system does not just produce selfish behavior, messy entrances and exits, and the cascading delays that result from routine moments of disorder. It spills over into qualitatively different categories of problems that are fostered by tense, chaotic, and ambiguous conditions on trains and platforms. These problems—for example, fainting spells and fights—amount to significant breakdowns in the normative infrastructure of the system, producing a feedback loop of escalating delays and growing distrust on the part of passengers, who respond by behaving even more poorly. In early 2017, a sobering new figure was released by the MTA. After rising to unprecedented levels the year before, ridership had actually declined slightly in 2016. Some public commentators pointed to the rise of ride-sharing platforms, such as Uber and Lyft, and the expansion of CitiBike, New York's bicycle-sharing program, as well as an increase in telecommuting. But among transit experts and advocates, an alternate possibility seemed just as plausible: conditions on the subway had gotten so crowded and so unreliable that New Yorkers were simply avoiding it.[55]

With crowding and delays reaching unprecedented levels, the MTA revisited a measure undertaken several times in the past. Platform guards, euphemistically referred to as "courtesy officers" were stationed along the platforms on some of the system's busiest lines. Wearing bright vests and wielding flashlights, the guards are intended to add a degree of formal social control to a space that typically relies on informal rule-following. Their role is to urge passengers to move into the cars and to discourage door holding—in short, to formalize and enforce the normative infrastructure. Once again, the

FIGURE 4.7. Normative infrastructure. Coordinating movement and navigating crowded conditions are basic behavioral requirements of the system, under the best of conditions. In 2017, overall subway ridership dropped, leading experts to wonder whether crowding and the resulting delays had become so severe that riders were abandoning the subway in favor of other, less stressful modes of transportation.

transit agency is attempting to buy space and time by convincing passengers to stick to the norms required for systemic efficiency. If there is no flexibility in the formal infrastructure—no room for improvements in the MTA's budget, and no leeway provided by the aging technology of the system—then the only apparent area of "give" is the normative infrastructure.

This view, born of desperation, is shortsighted. The history of the subway and its present social ecosystem tell the same story. The material and normative infrastructures of the subway are actually part of a complex, but coherent, sociomaterial system. When the technology of the subway fails—when the trains do not arrive on time or are rerouted owing to technical failure, or when they simply fall short of meeting the human demand—the normative infrastructure of the subway does not pick up the slack. It *also* breaks down, producing vicious circles of technological failure and social disorder.

In the New York subway, we learn something new about how people relate to material objects and technologies. We learn that the social life of the city is densely and inextricably intertwined with infrastructures that shape that social life, and rely on it in turn. The brief, superficial social interactions that take place in the subway, it turns out, are as crucial to the movement of trains through the system as the steel rails that lie beneath us as we rumble through the dark. In this sense, the subway does not just serve the public, it *is* the public.

PART III

Disappearance

5

The Newsstand

FIGURE 5.1. The newsstand.

It is early December. The darkness has fallen, and with it, the temperature. By 4:30 p.m., the gloom has transformed Ron's newsstand from a dingy steel box into a rectangle of golden light against the dim gray buildings of Downtown Manhattan. A cold breeze is blowing off the Hudson, but warmth emanates from the newsstand, even if it is just the figurative kind. Ron smiles down at me, eyes wide below bushy eyebrows and close-cropped black hair. He has just said something funny, which he does often, but I missed the punch line, distracted by a group of Italian tourists who had briefly stopped at the kiosk. "Sorry—I didn't catch that," I say. Ron stares at me, hands turned upwards in an exaggerated shrug. "Shark fishing!" he says.[1]

As an architectural form, the newsstand was born in these streets, a runty sibling of the subway and the skyscraper. For more than a century, these small sidewalk structures have existed in a kind of symbiotic relationship with the titans of New York City's landscape, cropping up in the shadows cast by glass or limestone towers, like a species of urban lichen. Spend enough time in New York City, and it is possible to develop a sixth sense for public objects like this—an urban telepathy, which allows one to correctly anticipate a news-stand that one has never actually seen before, just around the next corner, across from a park or a hotel. Amid the density and the urgency of the city, the newsstand makes sense. It offers a no-frills convenience to the hurrying masses—people whose hunger for media is matched by their scarcity of time. A quick exchange of information for money has always been the point.

Generically speaking, a newsstand is a type of kiosk, a public object that maximizes the convenience of economic activity by minimizing the time and space required. The purpose of a kiosk, simply put, is to reduce the friction of commerce. Unlike a brick-and-mortar convenience store, bodega, or maga-zine shop, a newsstand occupies well-trafficked public space and thus allevi-ates one of the primary transaction costs of economic exchange—namely, the amount of time and energy required to seek out a desired commodity. As writer Ariana Kelly notes, a kiosk is "an element of the fray . . . One can use it, theoretically at least, without breaking one's flow through space and time."[2]

In the case of Ron's newsstand, a desire for efficiency and economy is evident in the object's physical form. The front of the structure serves as both display and storage, holding rows of candy and stacks of newspapers. Strings of postcards and souvenirs cover practically every square inch of space around its rectangular opening. Ron has handwritten the prices on small pieces of cardboard, taped below each item. The guiding principle is to remove all mystery.[3] Pedestrians wandering by should be able to align their own needs with Ron's offerings in a fleeting instant—here is what is for sale, and this is how much it costs.

The affordances of this object, however, are actually somewhat nuanced. On the one hand, it is simply a container. Its purpose is to hold Ron and shelter him from the elements. Distilled to its material basics, a newsstand is really nothing more than a large steel box bolted to the sidewalk—a thing meant to hold more things, and a person who sells those things.

On the other hand, if we refocus on the human encounters that occur within and around this object, we see something different. All economic activity requires communication. In order to exchange commodities for currency, we need to also trade words, facial expressions, and hand gestures. With this in mind, the essence of this steel box is not what it encloses, but what it allows to pass through. Like a ticket booth or a checkout counter, a newsstand is an object built to facilitate a specific kind of social interaction. These interactions are typically minimal—a word or two of greeting, and a quick handling of money. In fact, even a token amount of verbal communication is optional if the buyer is in a rush, or if proprietor and customer do not share a spoken language, which, according to Ron, is a common situation.

I glance at my notebook. In the last forty-five minutes, seventeen people have paused at Ron's stand, and, while most of these interactions have been brief and transactional, many have not. My fieldnotes record the following:

> 3:37 p.m.: An East Asian man in his 50s asks for directions to a 7 Eleven. Ron tells him where the closest two are located, and gives him directions to each.
>
> 3:50 p.m.: Elderly Black woman stops to complain about the weather. She is one of Ron's many loyal customers. At 85 years of age, still working at a nearby office. She calls him Darling. He calls her "Dear." (He calls every woman this.) He asks her if she wants anything. She is annoyed by the question. "Darling if I wanted something, you would already know it."
>
> 4:00 p.m.: A white guy in his 40s or 50s asks Ron to charge his phone. He has a shopping cart covered with black plastic—he is perhaps unhoused, or a street vendor, or both. Ron nods and wordlessly obliges, plugging the phone in, while selling Lotto tickets to another customer.
>
> 4:13 p.m.: An office worker in his 20s—South Asian, like Ron— buys a Coke and lingers at the stand for about fifteen minutes. He talks about a recent vacation with his girlfriend, shows Ron and me pictures on his phone. Conversation goes to politics. Then back to vacations and swimming. (All three of us are poor swimmers it turns out.) Ron tells a joke about shark fishing.

Between and during these interactions, Ron has sold candy, lottery tick-ets, and bottled water with cheerful efficiency, acknowledging customers with a nod and a quick smile, and providing them what they need, even while engaged in conversation with other customers or passersby. He has effortlessly divided his attention, and this has allowed him to do the actual business of running a newsstand while engaging in a wide range of unremu-nerative activity. I wonder to myself where exactly his vocation begins, and where it ends. Ron does not waste a minute of his time, or of anyone else's. And yet, so much of what he does *at* work is not what he does *for* work.

At Ron's newsstand, the young office worker is still talking. He has moved on to another topic, and is now complaining about the subway, the lingua franca of New York City small talk. He pulls out his phone for the second or third time, and swipes and taps adroitly until he finds what he is looking for. "Look at this, man! This is heartless." He holds up his screen to show us the cover of today's *New York Post*, which depicts a rotten apple impaled on the spire of the Empire State Building. The image is meant to be a meta-phor for the city—"De Blasio's New York" the headline for the day. Moved by some vague instinct, I look down toward the base of the newsstand. At my feet, on the lowest shelf, lies a small stack of unsold copies of the *New York Post* displaying the very same image. These days, a stand like Ron's will sell perhaps fifteen or twenty newspapers in a day, down from thousands just a few decades ago. With the ascendancy of digital media, the material lifeblood of the newsstand has dwindled away. In his search for the *New York Post* cover, the office worker did not even consider the possibility that there might be a newspaper at a newsstand. I glanced sideways at Ron, who was shaking his head appreciatively at the young man's phone. If he sensed the irony of the situation, he gave no indication.

In this final section of the book, we consider objects that make trouble by disappearing, and in the process, removing their affordances from the landscape. Sometimes objects vanish abruptly, consumed by fire or floodwa-ter. Other times, they succumb to neglect or are slowly devoured by decay, gradually disintegrating into a natural or manmade landscape. But perhaps the most common reason for an object's disappearance involves a differ-ent kind of destructive force—a combination of technological innovation and profit seeking that Karl Marx and, later, economist Joseph Schumpeter referred to as the "creative destruction" of capitalism.[4] In order to generate profit, corporations produce a new commodity that is functionally equiva-lent to an older one, but that seems to offer some advantage to consumers. Maybe the new thing is more energy efficient. Or perhaps it is cheaper, faster,

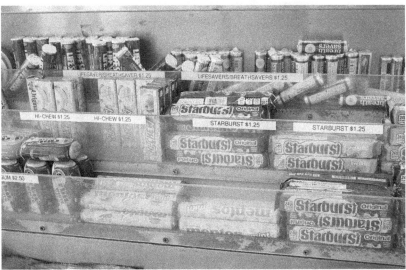

FIGURE 5.2. Removing mystery. Manhattan's newsstand operators maximize the efficiency and transparency of transactions through strategic placement of products and signage. The general organizing principle of items for sale is a hierarchy of visibility that corresponds to their popularity. This is an adaptation to the high-speed social life of the area's sidewalks, where the newsstand has to reduce friction, luring passersby out of the flow and quickly returning them to their desired path through urban space.

lighter, larger, and so on. Through this process, objects continually vanish from the public realm, replaced by newer and ostensibly better things. Most New Yorkers now carry an item in their pocket that makes the newsstand and the payphone redundant, a tiny device that places a vast network of digitized information at its owner's disposal.

Newsstands like Ron's were once ubiquitous across the city, and several hundred still can be found perched on street corners adjacent to busy intersections, near subway entrances, or close to tourist attractions. But in other respects, the city's newsstands occupy increasingly shaky ground. Like their cousins, the humble payphones that once punctuated the urban landscape, these public objects are threatened by a combination of technological change and a hostile regulatory environment. Both objects have been repeatedly targeted by city officials eager to declutter sidewalks and do away with unprofitable public artifacts, with the aim of making the city "smarter," cleaner, wealthier, and more modern. But what, if anything, does the city sacrifice when the newsstands vanish from the streets? How will the social life of the city change when these tiny islands of human connection withdraw, swept away by the tide of digital communication? And, more generally, what do we lose when a public object disappears?

Rationalizing the Sidewalk

If public telephones and newsstands do disappear entirely from city streets, technology will bear only part of the blame. Generically, the City of New York categorizes newsstands and payphones as forms of "street furniture," grouping them with street signs and garbage cans. This term is telling, as it reduces these objects to their materiality, surgically excising their human dimension—the people who use them, and the many things those people use them for. City officials have often viewed both the newsstand and the payphone through a lens that emphasizes their inert and aesthetic qualities—their ability to clog sidewalks and attract graffiti. A look back at the history of the newsstand offers insights into how this regulatory tunnel vision came about.

Until late in the nineteenth century, outdoor news sales were an informal enterprise, largely unregulated by the city. As long as they did not offend property owners or block busy sidewalks, vendors were free to sell newspapers anywhere they chose, propping a stack of papers on an overturned barrel or a wooden box. These improvised, portable objects were the city's first newsstands—their function was to elevate newspapers above the filth of the nineteenth-century streetscape and make them visible and accessible to passersby. Vendors typically set up them up in nooks and crannies along

FIGURE 5.3. Feeding an information-hungry city. New York City's first newsstands were simply tables, barrels, or crates that elevated printed matter off the city streets. They bore little resemblance to the brushed-steel and frosted-glass boxes that now adorn the city's street corners. Throughout the first half of the twentieth century, the permanence and the physical mass of newsstands increased, along with controversy over their entitlement to valuable sidewalk space. Photo: Lewis Wicke Hines, courtesy of National Child Labor Committee collection, Library of Congress, Prints and Photographs Division.

busy sidewalks, spaces that offered proximity and visibility to pedestrians, but that did not block foot traffic.

As the newsstand became a more common and familiar object across New York, its presence within the city's legal code increased as well. Shopkeepers were often at odds with sidewalk news vendors, and pushed for more stringent regulation. Partly in response to this constituency, officials created a permitting system that allowed temporary newsstands to be licensed for $1 per year. These structures had to be situated within the "stoop line" of street-facing buildings, where they would not obstruct the sidewalk, and could be constructed only with the property owner's permission. Later, the city extended the system to allow permanent newsstands, licensed for $5 per year. For twice that amount, a newsstand could be erected in the most valuable real estate of all—underneath the stairways of elevated train stations, a location that promised both free shelter and a steady stream of customers.[5]

Through the development and evolution of these licensing categories, the city constructed a definition of the newsstand that emphasized its materiality. The legal essence of the newsstand, according to the City of New York, was its capacity to impinge upon the city's most important scarce resource—its crowded sidewalks and streets. As legal scholar Mariana Valverde has pointed out, this is the oldest and most pervasive form of social control that municipal governments exert—the ability to categorize, measure, and license specific uses of urban space.[6] The permitting system legitimized sidewalk news sales, turning an informal practice into a formal enterprise, officially sanctioned and codified. In both legal and material terms, the newsstand had earned its place on the New York City sidewalk.

But the newsstand was doomed to be a controversial public object. Like other forms of street vending, the sidewalk news kiosk proved to be a victim of its own success, its popularity fueling periodic backlashes from city agencies, landlords, and the owners of "brick-and-mortar" storefront businesses. In the 1920s and 1930s, the newsstand's legitimacy was repeatedly contested, with aesthetic criticisms emerging alongside complaints about sidewalk congestion. Prominent civic organizations lamented the disheveled appearance of some newsstands in the city, proposing standardization.[7] Eventually, piggybacking on a controversy concerning the sale of pornography at public news kiosks, the city's license commissioner created a short-lived initiative to replace all newsstands in the city with modern, aesthetically pleasing metal models.[8] But efforts at aesthetic reform did not spread very far. At the height of the Great Depression, thousands of licensed and unlicensed newsstands dotted the city's sidewalks, their idiosyncratic, ad hoc appearance an indication of their humble origins.[9]

In the postwar period, newsstands continued to proliferate across Manhattan's commercial districts. The density of the city's core was increasing, growing in step with the financial services and advertising sectors. A man named Bernard Green, the closest thing to a newsstand tycoon New York has ever seen, recognized an opportunity in the escalating Midtown skyline. During the 1940s, he opened dozens of newsstands in Manhattan's forest of office towers, capitalizing on a national office construction boom. In the age before the smartphone or the Metrocard, Green's newsstands sold Manhattan's office workers everything needed for their evening commute—an afternoon newspaper, a bag of peanuts, and a subway token for the ride home.[10] By the 1950s, most blocks in Midtown and Downtown Manhattan had at least one newsstand on them.[11] In spite of the government's ambivalence toward the object, the newsstand had become a familiar fixture of the city's landscape and, inevitably, part of the social fabric of its sidewalk life.

But not long after the peak of the outdoor news-sales industry in New York City, the newsstand began a long, slow decline. A strike by the typesetters' union in the early 1960s had a prolonged effect on newspaper sales, and by the end of the decade, several of the largest daily newspapers in the city had stopped publishing. The following decade saw further decline in overall news sales. Shrinking newspaper circulation in the city deprived newsstands of much of their business. By 1980, the number of licensed newsstands in the city fell below three hundred—only one in five of the city's permitted newsstands had survived since the industry's heyday, three decades earlier.

Starting in the mid-1970s, however, this trend was temporarily reversed. Bowing to pressure from the newsstand industry, the city loosened the restrictions on what newsstands were permitted to sell. Although the price of items that could be sold at newsstands remained capped at $2, they were no longer restricted to printed matter, and they quickly diversified their offerings to include tobacco products, candy, and trinkets, such as costume jewelry or inexpensive souvenirs. These new sources of revenue helped to stabilize the industry. But another important factor in revitalizing the struggling newsstand business was demographic in nature. A wave of immigrants from India's Gujarat province brought new energy to sidewalk news sales across the city. Initially, many of these newcomers worked newsstands on behalf of nonimmigrant licensees, before purchasing a newsstand or opening their own. As this trend progressed, city officials perceptibly hardened their stance toward the newsstand, aligning themselves with property owners and merchants' associations that had long been opposed to the news sale industry.

A watershed moment in this transition occurred in 1991, when a local association of property owners and business owners on Manhattan's Fifth Avenue attempted to block an application by an Afghani immigrant to open a newsstand on the iconic shopping street. It soon came to light that the Department of Consumer Affairs had declined all newsstand applications on Fifth Avenue over a period of several decades. In the editorial pages of the *New York Times*, a former member of the New York City Arts Commission claimed that Fifth Avenue was "no place for newsstands," criticizing the proposed object as a "clumsy shed" whose "crude design" expressed indifference concerning its august location, "the city's premier location for window shopping, promenading, and boulevarding."[12] The chairman and the president of the Grand Central Partnership added their voices to this chorus, expressing concern about the brutal design of the newsstands, which were "blighting" Midtown

Streets.[13] According to Robert Bookman, a lawyer who has often represented newsstand owners in the city, the timing of these complaints was no coincidence. In a letter defending the Fifth Avenue newsstand, Bookman wryly noted that "newsstands were not the focus of such attacks when they were primarily operated by Caucasian veterans and the disabled. Opposition began when the industry became dominated by Asian immigrants."[14]

The newsstand's customer base changed during this time, as well as its workforce. Affluent and middle-class New Yorkers increasingly looked to home newspaper delivery and, later, the internet for their news. As a result, the newsstand became a progressively less crucial amenity for city residents from high socioeconomic strata. To the white-collar workers and professionals whose hunger for information had contributed to the rise of the newsstand, the street-corner kiosk was increasingly expendable. Newsstand operators looked to fill this gap by selling lottery tickets, magazines, and snacks, items with broader appeal among the city's working and lower-middle classes.

Over the ensuing decades, the city's regulatory position toward existing newsstands became steadily harsher, justified by officials who highlighted the newsstand's aesthetics and materiality—its capacity to look unsightly and get in the way. In 1988, the MTA demolished dozens of newsstands throughout the city's subway system, arguing that they obstructed police officers' views of the platform.[15] Concurrently, the city was developing a new, stentorian set of rules governing the licensing of newsstands. The revised regulations increased the licensing fee from $50 to $925, decreased the square footage available to newsstands, and moved them away from amenities that drive their presence, specifying a minimum clearance from subway and building entrances. These changes were favored by community boards, which claimed sidewalk congestion was a growing issue in the city. In a *New York Times* editorial, the paper surmised that the community boards were, in turn, pushed by business owners, who objected to competition from newsstands, now that they were permitted to sell nonprint items.[16]

Under the Giuliani administration, this trend intensified. Newsstands were unstandardized in their appearance and prone to graffiti, and these factors placed them squarely in the crosshairs of the new mayor's "broken windows" approach to addressing physical disorder in the city. Giuliani decried newsstands as a form of "clutter" on New York City sidewalks, and appointed Deputy Mayor Fran Reiter to a task force charged with freeing up the city's public space. The next year, the mayor signed an executive order setting out the objective of clearing every street corner in the city of unnecessary objects, a category that included newsstands.[17]

Simultaneously, the city began aggressively exploring the possibility of converting objects such as newsstands and bus-stop shelters into space for private advertising. In 1996, the Giuliani administration announced the Consolidated Street Furniture Franchise proposal. The initiative contracted out the design, construction, and maintenance of newsstands to a media company specializing in outdoor marketing, effectively converting existing structures into profitable advertising space.[18] The winning bidder on the contract would draw profit from advertising sales and return a percentage of the proceeds to the city. Meanwhile, the licensing system under which newsstands had operated since the 1800s would be replaced with a market-based system in which operators would bid competitively for the right to operate one of the newly built newsstands. Administration officials saw this as an important secondary source of revenue generated by the plan, publicly speculating that the city would receive $30,000 per year per newsstand by renting out public space to operators.

Similar plans had been undertaken in other cities. The outdoor advertising business was booming internationally, and had been reconfiguring urban landscapes across the globe for more than a decade. On the one hand, outdoor advertisements compete well in the attention economy of a digital world, because the built environment cannot be turned off or ignored in the same way that broadcast or print media can. Pedestrians, drivers, and transit riders are, to a degree, a captive audience. However, the industry's success can also be attributed to an increase in supply, as cities have aggressively sought to monetize public space through public-private partnerships with companies such as Cemusa or JCDecaux. These efforts typically involve increasing the viable advertising space within the city—by selling space on the sides of buses, for example—while suppressing alternate sources of public expression, such as graffiti or leafleting.[19]

The Giuliani administration abruptly abandoned the franchise plan after entertaining proposals for newly designed newsstands and bus stops from a number of large corporations and superstar architects.[20] But several years later, when new mayor Michael Bloomberg initiated a push to bring the Olympics to New York City, a similar proposal succeeded where Giuliani's had failed. Newsstand operators would be compelled to pay for the reconstruction of their own newsstands, which would be maintained by Cemusa, a Spanish corporation specializing in outdoor advertising. In the mid-2000s, existing newsstands began to undergo their corporate makeover. The idiosyncratic structures, whether constructed of clapboard or ornamented cast iron, began to disappear from city streets, only to reappear in the same

FIGURE 5.4. Printed news media on the decline. Throughout the twentieth century, newspaper and magazine sales drove the newsstand business. The decline of the market for printed media can be seen in the physical evolution of the newsstand, which now specializes in candy, beverages, and Lotto tickets. *Above*, image of a New York newsstand from 1953; *below*, the newspaper offerings of a contemporary newsstand.

1953 photo: Angelo Rizzuto, courtesy of the Library of Congress, Prints and Photographs Division, Anthony Angel Collection, LC-DIG-ppmsca-12345.

locations as uniform steel and glass boxes, whose rectangular surfaces lent themselves to large advertisements that could be run for tens of thousands of dollars per month. Previously, newsstand owners could collect advertising fees from ads posted on the outside of newsstands. Now, this revenue was to be split between Cemusa and the city.

Although newsstands have been physically reborn, reincarnated as a hybrid between a kiosk and a public advertising space, the economic outlook for the industry has only darkened in the last decade. Newsstand magazine sales had remained an important source of revenue, even as newspaper sales had diminished to a trickle, but in 2011 and 2012 the magazine business declined precipitously, as media consumers increasingly turned to digital sources.[21] Meanwhile, the city increased the aggressiveness of its regulation of newsstands, doubling the number of tickets issued to newsstand operators between 2009 and 2013, and more than quadrupling the overall fines collected.[22] In interviews with newsstand operators, the difficulty of making a profit out of the business was a common complaint. "This business is no good," a fifty-six-year-old Gujarati newsstand operator in Midtown told me in May, 2018. "It's not even a business anymore. It's a public service."

Throughout the troubled history of the relationship between the municipal government and the city's newsstands, officials have applied a variety of schemas to these objects, demonstrating a sort of taxonomic ambivalence: What exactly is a newsstand? Is it a material encumbrance akin to lampposts and fire hydrants? Is it an aesthetic object that could beautify city streets, but that has, throughout its history, often been accused of disarray and neglect? Or is it a moneymaker for the city? There is another possibility, which has not been explored nearly as extensively as the others. The newsstand has a set of sociological affordances that are separate from its material, aesthetic, or financial functions. My research suggested that these affordances, in fact, may be the most important of all. In order to understand what might be lost to us when a public object disappears from city streets, it is necessary to know, in social terms, what it does. This is, in fact, the same question, asked in different ways. In the next section, I turn my attention to the way newsstands enter into, and modify, the social life of the city.

Convenience

The most obvious social affordance of a newsstand is the one that arises directly from the object doing what it is overtly intended to do. The main purpose of a newsstand is economic—to supply a variety of products that meet an effective demand. These products are typically banal, their significance hiding in plain sight. But even the most mundane objects have meaning for the people who consume them. The objective, aggregate demand for the objects sold at a newsstand comprises thousands upon thousands of discrete, subjective moments that occur within an immediate social context. These moments are worthy of a closer look.

In a very busy subway station in Midtown, a medium-sized newsstand is wedged against the wall on the downtown platform, facing the tracks. On an October evening in 2019, Kamal, the news vendor, has been working for twelve hours and is at the end of his shift. His eyelids are heavy with fatigue, but he perks up when I stop by and ask him about the items he sells. "I solve problems," says Kamal. "Everybody who shops here, they have a problem. I try to solve as many problems as I can." Like many of the subway newsstands, Kamal's offers a very wide range of products. He carefully arrays these products around the interior of the newsstand, creating a visual inventory of artifacts, each of which speaks to a particular human need or desire.

Kamal sees my gaze wander across this bewildering collage of commodities and anticipates my next question. "You have a problem. Your problem is dry eyes. I solve it." He motions toward a bottle of eye drops. "You have a problem. Your glasses are broken. I solve it." An eyeglasses repair kit. "Something else broken. I solve it." Tiny bottles of super glue. And so on. "Your problem is you're hungry. . . . Your problem is you're tired. . . . Your problem is you want to have good sex tonight." Umbrellas, rain ponchos, sticky tape, lipsalve, mouthwash, cough drops, cigars, tissues, twenty-nine different puzzle booklets featuring sudoku or word searches. A large selection of pornographic magazines, as well as *National Geographic*, the *New Yorker*, and *F.E.D.S.*, a magazine that a media reporter once described as the "unofficial newsletter of urban crime culture." Kamal sells more than thirty different newspapers and pamphlets, including ethnic niche papers such as *Super Express*, the largest Polish-language newspaper in the United States; *Irish Voice*; and *America Oggi*, an Italian-language newspaper published in New Jersey for Italian immigrants. Alongside the *Wall Street Journal* and the *Financial Times*, Kamal sells the *Chief Leader*, a newspaper for city firefighters founded in 1897, which now covers issues of interest to the city's hundreds of thousands of unionized civil servants. From my fieldnotes:

> Behind Kamal is a long row of boxes containing over-the-counter remedies for various colds, flus, and digestive maladies. Immediately above

this array is an equally expansive collection of male sexual performance enhancers, boasting lurid packaging and names like Beast Platinum, Rhino, and Stiff Nights. These items are in the back of the newsstand, on the same level as the pornography, a positioning that makes these items less conspicuous. Above the sexual enhancement pills, Kamal has hung dozens of accessories for handheld digital devices: chargers, earphones, rechargeable batteries—multiple versions of each, for compatibility's sake. The front of the stand is reserved for impulse purchases—candy bars and gum—while the middle ground contains unglamorous necessities, which are readily visible to passerby, but neither foregrounded nor backgrounded by the organization of the array. This is where the Chapstick lives, along with the hand sanitizer, the Listerine, and the Kleenex packets.

Kamal's newsstand is an inventory of the needs of New York's subway riders, in all their diversity—both the early commuter and the late-night partygoer are represented here. The newly arrived immigrant or tourist desperately in need of an international calling card and a map of Midtown, as well as the lifelong New Yorker, who simply needs a book of crossword puzzles and a bag of chips for the long ride home. The common denominator is immediate necessity, which is often hard to distinguish from impulsive desire.

Kamal's particular business expertise lies in his ability to anticipate these needs, a talent that, in his case, is more science than art. In a worn notebook, he writes down the things people ask for that he does not carry. When experimenting with a new item, he places it out front, to make sure it is visible, and sees how it sells, in the same fashion that a supermarket chain might test a new product offering. This inductive empirical method has resulted in the current cornucopia of things found on the walls of his small underground shed. Small, independently operated kiosks like Kamal's thrive off convenience, and in the process, they inject the colorful business of everyday consumption into the city's diverse public spaces. Just by doing what they are intended to do, newsstands add a polyglot cultural richness to an often drab landscape of office buildings and subway platforms.

"How is business?" I ask, after getting the full rundown of his products. "Bad, bad, bad," Kamal says. "Now Amazon solves everyone's problems before they have them. They buy large quantities online, home delivery. I can't help people anymore. Why do they need me when they can buy ten of these [he gestured toward a tiny bottle of mouthwash] and keep them at home?" Online retailers are substituting one type of convenience for another, encouraging customers to preempt their momentary needs by having even the most trivial of items shipped to their home address. Chain pharmacies in large retail spaces pose additional competition, stocking everyday items that were formerly the bread and butter of corner stores, bodegas, and newsstands. Kamal mimics a person shopping online on a smartphone and shakes his head, alluding to a new delivery method under consideration by an online retailer. "I cannot compete with that. I sell things underground. It's not easy to do this. Now they will have drones that come from the sky."

Order

A separate category of social affordances follows less obviously from the newsstand's overt economic function. In economics, these side effects or by-products of economic activity are referred to as *externalities*. Pollution is a frequently offered example of a negative externality—one that is undesirable from a societal and environmental standpoint.[23] But externalities can be positive as well. Sometimes, an economic process has social benefits outside of the ability for an investor to turn a profit, or for a worker to earn a wage. One of the externalities of a newsstand stems from the fact that it locates a person—the news vendor—on a sidewalk for prolonged periods. A corner with a newsstand on it is seldom completely empty, and this may help suppress crime and social disorder on adjacent streets.

The theoretical grounding for this hypothesis comes from Jane Jacobs, who argued that order in urban environments is kept principally not by the police but by everyday people who inhabit public space and keep an eye on what happens there. The most important ingredient found in safe urban environments, according to Jacobs, is a sufficient quantity of "eyes on the street"—in other words, people who frequent the space and are generally aware of their surroundings.[24] In a residential area, neighbors can serve in this capacity. But among the best people to have around are "public characters"—people who hang around in public space more than most, and who take a keen interest in what happens there.[25] Newsstand operators are well positioned to serve as public characters, if they have the inclination to do so. Pedestrians come and go, but a newsstand is fixed. As a result, the typical newsstand operator spends a great deal of time occupying a specific patch of concrete, while stationed inside or outside of a large and permanent object. They spend many hours in public space and have a vested interest in the safety of that space.

Are blocks with newsstands safer than those without newsstands? It's quite possible that they are. In conversations during my fieldwork, newsstand owners recounted dozens of experiences that demonstrated a willingness to act to preserve the peace. On Wall Street, a longtime newsstand operator described breaking up a fistfight between two stockbrokers that erupted just down the street from his stand. An operator in Midtown described a recent incident in which he left his stand and tracked down a police officer after a purse snatching that left an Argentinian tourist sitting on the sidewalk, tears streaming down her face. Another operator in the West Village said he called 911 on repeated occasions, recalling a time when he reported an attempted robbery and another in which he called an ambulance after an elderly woman fell in the street.

But these firsthand accounts are inevitably flawed as a form of data. There is no way to measure the frequency of the types of events they describe, or the accuracy of their details. They might well be the exceptions that prove the rule, which leads us to a different line of questioning. On a day-to-day basis, does the presence of a newsstand increase the *perceived* safety of a block, according to the people who live and work on it? Perceptions are more consequential than they might seem. One of the linchpins of both Jane Jacobs's theory and the influential "broken windows" theory outlined by criminologist George L. Kelling and political scientist James Q. Wilson is that a public space will be safe if it is perceived to be safe by people who might frequent it.[26] Safety can be a self-fulfilling prophecy. When residents and visitors regard a street corner as secure, they will be more likely to linger, adding to the "eyes on the street" by their mere presence. With this in mind, an important consideration is whether the presence of a newsstand makes people *feel* safer.

Again, there is abundant evidence that it does. When newsstands have been removed or have faced removal, residents have protested, individually and en masse, on the grounds that the objects are beacons of safety in an uncertain urban environment. In 1988, when the MTA destroyed fourteen subway newsstands and closed dozens more, the Straphangers Campaign, a transit riders' advocacy group, held a press conference outside of one of the demolition sites, calling newsstands an "oasis" for subway riders.[27] Residents of the Park Slope neighborhood of Brooklyn reported a sensation of disorientation, grief, and insecurity after a local newsstand closed. The newsstand had typically remained open late into the night and made the corner feel more secure.[28] Similarly, when a West Village newsstand was abruptly removed in the mid-2000s, a resident described an immediate

FIGURE 5.5. Sidewalk beacons and eyes on the street. Newsstands are often open long after dusk, bringing light and activity to otherwise dark street corners.
Photo: "Newsstand at Night," Kazuko Oguma, licensed with CC BY 2.0. (To view a copy of this license, visit https://creativecommons.org/licenses/by/2.0/.)

effect on the tone of the block: "The old stand was open 24/7, and made the neighborhood safer. Without a newsstand, that corner did not become a good corner, late at night."[29] Elsewhere in the Village, residents reported an increase in vandalism, broken bottles, and drug paraphernalia after a newsstand was shut down.[30]

This anecdotal evidence is useful in describing the mechanism by which newsstands might enhance the sense of safety among residents. But, ideally, we would be able to test the direct link between a sense of safety and actual rates of social disorder and crime. The New York City Department of Consumer Affairs (DCA) licenses newsstands on an annual basis, which makes it possible to identify cases in which a newsstand opened or shut down. I used the DCA's 2013, 2015, and 2018 data to identify every street corner where there *was* a newsstand licensed in 2013, but *not* in 2015 or 2018.[31] There were twenty-one such corners in the city. I then looked up the number of criminal complaints that occurred at these intersections in 2013 and 2015, using crime data from the NYPD.[32] In 2013, when there were still operating newsstands on these corners, 582 crimes occurred at these twenty-one intersections, according to the NYPD data. In 2015, when there were no operating newsstand on these corners, 652 crimes occurred. In other words, there was an overall increase of 11 percent in crime on corners where newsstands were either removed or permanently shut down. On 65 percent of the twenty-one corners, crime either increased or remained consistent during this period. It is important to note that these numbers contrast sharply with citywide trends. During the three-year period spanning 2013 through 2015, violations, misdemeanors, and felonies actually declined by 7 percent across New York. Measured against this citywide baseline, crime on the corners that lost newsstands was 18 percentage points higher. This quantitative evidence is consistent with the idea that newsstands suppress criminal activity in the immediate vicinity. Shutting down or removing a newsstand may lead to an upswing in social disorder.

If newsstands do deter crime, this contribution is not integral to the business of running a newsstand. It is a positive social externality of the object—a side effect of the economic activity that comprises its primary purpose. And it is probably worth pointing out that serving in this capacity does not necessarily cost the newsstand operator anything at all. If a newsstand discourages street crime simply by remaining open late into the night, this work does not detract from its ability to sell newspapers, or, these days, chocolate bars and energy drinks. By focusing solely on the material and economic essence of this humble object, regulators may be missing something important.

Mobility

A second important positive externality of the newsstand is the opportunity it offers to a socially and economically vulnerable workforce. Interestingly, this benefit of the newsstand was widely recognized in the late 1800s and early 1900s, before a preoccupation with the material and aesthetic qualities of the object came to dominate the city's treatment of news vendors. Immediately following the Civil War, newsstands had offered an economic lifeline for impoverished New Yorkers in general and disabled war veterans in particular. Although selling newspapers on the street was not a particularly lucrative or prestigious trade, the work was less physically strenuous than other working-class occupations, and this led the city to regard the newsstand industry as a vocation of last resort for these vulnerable populations. In the late 1800s, veterans and the disabled were offered exemptions to street-vending regulations and priority in licensing, a provision that continues to this day.[33]

The materiality of the newsstand was central to its ability to provide a unique social benefit. Compact and self-contained, a newsstand could be effectively staffed by a disabled person with severe physical or sensory mobility constraints. A blind former news vendor explained to me how he sold newspapers from inside his stand for decades, using his senses of hearing and touch. He kept stacks of newspapers discernible by their size and thickness inside his stand, where they were protected against theft, exchanging them for coins identifiable in the same manner.

Throughout the early and mid-1900s, owing to the provisions described above, the city's newsstands were largely owned and operated by American-born men, many of whom were military veterans. In the 1970s and 1980s, the newsstand industry underwent a social transformation, as the languishing trade was resuscitated by an influx of immigrants hailing predominantly from western India. The newsstand continued to provide social support and mobility to an economically vulnerable category of American workers, helping these immigrants gain a foothold in the US economy. In 1965, the United States lifted the quota system that had restricted immigration for more than forty years, resulting in a burst of immigration from the Indian subcontinent. At first, these newcomers tended to have professional backgrounds, which granted them preferred status under immigration law. But chain migration soon produced a population of Gujarati immigrants with lower levels of human capital than their predecessors, who were similarly anxious to succeed in the United States.

Settling in growing Indian communities in Queens and Jersey City, these less-skilled workers found success in entrepreneurial occupations, where a relatively small amount of capital could be translated into substantial profit through hard work and canny investment decisions. According to a newsstand impresario quoted in the *New York Times*, the newsstand industry offered a rare combination of incentives to immigrant entrepreneurs: a low initial investment, rapid turnover of inventory, predictable profit margins, and no need to incur debt. Best of all, the demand for newspapers was inelastic over the short term. Although newspaper sales were gradually waning overall, interest in current events was not going out of style, and this meant a day-to-day consistency in revenue.[34]

Newly arrived immigrant men and women typically operated newsstands owned by other licensees until they could afford to build their own. When they themselves became owners, they benefitted from a steady stream of the same low-cost labor that they had previously provided.[35] Once a safe haven for veterans and the disabled, the newsstand now provided a different type of social benefit, offering a stepladder to the middle class for newly arrived immigrants. Sidewalk news sales received an infusion of new energy from a growing ethnic enclave, as a population of new American entrepreneurs threw a lifeline to a struggling industry and a dying sidewalk institution.

Friction

Finally, the newsstand offers one more social affordance. This one is a bit difficult to describe. The newsstand does something that is neither a direct or indirect result of the object performing its primary function so much as a result of the newsstand performing its function *imperfectly*. As mentioned at the start of this chapter, newsstands are intended to reduce the "friction" of commerce—specifically, to reduce the time and space necessary to purchase an item. But a newsstand does impose a degree of friction. It gets in the way of the very transactions that it is supposed to expedite. And this is a bad thing. Or is it? Looking closely at the inefficiencies of the newsstand as a mechanism of economic consumption brings into view some of the object's least obvious and most important sociological benefits.

Historically, a newsstand was a place to consume information on current events. But the very materiality of this process made it inefficient. The newspaper itself imposes its own kind of friction. It requires that its readers leaf through pages of undesired information in order to reach the good stuff—a movie review, perhaps, or a compelling story about current events. In the process of consuming the news, the reader is inevitably exposed to events and stories that lie outside of his or her prior frame of relevance. On our way to the sports section, we have no choice but to read a headline about nuclear disarmament, or cuts in public funding for education. Owing to its material form, a newspaper imposes "transaction costs" on a consumer of information, requiring time, effort, and, inevitably, the consumption of some unwanted facts.[36] But the inefficiency of the newspaper as a source of information actually produces a positive side effect—a more broadly informed readership, and citizenry.

In similar fashion, some of the most important social functions of a newsstand result from the obstacles that it places in the way of economic consumption. The most salient of these obstacles is the vendor, a human being who must be dealt with in order to make the exchange happen. Small talk is a potential by-product of this exchange. Some news vendors see incidental interaction with customers as a necessary part of their vocation. Others enjoy the social interaction. Over time, the accumulation of countless repeated episodes of small talk and the longevity of a newsstand operator on a city block can produce a relationship between the people who frequent the block and the news vendor—a familiarity and sociability that is, perhaps, less than friendship, but more than acquaintance. The resulting social capital is a direct consequence of the transaction costs of purchasing items at a newsstand, rather than, say, from an online retailer.[37]

The ability of newsstands to foster meaningful social ties is borne out by cases in which a newsstand has been closed down. In 2011, Jerry Delakas, a Greek newsstand operator in Cooper Square, was forced to shut down his newsstand because of a legal complication concerning his license. A *Daily News* reporter visiting the stand on its final days found school children's cell phones—banned at school—that Delakas stored for them at no cost during the day. He also found a rich history of relationships and rituals that had grown up around the newsstand. Owing to its proximity to the longtime headquarters of the *Village Voice*, a weekly newspaper with one of the most extensive classified ad sections in the city, job seekers would visit the newsstand on Tuesday nights to get an early copy and be the first to respond to job listings. Twelve hundred neighbors and regulars signed a petition to keep the stand open, supporting the newsstand's broader significance to the neighborhood. In the *Daily News* article, they mourned its closing in words that pointed to Delakas's role on the block: "Jerry's here rain, snow, sleet, blistering heat," said a sixty-eight-year-old man who lived nearby. "He's just a real important part of our community. We think the world of him." Some neighbors taped statements of support to the closed newsstand. One of them explained why the newsstand was so important in poignant terms: "This is a village," she said. "And Jerry is part of our fabric."[38]

On the other side of Broadway, in the West Village, a similar outpouring of grief and opposition had followed upon the closing of a newsstand several years earlier. The owners of the newsstand, two brothers from Queens, had developed strong ties with many of their regular customers. They signed for deliveries and stored packages for people on the block, and the newsstand itself, which had stood on the corner for seventy years, had become a "water cooler" for the neighborhood, hosting impromptu gatherings and encouraging low-stakes sociability among neighbors. "I always saw people standing in front of the newsstand with their dogs, talking about the lottery or that day's newspaper," said a resident who had lived above the newsstand for over three decades. "It gave color to the street corner."[39] When the newsstand closed, three hundred customers signed a petition pleading leniency from the DCA, to no avail. As these examples suggest, newsstands can be integral to place. This is particularly evident in the case of longtime operators, several of whom I encountered during my research for this chapter. From my fieldnotes from a field visit in early fall, 2018:

> I walked down to the financial district to meet with Arjun, a newsvendor who has been running a stand in downtown Manhattan for thirty-five years. Arjun was outside his stand when I arrived, arranging items on the shelves in the front. I was surprised when I met him, as he looks young for his age, with a strong, clear voice and a direct, energetic demeanor. His stand is frequented by Wall Street traders, and is immersed in the milieu and the history of the financial district, of which Arjun serves as a sort of human repository.

Arjun is able to recount, in intense detail, the most tumultuous episodes that the neighborhood has experienced in recent decades, because he enjoys telling stories, and, more importantly, because he was there to see them. Again, from my fieldnotes:

> He can describe the ashen faces of traders passing by on the sidewalk on Black Monday, the worst single-day stock market crash in the history of Wall Street. He has a vivid memory of the attacks of 9/11, which covered his newsstand in toxic ash, and recalls the day when a young white-collar worker jumped to his death several blocks away.

Any long-term owner of a local business might accumulate memories of such events, but other types of businesses are not situated on the sidewalk. Arjun's exposure to these episodes was visceral and direct—immersed in the collective emotional energy of the crowded streetscape that surrounds his kiosk, and the thousands of pedestrians who pass by his newsstand every day.

The sales at Arjun's newsstand are tied to the stock market, fluctuating in step with the prices of securities and commodities. This has given him rare insight into the mentality of his customers, making him a lay expert in behavioral economics and the psychology of risk. Even the most inexpensive items he sells—gum and hard candy—are forgone by traders when the markets falter and their commissions slip. Arjun wistfully recollects the days when daily newspapers published morning, afternoon, and evening editions, offering the most-current available source for the prices of stocks and publicly traded funds. "I used to sell 2,500 copies of the *New York Post* every single day to the traders," Arjun told me, shaking his head. "I would see the same guys over and over. I knew them well. Now it's mostly tourists and bottled water." Still, he views social interaction as integral to the job. "I like to talk to people," he confessed. "If I didn't, I would find something else to do."

Twelve blocks north, a stand is manned by an operator of similar longevity. George has been running his stand for approximately forty years, starting in the industry shortly after he immigrated to the United States from India. His eyes are growing clouded with age, but his face is animated and bright. He moved to New Jersey many years ago, when his children were still young, to the best school district where he and his wife could afford a house. Now, due to their professional success, he has no financial need to operate a newsstand, but he continues to come in three days a week to sit in a folding camp chair on the sidewalk, while his younger employee runs the stand. Like Arjun, George is a repository of block-specific history, but owing perhaps to the location of his newsstand, near City Hall, the nature of his recollections differs. George's favorite memories are dominated by protests and parades, including a victory parade for the New York Yankees, after which George's stand became briefly famous for holding fifty spectators on its roof.

Not all newsstand owners are gregarious. Not all enjoy socializing with customers. But for George, now well past the usual age of retirement, these aspects of his work are an extension of his personality, whether that personality led him into the newsstand business or was shaped by it. An excerpt from my fieldnotes, documenting a sunny afternoon in September, 2019:

I am sitting on a crate of bottled water next to George's chair. Been here for an hour and watched as an apparently ceaseless succession of customers and passersby stopped to have a conversation, exchange greetings, or have a quick laugh. This occurred every 5–10 minutes on average, as far as I could tell. The lunchtime rush has long gone, and there is rarely a line at the newsstand now, but some people seem to stop by just to say hi to George while others are just in the flow of the sidewalk and communicate with him in passing. The interactions range in duration and tone, from a serious conversation to jocular asides. "George, get up and get back to work!" a young West Indian woman told him with a smile, barely breaking her stride. George's nephew is manning the stand while George sits out front. I asked George why he still bothers to come into the city. Couldn't his nephew run his stand for him? "What will I do? Stay at home? My friends are here," George says, gesturing to the steady stream of pedestrians circulating on the busy sidewalk.

George's customers are mostly regulars. The blocks around the newsstand comprise limestone towers that house city, state, and federal government agencies, including the Internal Revenue Service. Workers in these offices stay in their jobs, and their jobs stay in these offices, George observes, so the same people have been shopping at his stand for decades. But George is not alone in this regard. In my conversations with newsstand operators, I routinely asked what percentage of their customers are regulars, and their answers were surprisingly high. Of the twenty-seven newsstand operators to whom I posed this question, the average was 82 percent.

Trust can emerge from repeated contact, and this trust permits newsstand operators to offer nonpecuniary services to their regular customers and neighbors. The new steel newsstands typically have an external electrical outlet, meant for powering the beverage refrigerator. Newsstand operators like Ron will lend this outlet on request to passersby who need to charge a phone or tablet. Informally offering credit to regular customers is also typical, as are small gifts—bottled water on a hot day, candy in winter. The favors are reciprocated by some regular customers. Ron has several elderly customers who will watch his stand while he takes a bathroom break. These informal exchanges are facilitated by the material form and position of a newsstand, which makes it feel more like a component of public space than a private commercial territory. Newsstand operators are visible and available in a way that convenience-store clerks are not, and this allows them to play a qualitatively different role, if they so choose. A newsstand can be more than simply an amenity for anonymous pedestrians. It can be an integral part of the social fabric of a block—an aspect of community, rather than a simple convenience.

In my field visits to newsstands this was confirmed repeatedly. Many newsstand owners, like George, position themselves outside their stands in order to interact with customers without the physical structure getting in the way. Here they are even more visible and available to people who live and work nearby, who often exchange greetings and acknowledgement on their way past. During an interview with a brusque Bangladeshi newsstand operator, who was leaning against a piece of construction scaffolding outside of his stand, a young boy of perhaps ten years old stopped and earnestly held out his fist, waiting to be bumped in greeting. The man's face, set in a scowl as he described the fines he had received in the last year, softened and brightened as he reciprocated the greeting. "Sometimes, the pain is worth it," he observed.

The friction imposed by a newsstand on exchanges of commodities and information doubtlessly plays a major role in the newsstand's decline. Why should consumers visit a metal box on the sidewalk to read an article that is already in their hand, a few clicks away? Ironically, however, behind the newsstand's inefficiency lies its most meaningful contributions to the sidewalk life of the city. A final example of this insight is the newsstand's contribution to urban wayfinding. Giving directions has always been one of the news vendors' unremunerated roles. For more than a hundred years, newsstand owners' occupation and their location on public sidewalks has made them available and led them to develop a degree of expertise on their surroundings, linking them to a social practice that breaks down the barriers of privacy and distrust that lie between visitors and the anonymous, impersonal big city.[40] Direction asking has become less common as mobile phones provide digital mapping applications and GPS systems that effectively preempt the informal practice and alleviate the need for social interaction, reducing the friction involved.

Surprisingly enough, my fieldwork revealed that newsstand operators still give directions scores of times per day. According to Ron, it is the most common reason why people stop by his stand apart from the purchase of lottery tickets and drinks. During my time observing his stand and George's, I saw dozens of cases in which the two men gave quick, competent directions to local government offices, businesses, subway stations, parks, and so on. "I have to know where most things are in the city," said George, "like a taxi driver." As writer Robert Sullivan notes, neighborhoods and cities lose something when people stop asking for directions.[41] But it turns out that the face-to-face institution of direction asking and giving is alive and well. People still *do* ask for directions. And they ask at newsstands.

How Things Disappear

So, these are some of the things that newsstands do, beyond selling magazines, gum, and lottery tickets, and they are some of the things that, perhaps, stand to be lost if newsstands vanish from the city's streets. The discussion above suggests that the ancillary sociological roles and meanings of a newsstand—its positive externalities—are not inconsequential. When an object that brings about social interaction on thousands of street corners and sidewalks gradually recedes from the public spaces of the city, it is inevitable that the character of those public spaces will be changed. If we view newsstands through a reductively market-centered lens, they seem to be losing an inevitable, Darwinian struggle against digital communication and online commerce. But if we view the newsstand's decline from the standpoint of the quality of public space in the city, we see a loss of convenience, safety, and vitality—qualities that researchers have found to be crucial to the well-being and economic vitality of urban neighborhoods. It seems a shame to allow the loss of a public object programmed for social interaction between strangers, neighbors, acquaintances. These social affordances are rare, and important—arguably more so than a marginal victory in the citywide pursuit of clean streets, unencumbered traffic, and unfettered markets.

What will this process look like, if it proceeds apace? Karl Marx used the word "annihilation" to refer to the death of things at the hands of capitalist innovation. But this word can be misleading. When markets produce a new object, the demise of the old one is frequently gradual, uneven, and incomplete.[42] The population that uses an antiquated technology shrinks and becomes more demographically specific, its membership a mirror image of new technology's early adopters. This is surely the case with the newsstand. Ask news vendors who continues to buy newspapers, and their answers are invariably the same: a dwindling population of older New Yorkers, who have not made the transition to digital media, or who continue to prefer the print version. In some cases, an object continues to be vital to a large constituency, long after it has been abandoned by trendsetters. This process reveals the social morphology of an object's user population, bringing into view the people who rely on it most. For an understanding of how this works, it is worth taking a fairly detailed look at the ongoing and gradual extinction of the payphone, the newsstand's diminutive cousin, which offers an interesting case study in the disappearance of public objects.

The payphone's decline began in the early 1990s, when the popularization of the cell phone began to reduce demand for the iconic sidewalk artifact. Mobile phones penetrated the upper socioeconomic strata first, leaving poor and working-class residents disproportionately reliant on a declining technology. Even more than the newsstand, the payphone was progressively socially stigmatized as it became less useful to affluent New Yorkers. Eventually, in wealthy neighborhoods, the use of a public telephone qualified as a mild form of social deviance sufficient to raise eyebrows and arouse suspicion. In Manhattan's wealthy Upper West Side, for example, residents protested the installation of new public phones, tying them with graffiti and drug dealing. By the early 2000s, debates over the role of the public payphone on city streets had taken on overt overtones associated with social class.[43]

Meanwhile, a large cross section of city residents continued to make use of public telephones, placing thousands of calls every day from the remaining kiosks and booths. *The Payphone Project*, a blog maintained by citizen journalist Mark Thomas, has been documenting the extensive use of the city's diminishing stock of functioning payphones for more than a decade, belying arguments that the payphone is a dying technology. In 2010, there were still more than sixteen thousand public payphones on New York City streets when a brave *New York Times* reporter staked out one of them, a heavily used payphone across the street from the Queens Criminal Court, which attracted more than one hundred callers per week. When the reporter interviewed some of the phone's users about their reasons for placing a call, the results amounted to a rare journalistic snapshot of the users of this disappearing object—mostly men who could not afford to keep a cell phone, or had had their phones confiscated. Their motivations for using the phone were mundane and universal, evincing a desire for information and human connection. In the lives of these payphone users, economic precarity or brushes with the law resulted in an inability to fully adopt a new communications technology. An obsolete public artifact offered a vital source of information and contact with loved ones.

In 2016, attempting to make the city's remaining payphones more profitable, the city struck a deal with a consortium of tech, communications, and advertising companies to replace the 7,500 existing payphones with LinkNYC kiosks. These slim, hypermodern pillars of brushed steel abruptly proliferated across the city, broadcasting free public Wi-Fi signals and digital advertisements, from which they generate revenue for the city and its corporate partners. An interesting feature of the LinkNYC kiosks is that they offer the ability to make free phone calls to anywhere in the United States. Thousands of calls per month were made on the state-of-the-art devices during the first years of the program.

The data generated by these phone calls give us an indication of who continues to rely on the public phone in the age of mobile communications. Citywide, the most frequently dialed number was the EBT hotline, a service for answering questions related to public nutritional assistance, or, food stamps.[44] The most heavily used kiosk in the city sits on the southwest corner of the intersection of West Fordham Road and Grand Avenue, in the Bronx, where nearly one out of every three residents lives below the poverty line, one in every two is foreign-born, and one in four is a noncitizen. In an eleven-month period starting in early 2016, over twelve thousand calls were placed from this kiosk, or roughly sixty calls per day, including twenty-eight emergency calls per month to 911. Other heavily used kiosks are in similarly high-poverty neighborhoods, or near locations where the city's unhoused population congregates, such as Port Authority or Penn Station.[45]

This brief analysis shows how a supposedly obsolete object can continue to be a vibrant and indispensable asset for a subset of the most vulnerable city residents. New technological artifacts do not cleanly and uniformly replace their predecessors. The process is messy and uneven, structured by variations in livelihood, living conditions, and lifestyle. New and old objects are very rarely functionally interchangeable. They offer different programs, or social affordances, and for this reason they serve different groups of users.[46] When a newsstand or a public phone disappears from a street corner, some cross section of local people—low-income, immigrants, the unhoused, the elderly—loses a source of information and social connection.

If the newsstand does lose its place on New York City's street corners, it will happen partly because the city government allows it to be so. After newsstand newspaper sales flagged in the 1960s and 1970s, the industry was revitalized in part by a loosening of the restrictions on what could be sold at a newsstand. By the same token, the decline of the newsstand in recent years has been accelerated by rising license fees, more stringent regulations, and steeper fines. Technological innovation has already eliminated much of the market for printed news media, but there are still many needs to be met, if the rules will allow it. Many of the venders I spoke to expressed a desire to sell hot drinks, like the coffee trucks that do a bustling trade on some street corners in the mornings. If the city government decides these quotidian street-corner objects are worthwhile, there is a chance that they will remain. If it continues to view them as a material and aesthetic nuisance, whose primary redeeming feature is a revenue stream shared with a multinational advertising company, then the objects may well disappear, or be fully converted into lifeless billboards.

When an object disappears, its affordances go along with it. When it comes to consuming information on current events, the cell phone offers an advantage in speed and convenience over the newsstand that can be easily quantified. But buying a newspaper from a newsstand involves modes of experience—tactile, temporal, social—that are themselves appealing or reassuring for many customers. For some consumers, the qualitative differences continue to matter. Perhaps the best argument for saving the newsstand is the range of counterintuitive social affordances that emerge indirectly and unintentionally from this fixture of New York City sidewalk life. The sense of security it confers on an anonymous street corner. The directions given. The cumulative weight of thousands of incidental, trivial interactions that take place through and around this modest object. The benevolent friction it imposes on the incessant commercial and social life of the city.

CONCLUSION

The Bench

FIGURE 6.1. The bench in Trump Tower.

On a bright, crisp November morning in 2019, I walked through the doors of 721 Fifth Avenue, otherwise known as Trump Tower. Three NYPD officers in helmets and body armor stood by the large glass doors as I entered, watching me with disinterest. They chatted to one another casually, assault rifles at their sides. I put my backpack on the conveyer belt at a security checkpoint and retrieved it when it emerged from the X-ray machine. To my left was a gold elevator bank and matching podium, in front of which stood a stocky private security guard in a dark suit. He silently scanned the lobby, eyes alert below a light brown crew cut, while speaking in hushed tones with one of many other building employees who moved through the atrium. On either side of me, pink marble walls rose vertiginously toward a high ceiling, where a massive American flag hung down. Like a cathedral, the atrium is intended to draw the eyes upward, where they can absorb the soaring grandeur of the space. The idea is to deploy the human capacity for awe, reminding visitors of something greater than themselves—in this case, the material wealth and power of the building's owner.

I had to ignore this reminder and look down to see the drab, low-lying object I was here to visit. A long, black bench fitted with metal slats and curved armrests sat at the base of the southern wall of the atrium, one of four identical such benches. A family of European tourists occupied part of the nearest bench, including a woman who looked to be in her late seventies or eighties. A teenager and a middle-aged woman next to her were glued to a phone, planning the next stop on their itinerary. The elderly woman patiently smiled into space, perhaps enjoying the white noise emanating from an indoor waterfall at the rear of atrium. I wandered over and sat down next to her.[1] I had reason to believe that Donald Trump hates this bench.

This concluding chapter begins with a detailed look at a final public object, one that disappeared (albeit temporarily) from the space in which it is located. Like the other objects considered in this book, the bench made trouble, becoming a flash point for contention and controversy. In this case, however, trouble arose not from how everyday users interpreted or used the bench, and not from how the city government classified or regulated this public object (at least, not principally). The bench made trouble for one man in particular—its billionaire owner. In the remainder of this chapter, I will tell the story of this battle between man and public object, which encapsulates the six overarching findings that emerged from the research described in this book. I will then conclude by summarizing these findings directly.

A strange thing happened in late 2016, while I was immersed in the research for this book, and it led me to this final case study. Donald J. Trump was elected president of the United States. For months, the media had been saturated with the drama surrounding this polarizing figure, a real-estate developer and reality-television star who used social media to recast himself as a fire-breathing, right-wing populist. His victory surprised almost everyone, it seems—professional pollsters, seasoned political journalists, and, according to some accounts, the president-elect himself. In the years since, scandals plagued Trump at every turn, as the president's actions repeatedly blurred the lines between the public good and his own private interest.

By late 2019, when I started writing this chapter, Trump was in the process of being impeached. Democrats in Congress alleged that he had withheld foreign military aid from Ukraine in order to further his own political prospects. Throughout this tumultuous period, public opinion in the United States became more and more divided. There seemed to be little, if anything, that most of us could agree about, and the acrimony of political discourse raised serious questions concerning the fate of American democracy. Against this backdrop of national turmoil, I began to wonder: Why should we even bother thinking about the sociology of mundane public objects? The story of Trump versus the bench helped me to answer this question.

When Trump built his eponymous tower, in the late 1970s, he took advantage of the bonus plaza program offered by the city, pledging to create and maintain a public space at street level. The atrium of his tower, like those of several other skyscrapers in Midtown, doubles as a sort of indoor plaza, or town square.[2] It is open to the public, accessible to anyone who chooses to use it. Building this public space was an unambiguous win for Trump. In exchange for creating the atrium, the city authorized him to extend his tower far higher into the sky than zoning would otherwise have allowed. He added twenty stories to the building, creating some of the most opulent residential space in the city—duplex condominiums and penthouses with sweeping park views, a block of real estate now valued at more than $500 million.[3]

The obligation to build a lavish, Trump-branded public space in Midtown Manhattan could not have been much of a sacrifice for the young developer. In the early 1980s, when the tower was completed, Trump was busily cultivating a reputation as a business tycoon of stratospheric wealth and decadent lifestyle. The atrium was central to the construction of this persona. It invited the public into the building and made it a tourist destination, elevating his national and global profile. The location of the public space on Fifth Avenue served to link Trump's brand with the power and prestige of the most famous luxury commercial corridor in the world. In fact, throughout his career, Trump has used the tower, and specifically its atrium, as a stage—a performative asset that reminds viewers of his status. The gold elevator bank provided an ideal prop for Trump's reality show, *The Apprentice*, symbolizing an imaginary rise up the corporate ladder (or descent, as the case may be). And in 2015, when Trump announced his presidential candidacy, he did so on a temporary platform constructed in front of the atrium's famous four-story waterfall.[4]

FIGURE 6.2. The view from the bench. In 2020, after Trump lost his reelection campaign, the bag check and NYPD security detail disappeared from the atrium. A massive American flag remained the sole reminder that the building's owner had held the nation's highest public office. The gold elevators and pink marble, however, retained their luster, reminding visitors of Trump's private wealth and economic power.

The importance of this space to Trump's public persona relies upon a symbolic conflation of the building and the man who built it. There is, of course, nothing subtle about this association. The atrium advertises the relationship between man and tower, bearing Trump's name, in capital letters, over the front entrance, and throughout the interior. In 2016, architecture critic Thomas de Monchaux noted that "not since Thomas Jefferson at Monticello or William Randolph Hearst at San Simeon has someone so near the summit of American political life been so closely identified with a single structure."[5] The atrium of Trump Tower sends a message about the profligacy of its owner with its surfaces and materials. Hundreds of tons of pink Italian marble were used in its construction, along with a profusion of gold paint. A generally favorable review by a well-known architecture critic suggested that the atrium demonstrated "not only a willingness to spend money, but also a knowledge of how to spend it correctly."[6] But others saw in the atrium only "pricey superglitz" and an interior suggestive of "posh ladies' powder room décor."[7]

Whatever the stylistic verdict might be, the atrium's agenda is clear—to aestheticize and display the private wealth of its owner. The fact that the atrium is, legally speaking, a public space, in exchange for which Trump received substantial public resources, is deeply paradoxical. As architecture scholar Kristine F. Miller writes:

> The bonuses from the [privately owned public space] program were only one part of an incredibly lucrative puzzle that included bonuses for all the building's retail square footage, transfer of air rights from a neighboring building, and generous city tax abatements for new housing. Beneath all the glitter and glass lies a suite of zoning bonuses that Trump parlayed into one of the most profitable real estate projects ever built in New York City. . . . The building's design "tells" us that Trump is richer than any of us will ever be. What it doesn't tell us is that Trump's fortune is founded on public money.[8]

To be clear, all privately owned public spaces are inherently contradictory. Much like the lawn in Brooklyn Bridge Park, the atrium embodies a financial-legal arrangement in which public use and private interest are intertwined. But instead of an association of property owners, the interest manifested in the atrium very clearly belongs to one man—and not just any man but a celebrity businessman who also happens to play a celebrity businessman on television. Trump is a walking, breathing simulacrum whose fortune has always relied on its own conspicuity. Because of this, there is perhaps no other space in the city where public and private are so perversely superimposed. The very idea that anyone other than Donald Trump might lay claim to this space is buried under the figurative weight of all that pink marble, polished brass, and gold veneer.

Which brings us to the matter of the bench. Public spaces are subject to a set of design provisions—among them, a stipulation that they contain ample public seating. Originally, the atrium contained a large marble bench, where the black metal benches currently sit, in order to satisfy this requirement. However, once he had benefitted from the bonus plaza provision, Trump began to undercut the public functions of the space, repeatedly closing the atrium for private events and instructing his private security guards to deny public access, a pattern that drew the attention of city regulators. In 1984, Philip Schneider, of the New York City Planning Department, paid an unannounced visit to the atrium of Trump Tower and found the large marble bench covered with flowerpots that prevented its intended use. After Schneider sent a letter requesting that the flowerpots be removed, Trump answered him personally in writing.

> We have had tremendous difficulties with respect to the bench—drug addicts, vagrants, et cetera have come to the Atrium in large numbers to sit and, in fact, to sleep on this bench. . . . [A]ll sorts of "horrors" had been taking place that effectively ruined the beautiful ambiance of a space which everyone loves so much.[9]

Adjusting for Trumpian hyperbole, it is clear that he viewed the bench as inconsistent with the ideas that the atrium was designed to convey. Whether anyone actually slept on the bench is impossible to say at this point, and mostly irrelevant. "Horrors" are another matter altogether. But even run-of-the-mill pedestrians and tourists, lingering in front of the building's gold elevators, may have been regarded by Trump as a profane intrusion on this temple to entrepreneurial excess. Eventually, after thousands of dollars of fines, Trump removed the flowerpots.

Later, however, the marble bench disappeared entirely. In its place appeared a massive kiosk of wood and glass labeled "Trump Store," where an attendant sold Trump-branded memorabilia and souvenirs. At the kiosk, visitors could purchase chocolate bars shaped like gold ingots, a $500 gold fountain pen, and later, when Trump ran for office, the distinctive, red "Make America Great Again" baseball caps. The removal of the bench was itself illegal, and so was the object that replaced it. Commercial structures in privately owned public space have to undergo a permitting process, and Trump's team had not bothered to apply for a permit. A legal battle with the city ensued.

FIGURE 6.3. A paradoxical public space. Behind the uniformed security guard and above the building's title, white block letters announce that Trump Tower is "OPEN TO THE PUBLIC." This signage is required of all New York City's public spaces. In this case, it extends a welcome that sharply contrasts with the trappings of private wealth and exclusivity both inside and outside of the atrium.

After the court ruled against Trump, the kiosk vanished, its contents moved to a retail space in the lower level of the atrium. The minimalist black bench—the humble public object on which I was sitting—appeared in its place.

What is this object? If we think about it for a moment, its symbolism is obvious. The bench is here as a grudging concession by a billionaire land-owner to a law that is intended to improve quality of life in the city. In this sense, the story of Trump versus the bench indicates his disregard for the public and, perhaps, for the rule of law itself, and his willingness to prioritize his own private interests. It is not too much of a stretch to suggest that the bench's temporary replacement with a Trump-themed gift shop forecasted one of the specific misdeeds that Trump (the president rather than the prop-erty owner) would later be accused of committing. In this analogy, both the bench and the military aid to Ukraine are public resources that Trump was willing to sacrifice for personal gain.

Perhaps the president's handling of his own building signaled how he would behave in the White House, for those willing to look closely at how humans treat everyday things. In October 2016, just weeks before Trump was elected, a prescient essay in the *New Yorker* suggested something like this. The author alluded to the prospect that Trump might actually win, and described the coming election as "a kind of threshold in time analogous to the shining gateway of Trump Tower itself, at which point the type of space encapsulated within—privately held, public in name only—might flow out into all the city and the country beyond."[10] By this logic, the bench on which I sat was not just a piece of furniture but an allegory for an America presided over by a hypothetical President Trump—a space governed via the unfet-tered privatization and personalization of the public realm.

This, more or less, is the symbolism of the bench. But metaphors do not support human weight. The bench, now restored to its rightful place thanks to a legal decision, does not just signify the protection of public goods against private enterprise, it materializes this reordering of values. By virtue of its physicality, it intervenes in society, making something happen, even if each of its discrete interventions is modest in nature—a moment of physical relief for an elderly tourist and a foot-weary sociologist. Like all of the things examined in this book, the bench is a point of contact with social forces that we tend to view as larger than us, and hence separate from subjective everyday experience.

Why bother thinking about everyday public objects? The bench offers an answer: it suggests that there are no social forces, no crosscurrents of political or cultural upheaval, so lofty and so remote that they do not produce telling reverberations in the material world around us, if we know where to look. Public objects, and the spaces and places in which we find them, bind macro and micro, linking the big and abstract stuff—ideology, inequality, power, history—to the textures, sights, and sounds of the small-scale world that occupies much of our conscious attention, much of the time. They provide an arena in which ordinary people experience these forces directly, viscerally, whether they know it or not, and whether they like it or not. At this micro level—localized, direct—objects shape our thoughts and actions in ways that were often unintended by their designers but that, nevertheless, reflect the sweeping political, social, cultural, and economic exigencies of our time. This is the social power of material things.

Reframed in this way, the story of the bench does not just embody a broader drama pitting private interest against public well-being. It illustrates the ability of material objects to translate such dramas into something far less grand, but also more tangible and more immediate. But this is not the only lesson the bench offers. The battle over public seating in Trump Tower encapsulates five other general qualities of interactions between people and things. It tells us about social control: at its heart was a contest over how people are permitted to use a small patch of public space. It tells us about inequality, pitting the financial interests of a billionaire landlord against the basic needs of ordinary New Yorkers. It illustrates the basic unpredictability of how material things will be received and acted upon, once introduced into public space. It shows us how public space is made more or less public by the objects that we find there. Finally, it points to the complex interactions between the social and the material that are integral to place—that make places what they are. The atrium of Trump Tower is made ambiguous, conflicted, and, arguably, fascinating by the contradictory affordances it contains: a place for regular New Yorkers and visitors to the city to sit in public and marvel at the material wealth of a very rich man. These six observations about encounters between people and things tie together all of the case studies in this book, and constitute its findings for research and practice. The remaining pages summarize these findings, one at a time.

1. THINGS HAVE IMMEDIACY

We should get the most obvious one out of the way first. This book reinforces what we already know (or think we know) about people's dealings with the material world around them. Namely, that they tend to be immediate and localized in nature, even as they reflect and engage broader social, political, or economic forces. How a person spends time in Brooklyn Bridge Park, it turns out, implicates centuries-old traditions in landscape architecture, ideas about public leisure and recreation that are tied to social class, and the conflation of private and public space under contemporary urban-planning regimes. But none of these factors trouble the consciousness of a teenager chasing a frisbee, or a retiree sitting on a bench and taking in the harbor breeze. A few folding chairs and tables might appear on a street corner, thanks to the city government's quest to make the city more livable. But what happens next depends upon how local people regard the basic act of sitting around in public. It turns out that the visions of Jane Jacobs and William H. Whyte, those venerated pillars of new urbanism, hold no sway over the hearts and minds of Sheepshead Bay. Being out in public and dealing with the objects you find there is not like voting, getting married, committing premeditated murder, or joining a religious cult. These acts involve what are commonly referred to as "big decisions": conscious choices in which there is much at stake, leading us to grapple reflexively and intentionally with large-scale social and cultural forces—ideology, tradition, class, morality, and the like. In our quotidian dealings with the material world outside our doors, these forces fade into the background, eclipsed by our habits, our sensory experiences, our passing desires or needs, as well as other, rarer states of mind—whimsy, curiosity, frustration, anxiety.

When we engage with public objects, we typically make small decisions, or no decisions at all. The material contents of our homes tell complex stories about us, as anthropologist Daniel Miller has shown,[11] but when it comes to how we move through public space, we are pragmatists, who seek to solve immediate problems using the materials that are closest at hand.[12] How should we get from here to there? What should we do with the final precious moments of our lunch hour? Which side of the street is shaded in the heat of a summer day? Which is darker, late at night? Bus or subway? Elevator or stairs? Throughout this book, we have seen evidence that people make sense out of the objects they encounter in the public spaces of the city drawing on interpretive frameworks that are heavily weighted toward the present, the proximate, and the practical.[13]

What does this mean for the people who design and regulate these objects, the architects and engineers and planners of public space? For one, it suggests that users' preoccupation with the here and now is likely to blind them to the larger considerations that these professions are compelled to take into account. Immediacy helps us to appreciate why, for subway commuters about to force their way onto a crowded 6 train, acting on behalf of the overall reliability of the subway system may be a hard sell. It tells us why, for city officials seeking to legitimize a crackdown on disorderly people or objects, invoking congested sidewalks is a comparatively easy one. Immediacy helps us to understand why the physical redesign of roads may be a more effective tool for reducing pedestrian risk than reeducating drivers. It shows us why eliminating a newsstand that is a fixture of a New Yorker's daily routine might be such a profoundly disorienting loss. We are starting with the most obvious finding of the case studies gathered here, and yet it bears repeating. Thinking clearly about people's interactions with material objects requires understanding the roles they play in the moment-by-moment consciousness of the people who use them.[14] Which brings us to the next finding of the research gathered in this book.

2. THINGS EXERT SOCIAL CONTROL

A second insight that emerged from the case studies gathered here is that public objects are always exerting forms of social control. Immersing ourselves in the world of public objects and their affordances has revealed the degree to which even the most innocuous of material artifacts influences the shape and direction of human affairs. A central contention supported by this book is that the social significance of the built environment hinges on this control capacity—its ability to enable or frustrate patterns of human action.

This capacity is perhaps most evident in the sections of the book in which coercive materiality looms large, and users are found to have little sway over the objects and places that surround them. Chapters 3 and 4 looked at cases in which people are relatively powerless in the face of massive infrastructural systems that, to varying degrees, fail to accommodate their requirements. For engineers and planners, striking a balance between allowing these users to move freely and constraining their action can be, literally, a matter of life and death.

To answer Langdon Winner's controversial question—yes, objects are political.[15] But, in the cases described in this book, power emerges more clearly into view via the aggregation of small-scale, everyday encounters between people and things.[16] Hundreds of school kids holding hundreds of subway doors, each for his or her own reason. Thousands of pedestrians struck by thousands of cars, each on her own subjectively meaningful trajectory through suburban space. As these individual users blur into a collectivity, idiosyncratic physical incidents coalesce, becoming coercive social facts. The multitude of momentary interactions between people and things in which human action is enabled or constrained, a perpetual process occurring across the city at all times of day and night—surely these encounters, in their summation, tell us as much about how power is structured in our society as does the design of a nuclear reactor or a parkway system, per Winner.[17]

In other cases examined in this book, fear of disorder emerges into the foreground, and the control capacity of public objects appears as a counterweight to the chaotic qualities of urban life. For example, anxiety about uncontrolled human behavior surfaced in the debates over the design of leisure and recreational spaces in Brooklyn Bridge Park, and in the neighborhood-level reactions to pedestrian plazas. At the heart of these reactions is a concern that urban space can exert too little social control, and allow for too much human agency. In chapter 5, we looked at the street-corner newsstand, an object that has itself been defined as disorderly and subjected to regulation, redesign, or removal by New York City. In the process, city agencies have ignored the social functions, processes, and meanings that have grown up around these fixtures of the New York City landscape, seeing disorder where there are forms of organic social order, including informal social control, that make this landscape safer, more social, and more humane. All of these cases highlight the capacity of objects to enable and constrain human behavior and, in doing so, to make different social worlds more or less possible.

One could argue that this boils down to what statisticians call selection bias. Admittedly, in researching this book, I sampled on the dependent variable, choosing to write about things that highlight the tension between enabling and constraining human action. I make no claim whatsoever to a generalizable sample of either people or things. A central argument running through the preceding chapters is that all manmade artifacts endorse certain patterns of thought and action and discourage others, but that under normal circumstances, this work, however consequential, is hidden from us. Rendering visible the social assumptions embedded in the built environment requires that we pay particular attention to public objects that make trouble. Problematic things have much to teach us—they dissipate the fog of a naturalized and internalized social order, offering clarity about what the material world actually does for us, just as we become newly aware of the importance of a household item when it first becomes available, or when it breaks, or when we run out of it. The sociology of public objects, then, has some strong parallels to our subjective experience of the material world in general. To further explore what things do, we should not ignore the evidence that lies in plain sight, in their ability to enable and frustrate human agency. Which brings us to the third general answer suggested by the case studies in this book.

3. THINGS ARE UNEQUAL

As objects shape and constrain human behavior, they favor some collective interests over others. At this point, individual encounters between people and things overlap with larger forces that are already quite familiar to social scientists—religion, gender, race, ethnicity, and, perhaps most of all, social inequality itself. When thinking about how objects relate to inequality, we often focus on material possessions: houses, automobiles, appliances, and other components of wealth that are unevenly distributed among the population. Other things come to symbolize inequality: the "poor doors" designed into affordable housing developments to segregate wealthy residents from those of modest means, or the barricades and security cameras that insulate gated communities from their surroundings. Still other things are so gratuitously expensive that, simply by existing, they refer to a lopsided societal distribution of wealth—personal wine cellars, private jets, gold-plated yachts (yes, apparently these do exist). But the case studies in this book highlight a different way in which material artifacts relate to inequality, which has to do with how they are used by different groups of people, and whether they are useful in the first place.

A telltale sign that a public object plays a role in social inequality is when it has starkly different functional implications for different groups. For single parents in surrounding neighborhoods who cannot afford after-school programs or extracurricular activities, the ornamental landscaping in Brooklyn Bridge Park implied a rent hike, while offering little in exchange. The inclusion of playgrounds, basketball courts, and playing fields on the other hand, provided affordances with tangible benefits. The entirety of chapter 2 was devoted to public spaces that have this polysemic quality, bearing distinct implications for different local collectivities. The divided roadways of Atlantic County are rife with objects—curbs, guardrails, shoulders—that are reasonable from the standpoint of motorists but that are deadly obstacles for those without the resources to own a car. Even the newsstands in chapter 5 can be seen in this light—their utility for many New Yorkers is in question, because of the diminishing popularity of printed media, but they remain safety beacons that assist vulnerable populations at night, they offer social contact to the solitary, socially isolated people of the city, and they are economic lifelines for immigrant workers.

In all of these cases, and innumerable others, the built environment stands to mitigate inequality or to make it more durable. Material artifacts that disempower already-marginalized or impoverished groups inscribe inequality in place, making it a feature of not just the socioeconomic landscape but the material one.[18] If, following social theorist Georg Simmel, objects "fix the contents" of society, this suggests a clear problem for an inequitable society. Our public objects lend permanence to a condition in which life is harder—riskier, less comfortable, less convenient—for some than for others.[19]

With this in mind, "for whom?" is a question that should be asked of virtually every material intervention in public space. Given existing levels of social inequality in New York City and, for that matter, across the country and around the world, "for everyone" is seldom an honest or accurate answer. Over the last half century, private developers have been routinely asked to invest in material amenities that will benefit not just home buyers but the community at large—to create parks, plazas, picnic grounds, public facilities, "for everyone." But to actually reduce existing inequality, private and public investment needs to go much further than this. Developers, architects, and planners who create and design public space need to ask specific questions in addition to the general one: Which material artifacts will make life more manageable for single, working parents? For unemployed or undocumented workers? For children whose housing is precarious, or whose home lives are troubled? For the unhoused? For the addicted? There are obvious reasons why private developers do not ask these questions of their own volition, so the city and state need to do more to require that they be asked.

4. THINGS ARE UNPREDICTABLE

These three qualities of interactions between people and things help to bring about a fourth quality that emerged from the research for this book. Immediate cultural and social contexts inject a degree of unpredictability or, to quote sociologist Terrence McDonnell, "entropy" into the processes through which people deal with things.[20] This quality is evident throughout the case studies in this book. The social world itself is heterogeneous and ever-changing, and this frustrates the ability of designers to predict how public objects will be used, particularly in a diverse or dynamic setting like New York City.

How should planners and designers account for this? The backdrop for chapters 1 and 2 is the popularization of participatory or community-based planning in American cities. The stories of the lawn in Brooklyn Bridge Park and the folding chair in Diversity Plaza suggest that granting local input into urban planning opens it up to competing local demands in ways that may make the resulting design more equitable, but that also make it more. In the design debates over Brooklyn Bridge Park, arguments about material form involved the construction of different imaginary publics. These fictional user populations embodied different ideas of whom the space should belong to, in a practical rather than a legal sense. As a result, the design process exacerbated the political fault lines between local neighborhoods and raised questions of social control that would affect the park itself, once built. Who would the park actually be for? The process, though certainly more democratic than the process behind, say, the design of Central Park, became more chaotic and less controllable by the park's planners as a result. A certain entropy was permitted into the design process by its participatory format, but at a deeper level, it was rooted in the nature of people's relationship to public objects—objects which, as I have suggested, exert control over their lives, and do so in uneven and potentially unequal ways.

A similar question troubled the NYC DOT's Neighborhood Plaza Program, shaping community-level reactions to a single material intervention, undertaken in drastically different neighborhood contexts across the five boroughs. City officials granted some power over these interventions to the public and, in doing so, sparked a series of neighborhood-level debates over the positive and negative implications of flexible public space—consequences that would hinge on the degree of social order and disorder within those communities, and how a few folding chairs and café tables might figure into a local social landscape that, in every case, is characterized by a unique set of tensions and recurring debates.

Design and planning, as argued in the introductory chapter, involves "theorizing about society."[21] When local communities get to participate in these processes, they actively, consciously theorize about themselves. Rather than negating or softening questions of social control, democratic inclusion brings these questions to the surface. This approach to planning can have a positive outcome from the standpoint of government agencies or financial or civic boosters. Corona's and Washington Heights' embrace of their new public spaces is hard to interpret as anything other than a success. And the lawns of Brooklyn Bridge Park, thanks in part to the prolonged, acerbic, and even legally conflictual design process, appear to have been adopted by the borough of Brooklyn, in all its diversity. But welcoming community input means decentralizing control over planning and design and implies a willingness to accept the results, whatever they might be. Given that people are affected in different ways by public objects, and see starkly different visions of themselves and others in the affordances they offer, a degree of uncertainty and unpredictability in the public reception of these objects is inevitable.

5. PUBLIC SPACE REQUIRES OPEN AFFORDANCES

A consistent theme in this book has been public space. In narrowly legalistic terms, for space to be public it has to be free to use and physically accessible to all. But looking closely at the affordances of public objects shows us that the material world prefigures and anticipates different human populations in ways that make public space more or less public, or, more accurately, that define "the public" differently. This means that for spaces to be genuinely public, affordances should not be too restrictive or inflexible, and this goes far beyond questions of accessibility. The tension inherent in the publicness of Brooklyn Bridge Park is evident in its closed affordances—its mosaic of micromanaged environments: a place to play volleyball (and only play volleyball), a place to look at the harbor (and only look at the harbor). The park's architects succeeded in designing a park that would attract a wide variety of visitors, but, in the process, they have likely sacrificed its ability to evolve and its openness to changing and unforeseen desires and needs. The White Horse and Black Horse Pikes, public spaces whose functions could not be more different from Brooklyn Bridge Park's, are similarly closed, their affordances rigidly imposed by the hard, durable surfaces of the landscape. Even the political struggle over the persistence of newsstands on public sidewalks is, in part, a question of open or closed affordances. Is the only function of a newsstand commercial? If so, the object seems to be failing, as its most lucrative trade, historically speaking, becomes less marketable and newsstands themselves become less profitable. In the municipal efforts to sanitize and regulate newsstands, we see the prioritization of competing affordances: sidewalks are for walking, not for vending (or standing and talking). But, as we have seen, newsstands serve a wide range of other social functions—they provide other social affordances. Whether they sell newspapers or lottery tickets, they are boxes that provide and accommodate social interaction, and, as such, they welcome the indeterminacy and variety of the social world. A more open approach to the regulation of public space, and a ceasefire in the classificatory struggle at the heart of the city government's dealings with newsstands, might allow these sociologically vital objects space to thrive.

There are, of course, limits to this line of argument. Closing off some of the affordances of the city's newly created pedestrian plazas was seen as necessary by the NYC DOT in order to keep these spaces viable as public space. This was done through material, symbolic, and institutional programming: painted boxes on the pavement at Times Square, along with ordinances stipulating where and when costumed buskers might solicit tips; rules concerning the dumping of garbage, or the placement of mattresses on the agency's property. If one affordance of a pedestrian plaza is a place to deposit household or commercial waste, then this affordance is likely to crowd out others, as few people will willingly sit and take in the scenery surrounded by bags of trash. But this, too, can be taken too far—the point is that there is an inherent tension between the closedness of affordances and the publicness of public space. Designers, planners, and regulators should think twice before micromanaging public behavior using the architectural and legal means at their disposal. Public space is only as public as it is flexible and adaptable—in other words, open to future adaptation, improvisation, and informality.

6. THINGS (AND PEOPLE) CREATE PLACES

The final and concluding finding that emerged from the research gathered here is that objects and people create places. Places, if you recall, are unique locations that contain specific material objects and have defined meanings. The case studies in this book show that the meanings of a place are heavily influenced by the encounters between people and things that take place there, and, more generally, the way the material and the social come together in a given location. As we will see in a moment, this argument sounds much simpler than it actually is. But we will start with the basics and move on from there.

Let us accept for a moment the idea outlined in the introduction of this book, that the material world stabilizes society and makes it more coherent and predictable. In this version of things, people and objects generally behave as we might expect, and the way they come together to "create" a given place becomes fairly easy to describe. A park (say, Brooklyn Bridge Park) is created by a collection of people who visit the park, and by the objects that compose the place and its surroundings, a combination of material elements (grass, trees, granite, steel picnic tables, distant skyscrapers) that offer certain affordances to the aforementioned people (jog here; bike there; sit here and admire the scenery). In this scenario, let us say that the objects perform as intended by an architect, and that the park's users also behave as expected, recognizing the park's affordances and availing themselves of the most salient possibilities. They jog here; they bike there; they sit and admire the scenery. So far so good. A handful of sentences and a few major assumptions about how the world works, and we have successfully constructed a place.

Complexity arises when we leave this fiction behind and visit a real place, where people and objects do *not* behave as we might expect. Released from our constraining assumptions, objects and people are now free to come together in asymmetrical, conflictual, and ambiguous ways. How the material and social elements of this kind of place shape and define the place itself becomes a more difficult process to describe. Contradictory or counterintuitive facts rise to the surface. Objects change, people change, or the relationship between objects and people changes, evolving over time or suddenly switching tracks. These and other inconvenient details make it ever-more obvious that the place is not just shaped by an architect's or planner's vision, but is subject to other, larger and less tangible things—competing ideologies, changing demographics, political interests, budget constraints.

Social theorists have devised complex metaphors to represent dynamic and unstable interconnections between the social and the material in scenarios such as this.[22] I have tried to keep things simple in this book but have still had to resort to coining my own complex idea, "normative infrastructure," to represent the mutually contingent and interlocking relationship between material objects and human behavior on the subway—a relationship that, incidentally, defines the subway as a place and helps give it meaning. In situations where objects or people make trouble, and do not behave as we might expect, it becomes harder to specify how people and things make places what they are.

Nevertheless, they do. Dysfunctional infrastructures and contradictory or unloved places are brought into being by problematic relationships between people and things. In our idealized version of Brooklyn Bridge Park, we might allow for the occasional malfunction, or moment of human error.[23] But some of the places described in this book are inherently, continuously unstable and contradictory, owing to endemic conflict between people and public objects. Thus is the nature of the subway, and of White Horse Pike, and of neighborhoods that hate their own pedestrian plazas, and of the atrium in Trump Tower. Even Brooklyn Bridge Park (the real one), departs from our fictional version, in its schizophrenic incorporation of a set of conflicting affordances—most notably, a private place to live and a public place to engage in leisure and recreation. These troubled places embody a degree of tension, incoherence, inconvenience, or danger. At the heart of such places are problematic or ambivalent encounters between people and things, which help to define how the places are experienced and understood by the people on hand.

Perhaps, when you finish reading this book, and leave the building you are in, you will find yourself in places like this—places where objects make trouble. As I suggested at the start of this book, when you go out into the public spaces of the city or town where you live, you will find things that have ideas about you. But maybe some of these ideas will be wrong, the objects' affordances unclear or unsuited for your needs. Maybe an object, in its definition of *the public*, will exclude you.

This should not be too surprising. Troublesome objects are not uncommon. The architects and planners who designed the places in which you find yourself might have imagined smooth and predictable relationships between people and things. But you are not a pixelated avatar in an advertisement, or an architectural rendering. You are not an anthropomorphic representation of an affordance that does not yet exist. Nor are you the happy emissary from some parallel universe, in which humans and their objects are perfectly codetermined, and always in synch. You are not a passive recipient of architectural or societal imperatives. You do not cross the street only inside of the crosswalks. You do not ride a perfectly functioning subway system, or live inside of a perfect public park. You are not a thought experiment in the world *as it might be*. You experience the world *as it is*, because this is the world you live in. And you are still in the midst of things.

ACKNOWLEDGMENTS

The idea for this book occurred to me while I was travelling south on New Jersey's Route 1, in Charles Varner's car (a.k.a. the "mobile research unit"), with Hana Shepherd and Stephanie Schacht, on our long semiweekly commute to Princeton. So, I would be remiss not to thank these three (and Charles's Honda) first. At around the same time, I would frequently sleep on a futon in a small, barely heated room in the Butler graduate student housing complex. The apartment was rented by Cristobal and Patricia Young, so they (and their futon) are next.

I benefitted from extraordinary mentorship from Paul DiMaggio and Kathy Newman at Princeton while embarking on this project. I still cannot believe my luck in having these two incredibly generous and supportive people around me at an early stage in my career. While studying at Princeton and living in Brooklyn, I took every opportunity to hang around uninvited at the sociology department of New York University, sitting in on urban sociology seminars and workshops. The reason for my interloping was the inimitable Harvey Molotch, who had a massive influence on my thinking about people and things. Harvey, your unflagging sociological curiosity and good humor provided the fuel for this book. I really hope you like it. During this time, conversations with a wider network of Princeton graduate students and faculty helped shape the ideas that appear here, or provided inspiration, solidarity, and other scarce resources that are vital to social research. Thanks to Len Albright, Sofya Aptekar, Mitch Duneier, Doug Massey, Alex Murphy, and Ethan Schoolman.

Once happily ensconced in the Sociology Department at Hunter College, I received enormous support from all of my City University of New York colleagues, which allowed me to write this book. I owe a special debt of gratitude to Lynn Chancer and Erica Chito Childs, for being absolutely the best department chairs I could have had during this time. Thanks as well to Peter Tuckel and William Milczarski for collaborating on the subway research, and to Tom DeGloma, Mark Halling, and Howard Lune for helpful feedback on early chapter drafts. A writing workshop convened by Andy Polsky and Rob Cowan provided a much-needed boost at a crucial stage. Conversations at the Graduate Center with Setha Low, Rich Ocejo, Greg Smithsimon, and Sharon Zukin were invigorating and always interesting, as were chats with scholars outside my CUNY network—notably, Hilary Angelo, Gordon Douglas, Noah McClain, Terrence McDonnell, and Stéphane Tonnelat. Stéphane's workshop on transit ethnography provided a rare chance to commune with scholars from around the globe who were working on related topics, and I would like to thank the participants in that workshop for a productive weekend that was crucial to my research in the subway.

My research benefitted from the assistance of some extremely bright graduate and undergraduate students at Hunter. Special thanks to my Macaulay Honors College students, a kind and talented group of people, who have shown themselves to be at least as supportive of me as I am of them. Brian Lamberta, Joy Nuga, and Jisun Reiner helped me with site visits at various points in my research. A team of graduate students at Hunter's Master's Program in Applied Social Research gamely ventured into the subway with me to observe and analyze passenger behavior. Farimata Caruso, Michelle DeCurtis, Prahelika Gadtaula, Matt Herman, Nicholas MacDonald, Nicholas Silipo, and Daniell Singh were a joy to work with.

Many thanks to Jacqueline Delaney, Meagan Levinson, Maia Vaswani, and the team at Princeton University Press, and much gratitude as well to several anonymous readers, whose feedback was very helpful. I am grateful to the New York City Transit Museum for permitting me to reprint several digital images from their archives, which appear in Chapter 4. Portions of Chapter 3 were previously published in Mike Owen Benediktsson, "Where Inequality Takes Place: A Programmatic Argument for Urban Sociology." *City & Community*, 17.2 (2018): 394–417, and appear courtesy of the American Sociological Association. Other parts of the chapter were previously published in Mike Owen Benediktsson, "Beyond the Sidewalk: Pedestrian Risk and Material Mismatch in the American Suburbs." *Mobilities*, 17.1 (2017): 76–96, and appear courtesy of Taylor & Francis. I would also like to extend my appreciation to my friends outside of academia, who contributed in a variety of ways, tangible and intangible, to this project. Thanks to The Forum for twenty-five years of friendship and unserious debate. Thanks to Leigh, Kevin, Niki, Rob, Joel, Gemma, and my many beloved neighbors at 1818 Newkirk and on Meadowbrook Lane for unpaid childcare, top-notch pandemic home cookery, and strong, enduring friendship. Thanks to Ehris, for being the best of "little brothers" while I was finishing this book. And the deepest appreciation as well to my family. Thanks to Pete Newman, Livia Scott, and Tina Kelley, and to my parents, Lynn and Tom Benediktsson, for supporting me in everything, at all times, regardless of how unpleasant I am about it. Thanks to Felix and Phoebe for absolutely nothing. All you guys did was distract me from my writing, especially over the last twenty-four months. But it's okay—I love you both anyway. Indescribable gratitude to my wife Kate. I would dedicate my entire life if the opportunity presented itself. But, for now, this book will have to do.

Finally, I owe a dept of gratitude to all the people, places, and things that appear in this book. But particularly to the people, who shared their experiences and ideas with me largely out of an unselfish desire to improve the city and its suburbs as a place to live or work. Without their generosity, this book could not have been written.

NOTES

Introduction

1. Herbert J. Gans, *The Levittowners: Ways of Life and Politics in a New Suburban Community* (New York: Pantheon Books, 1967), 13. On gender and the materiality of the suburban home, see Dolores Hayden's *Redesigning the American Dream: The Future of Housing, Work, and Family life* (New York: W.W. Norton, 1984).

2. Pierre Bourdieu, *The Logic of Practice* (Palo Alto, CA: Stanford University Press, 1990), 190, 215, 272. On the cultural and social significance of personal possessions, see Daniel Miller's *The Comfort of Things* (Cambridge, UK: Polity, 2008).

3. Thomas S. Kuhn, *The Structure of Scientific Revolutions* (Chicago: University of Chicago Press, 1962). To be clear, many fascinating books and articles about objects and materiality have been written by sociologists. I was inspired by this work, and make reference to it throughout this book. But this body of research and theory does not cohere into a discernible subdiscipline or "school" of research, and is well outside of the sociological mainstream. To my knowledge, there are no academic journals or edited volumes devoted to material sociology, and few, if any, courses in material sociology are offered at US colleges or universities. The American Sociological Association (ASA) has subsections devoted to the study of "rationality and society," "evolution, biology, and society," and "animals and society," but there is currently no section on "objects and society." As it stands, there appears to be no formal community of sociologists, in the United States or in any other country, expressly devoted to the study of how people relate to things. None of this matters, if you happen not to be a sociologist. The primary point here is simply that the social role of material objects remains unsettled and ambiguous among experts, and secondarily, that this is largely because people (not just sociologists) look past the material world when thinking about and describing social processes. The most compelling argument for this omission remains Bruno Latour's, in "Where Are the Missing Masses? The Sociology of a Few Mundane Artefacts," chapter 8 in *Shaping Technology\Building Society*, edited by Wiebe E. Bijker and John Law (Cambridge, MA: MIT Press, 1992), and *Reassembling the Social: An Introduction to Actor-Network-Theory* (Oxford: Oxford University Press, 2005).

4. David Frisby and Mike Featherstone, eds., *Simmel on Culture: Selected Writings* (New York: Sage, 1997), 146–51.

5. Namely, urban sociology and geography; dramaturgical and symbolic interactionist sociology; the broad, interdisciplinary field generally referred as science, technology, and society (STS); and the narrower one known by the moniker actor network theory (ANT); as well as the study of material culture in anthropology and sociology.

6. Control is meant here not necessarily in the sense of intentional or insidious social control, but rather a neutral form of power that orders social relations and enables or constrains specific patterns of human behavior.

7. The concept of affordances originated in the work of psychologist James J. Gibson, where he defined the term as one that refers to both an animal and its environment "in a way that no

existing term does." According to Gibson, "the affordances of the environment are what it offers the animal, what it provides or furnishes, either for good or ill": *The Ecological Approach to Visual Perception* (Hillsdale, NJ: Lawrence Erlbaum Associates, 1986): 127. A rock, for example, might provide a place to sit or stand. The idea of affordances, sometimes referred to as "scripts" or "programs," has since been adopted by social scientists who study the societal implications of material artifacts. For well-known examples, see Madeleine Akrich's "The De-scription of Technical Objects," chapter 7 in Bijker and Law's *Shaping Technology\Building Society*, and Latour's "Where Are the Missing Masses?" For more on the use and evolution of the concept of affordances, see Alan Costall, "Socializing Affordances," *Theory and Psychology* 5, no. 4 (1995): 467–81.

8. More recently, "affordance theory" has been extended to nonmaterial objects, such as laws and even music genres: Clayton Childress, Shyon Baumann, Craig M. Rawlings, and Jean-Francois Nault, "Genres, Objects, and the Contemporary Expression of Higher-Status Tastes," *Sociological Science* 8, no. 12 (2021): doi:10.15195/v8.a12.

9. Although humans have, on occasion, been compelled to eat their shoes, relieving hunger is not typically an affordance of a shoe. One affordance of a shoe is protecting one's foot; another is following an important social convention pertaining to attire. In other words, affordances involve an alignment between the materiality of an object and existing human desires or needs. The alignment is embodied in a likely course of human action that satisfies the human need and is possible—even encouraged—by the design of the object; in this case, wearing a shoe on one's foot. After several weeks on a desert island with no food, other affordances of the shoe might materialize. But until then, they effectively do not exist.

10. The term as I use it overlaps somewhat with the meaning of the word as it is used in computer science and architecture, where the "programming" of a building or a built space is (roughly) its accommodation of a set of desired affordances, or the various activities that it would offer to an inhabitant or user. Once programmed, an object or place can constrain behavior and foreclose certain options. In this regard, deviating somewhat from the concept of affordance, programming can indicate not just what could be done but also what strictly cannot or should not be done.

11. Rules concerning how objects are to be used are "institutionalized" *not* because formal institutions make or enforce these rules, although sometimes they do, but because people implicitly acknowledge the rules. Put differently, even informal norms are social "institutions," in the sense formulated by Peter Berger and Thomas Luckmann in their classic work on the sociology of knowledge: *The Social Construction of Reality: A Treatise in the Sociology of Knowledge* (London: Penguin UK, 1966), 72–85. Implicit, informal assumptions about behavior have long fascinated sociologists, in part because they seem to compose much of the cognitive and social infrastructure of collective behavior. Typically, we think of unspoken behavioral rules as norms that stabilize interactions between people, but if we shift our attention to the material objects implicated in social norms, we see complex systems of informal regulations concerning how objects themselves are to be used, and by whom. In his well-known essay on deference and demeanor, for example, Erving Goffman describes the behavior of a psychiatric ward's staff: "Doctors had the right to saunter into the nurses' station, lounge on the station's dispensing counter, and engage in joking with the nurses; other ranks participated in this informal interaction with doctors, but only after doctors had initiated it"—Erving Goffman, *Interaction Ritual: Essays on Face-to-Face Behavior* (New York: Pantheon Books, 1967), 79. For Goffman, the point is that disregarding formality can be a privilege held by those with formal authority. But if we shift our focus from the doctor to the dispensing counter, we see that the object has different affordances, or programs, for different people: it's not just a functional object, but a prop for a doctor wishing to convey a jocular sense of ownership and power over his surroundings. This program is contained within the object—a latent potentiality waiting for someone to take advantage of it—in this particular social context. Similarly, in Harold Garfinkel's famous experiment, when he instructed his students to act like guesthouse

boarders in their own homes, the students became sensitized to an instability in how they should behave, not just toward their family members but toward the objects in their homes. "Familiar objects—persons obviously, but furniture and room arrangements as well—resisted students' efforts to think of themselves as strangers. Many became uncomfortably aware of how habitual movements were being made; of *how* one was handling the silverware, or *how* one opened a door or greeted another member"—Harold Garfinkel, *Studies in Ethnomethodology* (Malden, MA: Polity, 1967), 46. Having familiarized themselves to using household objects in an informal and intimate manner, it proved difficult to behave formally toward them—to "estrange themselves," as Garfinkel puts it (37). These examples illustrate what I call *institutionalized programs*—implicit or explicit social rules for how objects are to be used by different classes of people—but they also underscore one of the central points in this introduction: that social interactions are mediated by material objects that are typically ignored, but that do a lot of heavy lifting when it comes to making, again in Garfinkel's words, a "common sense world" possible (36).

12. Latour, "Where Are the Missing Masses?"

13. Throughout this book, I use language (e.g., "stability," "break down," or "dysfunction") that might seem to suggest a theoretical commitment to functionalism, or, relatedly, an endorsement of the idea that the social world empirically tends toward stasis or equilibrium. The concept of affordances has functionalist undertones, as it recasts objects in terms of their apparent social uses. In the chapters that follow, the functions or uses of things are meant to be understood only as relative to other proximate elements of a sociotechnical or cultural system, place, or space, not as general laws. There is no grand theory here. If there is functionalism, it is of the "middle range" variety—Robert Merton, *Social Theory and Social Structure* (New York: Free Press, 1968), 39–72. For example, the subway door-closing device known as an "actuator" (mentioned at the beginning of chapter 4) has a "function" relative to the subway door, which in turn has a function relative to the train, which has a function with regard to the stated objectives of the transit agency and its governing bodies. Beyond the roles objects play within a bounded system of this sort, there is no need to ascribe broader societal functions to an object or a human action. And, as should be clear from the main arguments of chapters 3 and 5, the social affordances of objects within a particular place and time often run contrary or orthogonal to their explicit functions within a larger social system.

14. Harold Garfinkel, "Studies of the Routine Grounds of Everyday Activities," *Social Problems* 11, no. 3 (Winter 1964): 225–250. I am taking some liberties here: Garfinkel was talking about intentionally violating social norms in order to make visible the underlying behavioral assumptions that made possible a "common-sense" or taken-for-granted social world. But my approach is in the same spirit. Misbehaving or novel material objects are like Garfinkel's breaching experiments, in the sense that they momentarily estrange us from the material world and make us aware of the role everyday things play in our lives.

15. Bruno Latour, *Reassembling the Social: An Introduction to Actor-Network-Theory* (Oxford: Oxford University Press, 2005), 80

16. Thomas F. Gieryn, "What Buildings Do," *Theory and Society* 31, no. 1 (2002): 42–43.

17. See William Russell Ellis and Dana Cuff, *Architects' People* (New York: Oxford University Press, 1989); Gieryn, "What Buildings Do"; Harvey Luskin Molotch, *Where Stuff Comes From: How Toasters, Toilets, Cars, Computers, and Many Others Things Come to Be as They Are* (New York: Routledge, 2003); Nelly Oudshoorn and Trevor J. Pinch, *How Users Matter: The Co-construction of Users and Technology* (Cambridge, MA: MIT Press 2005).

18. John Chris Jones, *Design Methods* (New York: John Wiley and Sons, 1992), 9.

19. See David K Miller, "Theories, Paradigms, and Planning," in *Professionals and Urban Form*, ed. J. R. Blau, M. La Gory, and J. Pipkin (Albany, NY: State University of New York Press, 1983), 134–45.

20. Herbert J. Gans, *People and Plans: Essays on Urban Problems and Solutions* (New York: Basic Books, 1991).

21. Claude S. Fischer, *America Calling: A Social History of the Telephone to 1940* (Berkeley: University of California Press, 1994): 69–72, 185–87.

22. Terence E. McDonnell, *Best Laid Plans: Cultural Entropy and the Unraveling of AIDS Media Campaigns* (Chicago: University of Chicago Press, 2016).

23. Michael Ian Borer, "The Location of Culture: The Urban Culturalist Perspective," *City and Community* 5, no. 2 (2006): 173–97; Borer, *Faithful to Fenway: Believing in Boston, Baseball, and America's Most Beloved Ballpark* (New York: New York University Press, 2008).

24. On the neglected importance of "repair and maintenance" in social theory, see Stephen Graham and Nigel Thrift's "Out of Order: Understanding Repair and Maintenance" (*Theory, Culture and Society* 24, no. 3 [2007]: 1–25). Also see Latour's *Reassembling the Social* on "accidents, breakdowns, and strikes" (81), and Susan Leigh Star's "The Ethnography of Infrastructure" (*American Behavioral Scientist* 43, no. 3 [1999]: 382) on "breakdown."

25. Urban planners call these "desire lines"—traces of informal uses that evince a desire to use a space contrary to its programming.

26. Langdon Winner, "Do Artifacts Have Politics?," *Daedalus* 109, no. 1 (1980): 121–36.

27. Sofya Aptekar, "Looking Forward, Looking Back: Collective Memory and Neighborhood Identity in Two Urban Parks," *Symbolic Interaction* 40, no. 1 (2017): 101–21; Michael Ian Borer, "From Collective Memory to Collective Imagination: Time, Place, and Urban Redevelopment," *Symbolic Interaction* 33, no. 1 (2010): 96–114.

28. See, for example, Wendy Griswold, Gemma Mangione, and Terence E. McDonnell, "Objects, Words, and Bodies in Space: Bringing Materiality into Cultural Analysis," *Qualitative Sociology* 36, no. 4 (2013): 343–64; Terence E. McDonnell, "Cultural Objects as Objects: Materiality, Urban Space, and the Interpretation of Aids Campaigns in Accra, Ghana," *American Journal of Sociology* 115, no. 6 (2010): 1800–1852; Colin Jerolmack and Iddo Tavory, "Molds and Totems: Nonhumans and the Constitution of the Social Self," *Sociological Theory* 32, no. 1 (2014): 64–77.

29. See Richard Sennett, *The Fall of Public Man* (New York: Alfred A. Knopf, 1976); Marshall Berman, *Modernism in the Streets: A Life and Times in Essays* (New York: Verso, 2017); Henri Lefebvre, *The Urban Revolution* (Minneapolis: University of Minnesota Press, 2003), 18–21.

30. Michael Sorkin, *Variations on a Theme Park: The New American City and the End of Public Space* (New York: Hill and Wang, 1992); Setha Low and Neil Smith, *The Politics of Public Space* (New York: Routledge, 2013); Don Mitchell, *The Right to the City: Social Justice and the Fight for Public Space* (New York: Guilford, 2003); Benjamin Shepard and Gregory Smithsimon, *The Beach beneath the Streets: Contesting New York City's Public Spaces* (Albany, NY: State University of New York Press, 2011).

31. Thomas F. Gieryn, "A Space for Place in Sociology," *Annual Review of Sociology* 26 (2000): 463–96.

32. For sociological definitions or applications of the concept of place, see: John Urry, *Consuming Places* (New York: Routledge, 1995); John R. Logan and Harvey Luskin Molotch, *Urban Fortunes: The Political Economy of Place* (Berkeley: University of California Press, 1987); Doreen Massey, *Space, Place, and Gender* (Cambridge: Polity, 1994); Ray Oldenburg, *The Great Good Place: Cafes, Coffee Shops, Bookstores, Bars, Hair Salons, and Other Hangouts at the Heart of a Community* (Cambridge, MA: Da Capo, 1999); John Urry, "The Place of Emotions within Place," in *Emotional Geographies*, ed. Joyce Davidson, Liz Bondi, and Mike Smith, 77–86 (New York: Routledge, 2016); Borer, "Location of Culture"; Sharon Zukin, "Reconstructing the Authenticity of Place," *Theory and Society* 40, no. 2 (2011): 161–65.

33. The term was coined by William I. Thomas in *The Unadjusted Girl* (Boston: Little, Brown, 1931, 41), and is associated with symbolic interactionism. But it was Erving Goffman who pointed

to the importance of material objects to our "definition of the situation" in his classic work of dramaturgical sociology: *The Presentation of Self in Everyday Life* (New York: Doubleday, 1959).

34. For example, in addition to the cases covered in this book, protracted political and legal controversies have surrounded proposals to create a bike lane in Park Slope, Brooklyn, and a bicycle corral in Crown Heights, to relocate the fountain in Washington Square Park, and to install separate doors for affordable housing residents ("poor doors") in mixed-income apartment buildings. The small, quotidian nature of these cases illustrates the overt politicization of urban architecture and design decisions that formerly took place behind closed doors.

35. Robert A. Caro, *The Power Broker: Robert Moses and the Fall of New York* (New York: Knopf, 1974), 611, 741, 837–94, 968–72.

36. Even in cases, such as large public housing complexes, where the physical environment for an entire community was built literally from scratch, the material needs specific to that community were not incorporated into the design process. The most comprehensive design manual for low-income public housing published by the National Housing Authority during the heyday of urban renewal contains scores of photographs of white residents engaged in various domestic routines, and justifies its recommendations with blanket claims regarding the needs of low-income families with children. In the entire 294-page document, a single page outlines the need to accommodate the "particular characteristics" of tenants, which derive from nationality and "local custom." "Each community must study and know its local problems and must meet them as it sees best in each case," the manual reads, but no advice is offered concerning the procedures for taking community needs into account: National Housing Authority, *Public Housing Design: A Review of Experience in Low-Rent Housing* (Washington, DC: Government Printing Office, 1946), 86.

37. David Halle and Elizabeth Tiso, *New York's New Edge: Contemporary Art, the High Line and Megaprojects on the Far West Side* (Chicago: Chicago University Press, 2014); Alan A. Altshuler and David E. Luberoff, *Mega-Projects: The Changing Politics of Urban Public Investment* (Brookings Institution Press, 2004).

38. Jacobs framed her manifesto on the value of informal street life as an attack on the very enterprise of city planning, which ignored the small, socially cohesive spaces of the city, disregarding, as she put it, the "human scale": Jane Jacobs, *The Death and Life of Great American Cities* (New York: Random House, 1961). Meanwhile, on the other side of the Atlantic Ocean, Henri Lefebvre struck a nerve when he argued that the users of urban space have a "right to the city"—a right to shape their own lives by having a hand in the social and political processes that create and modify urban space: Henri Lefebvre, "The Right to the City," in *Writings on Cities*, ed. Eleonore Kofman and Elizabeth Lebas (Malden, MA: Blackwell, 1996), 63–181. For other influential contemporary critiques of modernist planning, see Lewis Mumford's *The Urban Prospect* (San Diego: Harcourt, Brace, and Wold, 1968) and William H. Whyte's *The Social Life of Small Urban Spaces* (Washington, DC: Conservation Foundation, 1980); for a fascinating historical look at how the authority of twentieth-century planners evolved during this period, see Stephen Bocking's "Constructing Urban Expertise: Professional and Political Authority in Toronto, 1940–1970" (*Journal of Urban History* 33, no. 1 [2006]: 51–76).

39. The filing of an Environmental Impact Statement, for example, a regulatory requirement adopted in the early 1970s in order to mitigate negative environmental impacts, has increasingly served as a moment in which the social as well as environmental impacts of a new development are subject to explicit, public debate.

40. In recent decades, completed city design projects or infrastructural changes have increasingly been proposed by community actors. A nonprofit organization that tracks such projects, the Municipal Arts Society, mapped eighty-seven community-based plans completed between 1989 and 2008.

41. Whyte, *Social Life*.

42. Amanda Burden, "Jane Jacobs, Robert Moses, and City Planning Today," *Gotham Gazette*, November 6, 2006, https://www.gothamgazette.com/index.php/development/3402-jane-jacobs-robert-moses-and-city-planning-today.

43. For summaries of Mayor Michael Bloomberg's physical legacy, see Brian Peteritas's "Will the Next NYC Mayor Continue Bloomberg's Urban Planning Legacy?" (*Governing*, February 16, 2013, https://www.governing.com/archive/gov-nyc-mayor-bloombergs-urban-planning-legacy.html) and Jim Dwyer's "The Impossible Mayor of the Possible" (*New York Times*, August 16, 2013, https://archive.nytimes.com/www.nytimes.com/2013/08/18/nyregion/the-impossible-mayor-of-the-possible.html).

44. For example, Anna Lowenhaupt Tsing, *The Mushroom at the End of the World* (Princeton, NJ: Princeton University Press, 2015); Sidney Wilfred Mintz, *Sweetness and Power: The Place of Sugar in Modern History* (New York: Penguin, 1986); Mark Kurlansky, *Salt* (New York: Random House, 2011).

45. See, for example, Fischer, *America Calling*; Wiebe E. Bijker, *The Social Construction of Bakelite: Toward a Theory of Invention* (Cambridge, MA: MIT Press, 1987); Bijker, *Of Bicycles, Bakelites, and Bulbs: Toward a Theory of Sociotechnical Change* (Cambridge, MA: MIT Press, 1997).

46. See Daniel Miller, *Comfort of Things*.

47. Identifying documented instances of "trouble" (malfunction, disorder, disaster), describing these cases sociologically, and, in some cases, coming up with a social explanation is an established approach to social research. There is a strong basis for this pragmatic, opportunistic method in some of the oldest schools of social research—functionalism, American pragmatism and abductive analysis, ethnomethodology and conversation analysis, grounded theory, etc. Analyzing trouble means sampling on the dependent variable. Nevertheless, detailed qualitative accounts of trouble have produced valuable insights when applied to such varied topics as heat waves, (Eric Klinenberg, *Heat Wave: A Social Autopsy of Disaster in Chicago* [Chicago: University of Chicago Press, 2003]), floods (Kai T. Erikson, *Everything in Its Path* [New York: Simon and Schuster, 1972]), episodes of conflict or violence (Randall Collins, *Violence: A Micro-Sociological Theory* [Princeton, NJ: Princeton University Press, 2009]), and technological malfunction or failure (Diane Vaughn, *The Challenger Launch Decision: Risky Technology, Culture, and Deviance at NASA* [Chicago: University of Chicago Press, 1996]; Bruno Latour, *Aramis; or, The Love of Technology* [Cambridge, MA: Harvard University Press, 1996]).

48. In cases where my informants served in formal capacities with regard to an organization mentioned in the book, I use their actual names. I use pseudonyms to refer to the newsstand operators described in chapter 5, and informal users of the objects and spaces mentioned throughout the book.

Chapter 1

1. Small, simple things are indisputably objects: a pebble, a maple leaf, a paper clip. We tend to categorize large and/or complex things in a different way, as containers or settings for human activity. Something as large and as complicated as an automobile might still be seen as an object, but a house is typically not. A bucket is an object, but a swimming pool is not. A natural lake is even less of an object. The categorical distinctions at work here are fuzzy, but they seem to involve whether the thing in question is large enough for us to fit inside of it, which is not a particularly satisfying criterion. In this book, I take the stance that the point at which "objects" give way to larger, more complex things is mostly a matter of semantics. We are either concerned with the materiality of a thing (large or small) or we are not. Having said that, if a reader would prefer to think of a lawn as a "space" or an "environment," this is fine—it makes little difference for the argument in this chapter.

2. Frederick Law Olmsted and Calvert Vaux, "Preliminary Report to the Commissioners for Laying out a Park in Brooklyn, New York: Being a Consideration of Circumstances of Site and Other Conditions Affecting the Design of Public Pleasure Grounds" (1866), in *Landscape into Cityscape: Frederick Law Olmsted's Plans for a Greater New York*, ed. Albert Fein (Ithaca, NY: Cornell University Press, 1968), 97–98.

3. Olmsted acknowledges the enjoyment that people take in being with other people, and designed his parks to afford spaces and occasions for people-watching. The sides of Prospect Park's Long Meadow, for example, slope upward toward wooded hills, offering a natural amphitheater from which to view not just the pastoral landscape but the human activity that would occur within it. Prospect Park and Central Park, Olmsted wrote:

> are the only places in [Manhattan and Brooklyn] where . . . you will find a body of Christians coming together, and with an evident glee in the prospect of coming together, all classes largely represented, and with a common purpose, not at all intellectual, competitive with none, disposing to jealousy and spiritual or intellectual pride toward none, each individual adding by his mere presence to the pleasure of all others, all helping to the greater happiness of each. You may thus often see vast numbers of persons brought closely together, poor and rich, young and old, Jew and Gentile. . . . I have looked studiously but vainly among them for a single face completely unsympathetic with the prevailing expression of good nature and light-heartedness. (Frederick Law Olmsted, "Public Parks and the Enlargement of Towns" [1870], in *Civilizing American Cities: Writings on City Landscapes*, ed. S. B. Hutton [New York: Da Capo, 1997], 75)

4. Intuition is backed up by the many studies of overt social exclusion through architecture. For more, see Peter Marcuse on urban "citadels" in "The Enclave, the Citadel, and the Ghetto: What Has Changed in the Post-Fordist US City" (*Urban Affairs Review* 33, no. 2 [November 1997]: 228–64), Setha Low on gated communities in *Behind the Gates: Life, Security, and the Pursuit of Happiness in Fortress America* (New York: Routledge, 2004), and Mike Davis on "panopticon shopping malls" in *City of Quartz: Excavating the Future in Los Angeles* (New York: Vintage, 1990). Restrictive local codes regulating public behavior can also be deployed in order to earmark public space for one group of users or another. See Nicholas Blomley, "Civil Rights Meet Civil Engineering: Urban Public Space and Traffic Logic," *Canadian Journal of Law and Society* 22, no. 2 (August 2007): 55–72; Mariana Valverde, *Everyday Law on the Street: City Governance in an Age of Diversity* (Chicago: University of Chicago Press, 2012).

5. For detailed historical accounts of the legal, financial, and political process behind Brooklyn Bridge Park, see Joanne Witty and Henrik Krogius's *Brooklyn Bridge Park: A Dying Waterfront Transformed* (New York: Fordham University Press, 2016) and Nancy Webster and David Shirley's *A History of Brooklyn Bridge Park: How a Community Reclaimed and Transformed New York City's Waterfront* (New York: Columbia University Press 2016).

6. Julian E. Barnes, "Disparate Visions for a New Park: Accord Is Sought among Clashing Views in Brooklyn," *New York Times*, December 12, 1999.

7. Although the areas in and around the chosen site for Central Park were quite low in density, they were not uninhabited, as this quote seems to suggest. More than 1,500 people were displaced to make space for the park. Nor was there "public agreement about what parks were supposed to be." According to Roy Rosenzweig and Elizabeth Blackmar in *The Park and the People: A History of Central Park* (Ithaca, NY: Cornell University Press, 1992), the design of the park was hotly debated in the press, and the selection of both the commission in charge of the design competition and the winning design itself were widely regarded as political. Finally, it is not true that Olmsted and Vaux were unencumbered by specific programmatic demands—the design competition actually stipulated a series of required elements for the

park. These elements complicated Olmsted and Vaux's design and compelled them to make aesthetic compromises.

8. Witty and Krogius, *Brooklyn Bridge Park*, 35.

9. Jess Wisloski and Neil Sloane, "A-Park-Ments," *Brooklyn Paper*, January 8, 2005.

10. A newly created organization, the Brooklyn Bridge Park Defense Fund (BBPDF) claimed that the inclusion of housing in the park violated the public trust doctrine, which requires that public parkland be used exclusively for the public good. In dismissing the case, a county Supreme Court judge countered that the grounds of BBP were not actually "public parkland, have never been parkland, and were never designated to be parkland." See Jen Chung, "Judge Tosses Brooklyn Bridge Lawsuit," *Gothamist*, November 29, 2006, https://gothamist.com/news/judge-tosses -brooklyn-bridge-park-lawsuit.

11. To be fair, similar arguments were made concerning Central Park as well. As upscale high-rise apartment buildings were built up around the park, the view of the park was increasingly regarded as an amenity of these spaces, with property owners lobbying for landscaping changes that would, in their minds, improve their view. Rosenzweig and Blackmar note that these apartment buildings created "a new constituency of park users who never passed through the gates" (*Park and the People*, 377).

12. Mary Pat Thornton to Wendy Leventer, November 2, 2005.

13. Olmsted, an early proponent of lawns in residential settings as well as public recreational settings, envisioned the suburban front lawn as providing a communal, park-like feeling—one that was consistent with American egalitarian ideals and that contrasted with stodgy European landscapes carved up by hedgerows and rock walls. But the lawn took on a different meaning as it was popularized in the early twentieth century. On the evolving cultural associations of the front lawn in America, see Virginia Scott Jenkins's *The Lawn: A History of an American Obsession* (Washington, DC: Smithsonian Institution, 2015), Fred E. H. Schroeder's *Front Yard America: The Evolution and Meanings of a Vernacular Domestic Landscape* (Bowling Green, OH: Popular Press, 1993), and Christopher Grampp's *From Yard to Garden* (Chicago: Center for American Places at Columbia College Chicago, 2008).

14. Julian E. Barnes, "As Some Fight a Park Plan, Its Supporters See Elitism," *New York Times*, August 16, 2000. The Napoleon's army comment is quoted in Witty and Krogius, *Brooklyn Bridge Park*, 75.

15. Witty and Krogius, *Brooklyn Bridge Park*, 68, 78.

16. Richard D. Lyons, "In Brooklyn Heights, a Spotlight on 87 Neglected Acres," *New York Times*, October 27, 1985.

17. See Paul Boyer, *Urban Masses and Moral Order in America, 1820–1920* (Cambridge, MA: Harvard University Press, 1992); John F. Kasson, *Amusing the Million: Coney Island at the Turn of the Century* (New York: Hill and Wang, 1978); Roy Rosenzweig, *Eight Hours for What We Will: Workers and Leisure in an Industrial City, 1870–1920* (Cambridge: Cambridge University Press, 1985); Dorceta E. Taylor, "Central Park as a Model for Social Control: Urban Parks, Social Class and Leisure Behavior in Nineteenth-Century America," *Journal of Leisure Research* 31, no. 4 (1999): 420–77; Rosenzweig and Blackmar, *Park and the People*.

18. Rosenzweig and Blackmar, *Park and the People*, 110–11.

19. Tom Boylan, "One Brooklyn Bridge Park Commercial," YouTube, February 26, 2010, https://www.youtube.com/watch?v=qQCTIo1YlNE.

20. Constance Perin, *Everything in Its Place: Social Order and Land Use in America* (Princeton, NJ: Princeton University Press, 1977).

21. Grampp, *From Yard to Garden*.

22. Jane Jacobs, *The Death and Life of Great American Cities* (New York: Random House, 1961).

23. "Brooklyn Bridge Park's Committee on Alternatives to Housing Public Hearing, Part I," Brooklyn Bridge Park Corporation (website), accessed October 1, 2014, p. 94, www .brooklynbridgeparknyc.org.

24. "Brooklyn Bridge Park's Committee on Alternatives to Housing Public Hearing, Part II," Brooklyn Bridge Park Corporation (website), accessed October 1, 2014, p. 114, www .brooklynbridgeparknyc.org.

25. Michael Van Valkenburgh, "Brooklyn Bridge Park," 100th Annual Meeting of the Brooklyn Heights Association, keynote address, Brooklyn Heights Association, February 23, 2010.

26. Witty and Krogius, *Brooklyn Bridge Park*, 69.

27. For example, see Sarah Amelar, "Brooklyn Bridge Park by Michael Van Valkenburgh Associates," *Architectural Record*, January 16, 2011, https://www.architecturalrecord.com/articles /7857-brooklyn-bridge-park-by-michael-van-valkenburgh-associates.

28. Van Valkenburgh, "Brooklyn Bridge Park."

29. Rosenzweig and Blackmar, *Park and the People*, 130–39, 365.

30. State of New York Executive Chamber, "BBPDC Lease Agreement," press release, Brooklyn Bridge Park Corporation (website), June 6, 2009, https://www.brooklynbridgepark.org/about /press-releases/bbpdc-lease-agreement/.

31. All comments by Cobble Hill residents and activists quoted in this section were drawn from transcripts of two public hearings held in November and December, 2010, or from written testimony submitted by Cobble Hill residents in conjunction with the hearings. The subject of the hearings was the plan to finance the park using payments generated by the inclusion of private housing in the park. They were organized by a consultant, Bay Area Economics, contracted by the Brooklyn Bridge Park Corporation, and were hosted by the corporation's Committee on Alternatives to Housing. Transcripts of the hearings were posted on the Brooklyn Bridge Park website, www.brooklynbridgepark.org, where they were accessed on October 1, 2014.

32. "A-Park-Ments," *Brooklyn Paper*, January 8, 2005.

33. Van Valkenburgh, "Brooklyn Bridge Park." Other members of Van Valkenburgh's team were less diplomatic in describing their work. Speaking to reporter Nancy Scola, one of the principal architects on the project described the public input as a factor that constrained the design team's ability to act on behalf of the community's unknowing needs and desires. "I'm the designer. . . . We're not an instrument of the community. This park is so responsive to their needs, even if they don't know it." Later in the interview, the architect struck a patronizing tone regarding the community input into the design: "This isn't for amateurs. We pretend it is, to be nice, but it's not"— quoted in Nancy Scola, "Sward into Playgrounds: What All the Fuss over Brooklyn Bridge Park Is Actually About," *Politico New York*, August 29, 2011, https://www.politico.com/states/new -york/albany/story/2011/08/sward-into-playgrounds-what-all-the-fuss-over-brooklyn-bridge -park-is-actually-about-070248.

34. On an afternoon in spring 2016, two undergraduate research assistants counted all 642 benches in the park, 360 of which point outward, away from the park's public spaces and toward the harbor, the Brooklyn Bridge, the Statue of Liberty, or the downtown skyline.

35. Ginia Bellafante, "Suddenly, a Police Presence Comes to Brooklyn Bridge Park," *New York Times*, April 24, 2015.

36. The results of these user surveys, corroborated through conversations with park officials, as well as my own participation in the official user count conducted by the Brooklyn Bridge Park Corporation and Conservancy in 2015, provided valuable details on the demographics of park users at several points in time.

37. According to American Community Survey (ACS) data for 2013, the White non-Hispanic population share of the three tracts adjacent to the park ranged from 72% to 82%, while White non-Hispanics composed only 36% of the Brooklyn population as a whole. (The Black non-Hispanic

share of Brooklyn's population was 36%, the Hispanic share was 20%, the Asian share 11%, and the racially mixed share 2.3%.) If a third of park users represented the neighboring tracts, a third represented other Brooklyn neighborhoods, and the last third represented New York City as a whole, then the numbers actually suggest that the park was more likely to attract people of color than White non-Hispanics, given their prevalence within each of these respective populations. US Census Bureau, "Race, 2013," ACS 2013 (5-Year Estimates), prepared by Social Explorer, accessed April 12, 2018, https://www.socialexplorer.com/tables/ACS2013_5yr.

38. See Nicolai Ouroussoff, "Proposed Brooklyn Park Draws Class Lines," *New York Times*, September 19, 2005; Ouroussoff, "The Greening of the Waterfront," *New York Times*, April 1, 2010.

39. Ethan Kent, "Brooklyn Bridge Park," Hall of Shame Archive, Project for Public Spaces, July 21, 2006, https://www.pps.org/places/brooklyn-bridge-park.

40. Bellafante, "Suddenly, a Police Presence."

41. Rosenzweig and Blackmar, *Park and the People*, 469. A similar process of democratic adaptation has occurred in Prospect Park, as informal gathering spaces serving specific constituencies were absorbed into the park's material and symbolic programming. The African drummers who congregated on the southeastern corner of the park on Sunday afternoons were given their own grove. Dog owners eventually won the right to let their dogs off the leash at times. See chapter 3 in Setha Low, Dana Taplin, and Suzanne Scheld's *Rethinking Urban Parks: Public Space and Cultural Diversity* (Austin: University of Texas Press, 2009).

42. Stewart Brand, *How Buildings Learn: What Happens after They're Built* (New York: Viking, 1994).

43. This tradeoff is increasingly widespread in the era of privately financed public goods. According to the advocates of public-private partnerships, private financing gives public parks, libraries, schools, etc., a more certain future, insulating them from future fiscal crises and austerity regimes that could imperil public funding. But the needs of private entities and their ability and willingness to fund public amenities will also inevitably evolve over time and change in response to exogenous events, and because they are not democratically accountable or mandated to serve the public good, it is uncertain how the provision of those goods will be affected by this relationship over time.

44. Admittedly, in the decades that followed the construction of Central Park, this capacity was tested. The lawns were victims of their own success. Picnicking and strolling—two of the wholesome activities with universal appeal that Olmsted intended the lawns to encourage—destroyed the grass, forcing park administrators to limit their use. Even more ironically, their success as venues for a variety of incompatible activities (e.g., ball playing, croquet, picnicking) led to the adoption of a system of color-coded pennants that marked the lawns for different uses (and hence, different groups of users) at different times of day or week. The lawns were, in a sense, found by park administrators to be too democratic, accommodating incompatible uses that had to be scheduled and demarcated through signage and regulation. By providing the people of the city with an unobstructed expanse of green turf, Olmsted and Vaux gave them a space that they could make their own, occupying it as they saw fit, often in ways that sharply contradicted the designers' imagined programs for the space. See pp. 307–40 in Rosenzweig and Blackmar, *Park and the People*.

Chapter 2

1. For a fascinating social history of the chair, see Witold Rybczynski's *Now I Sit Me Down: From Klismos to Plastic Chair: A Natural History* (New York: Farrar, Straus, and Giroux, 2016).

2. When sociologist William H. Whyte studied how people use moveable seating in public plazas, he made an interesting discovery. People nearly always take advantage of the affordance of mobility and flexibility, relocating or adjusting a chair before sitting in it. In the grainy footage

of Whyte's well-known documentary, this practice is exploited for its comedic effect. Oblivious to the fact that they are being recorded, men in suits can be seen making minute adjustments in the position of a chair, shifting it a few inches to the right or left, in an unthinking gesture of mastery over their environment.

3. The seven hours were not continuous. I was distracted from time to time by other events in the plaza and took a short break for lunch, but kept an eye on the chair for a full seven hours throughout the day, logging separate entries for each time the chair was used.

4. *PlaNYC: A Stronger, More Resilient New York* (New York: City of New York, 2013), 29–37.

5. Noah Kazis, "New York Has 81,875 Metered Parking Spaces, and Millions of Free Ones," *StreetsBlog*, March 22, 2011, https://nyc.streetsblog.org/2011/03/22/new-york-has-81875-metered-parking-spaces-and-millions-of-free-ones/.

6. For a history and analysis of privately owned public space in New York City, see Jerold S. Kayden's *Privately Owned Public Space: The New York Experience* (New York: John Wiley and Sons, 2000).

7. William H. Whyte, *The Social Life of Small Urban Spaces* (Washington, DC: Conservation Foundation, 1980).

8. See Steven Flusty, *Building Paranoia: The Proliferation of Interdictory Space and the Erosion of Spatial Justice* (West Hollywood: Los Angeles Forum for Architecture and Urban Design, 1994), 18.

9. See Whyte, *Social Life*, and Jane Jacobs, *The Death and Life of Great American Cities* (New York: Random House, 1961). In their writing, Whyte and Jacobs argued that informal urban society was capable of thriving on its own, given the right material conditions: visibility from the sidewalk, a mix of surrounding land uses, a level of population density that is not too low, nor too high, and a mix of sun and shade. In downtrodden ghettos and in immigrant slums, they suggested, just as in upscale neighborhoods, people already know how to create and maintain successful public spaces. The primary task for architects, designers, and planners is to get out of the way and provide the flexibility for these informal social processes to take place.

10. Andrew Wiley-Schwartz, interview with author, 14 July 2016.

11. Andrew Wiley-Schwartz.

12. Janette Sadik-Khan, "New York City's Streets? Not So Mean Any More," filmed September 20, 2013, in New York City, TED.com, September 2013, https://www.ted.com/talks/janette_sadik_khan_new_york_s_streets_not_so_mean_any_more?language=en.

13. Quoted in Sewell Chan, "Parking Lot in Dumbo Becomes a Public Plaza," *City Room* (blog), August 9, 2007, https://cityroom.blogs.nytimes.com/2007/08/09/parking-lot-in-dumbo-becomes-a-public-plaza/.

14. Michael M. Grynbaum, "Tourists and New Yorkers Take a Rubber Seat in Times Square," *New York Times*, June 10, 2009.

15. See Steve Cuozzo's columns in the *New York Post* during this period. For example, "Idiotic DOT Takes a Walk on the Wild Side," *New York Post*, November 13, 2008.

16. Grynbaum, "Tourists and New Yorkers"; Mike Lupica, "Mayor Bloomberg Does in Times Square What He Could Not with Congestion Pricing," *New York Daily News*, June 8, 2009, https://www.nydailynews.com/news/mayor-bloomberg-times-square-not-congestion-pricing-article-1.375811.

17. Shari Logan and Tom Namako, "It's Slimes Square!—Piggy Pedestrians Trashing Car-Free Plazas," *New York Post*, June 9, 2009.

18. Steve Cuozzo, "Times Square Yawn Chairs—Revamp Doesn't Save this Broadway Flop!" *New York Post*, August 18, 2009.

19. Matt Lysiak and Leo Standora, "What the H-Elmo, Man? Surly 'Sesame' Character Hassles Times Square Tourists," *New York Daily News*, August 22, 2009.

20. Antonio Antenucci, "Times Square Gropefest: Mario Wasn't the First: NJ Tourist," *New York Post*, December 23, 2012.

21. Shayna Jacobs, Joseph Stepansky, and Steohen Rex Brown, "Crumb Bum: Cookie Creep Shoved Tot, Swore at Us—Ma," *New York Daily News*, April 9, 2013.

22. James C. McKinley Jr., "Accused of Unheroic Acts, a Spider-Man Claims Self Defense," *New York Times*, June 18, 2014.

23. Thomas Tracy, "Spidey Faces Chair-Toss Rap," *New York Daily News*, March 19, 2006.

24. A survey taken by the Times Square Alliance found that 45% of people who work in Times Square area had experienced or witnessed an unpleasant interaction with one of the costumed characters or desnudas—Patrick McGeehan, "Mayor Says Topless Women Need to Be Reined In," *New York Times*, August 19, 2015.

25. James C. McKinley Jr., "Topless in Times Square: A Legal View," *New York Times*, August 20, 2015.

26. Michael Wilson, "Enforcement a Little Fuzzy on Elmos," *New York Times*, June 30, 2012.

27. Mark Cunningham, "Missing the Naked Cowboy: A New Times Square Menace," *New York Post*, April 9, 2013.

28. Michael Gartland and Stephanie Pagones, "Angry Cartoons, Naked Girls, Maddening Crowds, Times Square Has Become the Great Blight Way," *New York Post*, July 13, 2014.

29. Jennifer Fermino, Rocco Parascandola, and Corky Siemaszko, "Start from Square One: Blaz's Radical B'Way Idea: Cars May Drive Scum Out," *New York Daily News*, August 21, 2015.

30. Emily Weidenhof, interview with the author, August 1, 2016.

31. An analysis of American Community Survey data by the Furman Center at New York University found that in 2019, in more than 11% of Corona's renter households the crowding qualified as "severe," the highest rate of any district in the city: "Elmhurst/Corona QN04," NYU Furman Center, accessed July 21, 2021, https://furmancenter.org/neighborhoods/view/elmhurst-corona.

32. Prerana Reddy, interview with the author, November 2, 2016.

33. Prerana Reddy.

34. Direct observation supported this, as well as my interviews with Priana Reddy and Ricardo Calixte.

35. Here, Reddy refers to Jane Jacobs's concept of "eyes on the street": Jacobs, *Death and Life*, 35.

36. Two seminal sociological texts on this idea are Michael Schudson's "How Culture Works" (*Theory and Society* 18, no. 2 [1989]: 153–80), and David Snow and Robert Benford's "Ideology, Frame Resonance, and Mobilization" (*International Social Movement Research* 1 [1988]: 97–217). In cognitive science, which overlaps with cultural sociology in many respects, resonance is understood in psychological terms, as the degree to which a new idea fits with prior mental schemas, categories, or frames. See Paul DiMaggio, "Culture and Cognition," *Annual Review of Sociology* 23 (August 1997): 263–87.

37. Prerana Reddy, interview.

38. Terence E. McDonnell, Christopher A. Bail, and Iddo Tavory, "A Theory of Resonance," *Sociological Theory* 35, no. 1 (March 2017): 1–14.

39. Prerana Reddy, interview.

40. Julianne Cuba, "Road Rash! Locals: City Burning Us with Unpopular Sheepshead Bay Road Changes," *Brooklyn Daily*, April 22, 2016, http://www.brooklyndaily.com/stories/2016/17/bn-the-new-sheepshead-bay-road-2016-04-22-bk.html.

41. There are forty-four discernible figures in the mural, and all of them appear to be White.

42. Jake Mooney, "Homegrown Beauty, Interrupted," *New York Times*, March 27, 2005, https://www.nytimes.com/2005/03/27/nyregion/thecity/homegrown-beauty-interrupted.html.

43. Steve Barrison, interview with author, July 25, 2016.

44. Theresa Scavo, interview with author, July 10, 2017.

45. Quotes from fieldnotes logged by Sofya Aptekar who was conducting fieldwork in Astoria at the time.

46. Ephraim Neirenberg, interview with author, July 12, 2017.

47. Herman Rothberg interview with author, May 12, 2017.

48. Eli Rosenberg, "Midwood Residents Will Have to Wait to Find Out the Fate of the Controversial Pedestrian Plaza," *Brooklyn Daily*, April 27, 2012, http://www.brooklyndaily.com/stories/2012/18/kc_elmplazapostponed_2012_04_27_bk_copy.html.

49. The agora, an open public square that served a variety of social, political, and economic functions in the cities of ancient Greece, has become a metonym for unrestricted urban sociality. Although some agoraphobes fear wide-open areas, others fear the crowded, uncontrolled conditions that occur in urban public space.

50. Richard Sennett, *The Fall of Public Man* (New York: Alfred A. Knopf, 1976), 265–72. Sennett describes some of the behavioral and architectural tactics that developed during this period: urban social norms demanding silence between strangers, for example, as well as spaces that materialize these norms—for example, train cars that contain rows of seats facing forward. As the public realm became more problematic for wealthy and middle-class urban dwellers, privacy emerged as a correspondingly more important part of a privileged lifestyle.

51. Lyn H. Lofland, *A World of Strangers: Order and Action in Urban Public Space* (New York: Basic Books, 1973), 69–73; Arthur Stinchcombe, "Institutions of Privacy in the Determination of Police Administrative Practice," *American Journal of Sociology* 69, no. 2 (September 1963): 150–60. As the middle class was increasingly "affiliated", drawn into schools, jobs, homes, and forms of organized recreation, lack of affiliation itself became threatening. As Stinchcombe points out, a legal order and an enforcement apparatus developed in order to police public behaviors that continued to be perfectly legal when they took place in a private domicile. Unhoused people of course, have no choice but to run afoul of this order. Their very existence is criminalized by ordinances that prohibit the public enactment of behaviors vital to their survival: sleeping, urinating, cooking, etc. A similarly perverse relationship holds between homelessness and the privatization of public space. Unhoused people can be legally evicted from any privately owned property, so as genuinely public space becomes a scarcer commodity, they become more concentrated within and reliant upon existing public spaces, increasing the symbolic and rhetorical association of unhoused people with public parks, plazas, and sidewalks. In recent decades, the public realm itself, as the zone in which classes mingle, has been subject to increasing social control. There has been a systematic decline in the quantity of public space in North American cities, as well as a proliferation of local laws that specify precisely when, where, and how a person may legally occupy public space, often prohibiting sitting for prolonged periods or lying down on sidewalks or in public parks. See Nicholas Blomley, "Civil Rights Meet Civil Engineering: Urban Public Space and Traffic Logic," *Canadian Journal of Law and Society* 22, no. 2 (August 2007): 55–72; Blomley, "How to Turn a Beggar into a Bus Stop: Law, Traffic and the 'Function of the Place,'" *Urban Studies* 44, no. 9 (August 2007): 1697–712; Anastasia Loukaitou-Sideris and Renia Ehrenfeucht, *Sidewalks: Conflict and Negotiation over Public Space* (Cambridge, MA: MIT Press, 2009); Don Mitchell, *The Right to the City: Social Justice and the Fight for Public Space* (New York: Guilford, 2003), 160–63.

52. Streets and sidewalks accommodate a bewildering variety of social activities, but ones that are physically designed and legally designated for transportation. Within these spaces immobility is, in a sense, regulated. Restrictions on use are typically legitimized by what legal geographer Nicholas Blomley in "Civil Rights Meet Civil Engineering" refers to as "traffic logic": an argument that prioritizes the free flow of people or things. This makes sidewalks legally precarious for the people forced to live and work on them. In a growing number of American cities, traffic logic has been used to defend legal restrictions on the amount of time that one can spend sitting or lying

on a public sidewalk—ordinances that clearly target panhandlers, street vendors, buskers, and unhoused people.

53. Allegra Hobbs, "One Way? No Way!: CB15 Pans City Plan for Sheepshead Bay Road," *Brooklyn Paper*, June 19, 2015, https://www.brooklynpaper.com/one-way-no-way-cb15-pans-city-plan-for-sheepshead-bay-road/.

54. Blomley, "Civil Rights Meet Civil Engineering."

55. W. I. Thomas and D. S. Thomas, *The Child in America: Behavior Problems and Programs* (New York: Knopf, 1928), 571–72. For a full genealogy of the theorem, see Thomas Merton's "The Thomas Theorem and the Matthews Effect" (*Social Forces* 74, no. 2 [December 1995]: 379–424).

56. Andrew Wiley-Schwartz, interview with author, July 14, 2016.

57. Laura Hansen, interview with author, July 20, 2016.

58. Andrew Ronan, interview with author, August 25, 2016.

59. Roughly $30,000 was raised at the plaza to help victims of the earthquake—Cristina Schreil, "New Diversity Plaza DOT Plans Unveiled," *Queens Chronicle*, May 14, 2015, https://www.qchron.com/editions/western/new-diversity-plaza-dot-plans-unveiled/article_70914ee3-07a7-5440-8975-4fd3231e5ebf.html).

60. Karl Vick, "One City Block Holds the World," *Time*, July 11–18, 2016, 48–49.

61. FAB is a BID, a nonprofit organization that levies a fee on property owners in a district and provides amenities and services to enhance local commercial activity and quality of life. In New York City, property owners make up the majority on any BID's board of directors, so the organizations can be seen as having a stake in local property values.

62. This drug trade was avidly chronicled by Brooklyn blog Brownstoner. See, for example, "Turning Up the Pressure on Grand and Putnam," *Brownstoner*, June 29, 2006, https://www.brownstoner.com/brooklyn-life/turning-up-the/. Coincidentally, I lived near this intersection for four years in the early 2000s, and observed drug- and/or gang-related criminal activity on a regular basis, including a fatal shooting on the sidewalk in front of the building where I lived.

63. Phillip Kellog, interview with author, August 3, 2016.

Chapter 3

1. According to the tortured prose of the NJDOT design standards, the divider is part of "a longitudinal system used to prevent an errant vehicle from crossing that portion of a divided highway separating traveled ways for traffic in opposite directions": Department of Transportation of the State of New Jersey, *Roadway Design Manual 2015* (Trenton: NJDOT, 2015), sec. 3.2.

2. Langdon Winner has written that the most politically weighty material objects are often conceived through a combination of human agency and coincidence, such that the originating ideas behind these objects cease to be relevant—"Do Artifacts Have Politics?," *Daedalus* 109, no. 1 (1980): 121–36. Things like nuclear reactors and railroads, Winner suggests, "transcend the simple categories 'intended' and 'unintended' altogether." "Rather, one must say that the technological deck has been stacked long in advance to favor certain social interests, and that some people were bound to receive a better hand than others" (125–26).

3. Clay McShane, *Down the Asphalt Path: The Automobile and the American City* (New York: Columbia University Press, 1994).

4. Jill Maser, *The Black Horse Pike* (Chicago: Arcadia, 2008); Maser, *The White Horse Pike* (Chicago: Arcadia, 2005).

5. Lizabeth Cohen, *A Consumer's Republic: The Politics of Mass Consumption in Postwar America* (New York: Vintage Books, 2004).

6. Barry Checkoway, "Large Builders, Federal Housing Programmes, and Postwar Suburbanization," in *The City: Critical Concepts in the Social Sciences*, ed. Michael Pacione, 37–60 (New

York: Routledge, 2002); Dolores Hayden, *Building Suburbia: Green Fields and Urban Growth, 1820–2000*, 1st ed. (New York: Pantheon Books, 2003), 185–257; Andres Duany, Elizabeth Plater-Zyberk, and Jeff Speck, *Suburban Nation: The Rise of Sprawl and the Decline of the American Dream* (New York: North Point, 2000).

7. Hayden, *Building Suburbia*, 164–89.

8. As state roads crossing through and between small suburban townships, The Black Horse and White Horse Pikes were designed in accordance with by NJDOT road design standards and traffic engineering specifications. At best, standards institutionalize good sense, overcoming local idiosyncrasies that stand to have a negative impact on efficient or safe use. But rather than resolving the contradiction in the social function of the two pikes, the NJDOT standards acknowledged and reinforced it. The White Horse and Black Horse Pikes are listed as "Other Principal Arterial" roads, a class indicating that the road serves as a high-speed "corridor" and that it offers access to homes and businesses. The standards resolve this contradiction in favor of high-speed traffic: "because of the function of principal arterial highways, the concept of service to abutting land should be subordinate to the provision of travel service to major traffic movements." Department of Transportation of the State of New Jersey, *Roadway Design Manual 2015* (Trenton: NJDOT, 2015), sec. 2.2.2. In other words, the needs of high-speed motor-vehicle traffic are to be prioritized above the needs of people—both drivers and pedestrians—who require access the businesses along the road. In this way, engineering standards institutionalize a bias in favor of high speed travel and make this bias a guiding principle for the material configuration of an entire environment, in spite of the fact that several different classes of users share this environment.

9. From the 1950s through the mid-1970s, median income levels in suburban communities steadily increased relative to urban centers. See William H. Frey and Alden Speare, *Regional and Metropolitan Growth and Decline in the United States* (Russell Sage Foundation, 1988). Researchers have identified a diverse array of secular trends behind the increase in suburban poverty, including population loss and population aging, a decline in the value of postwar suburban housing, surpluses of new housing at the expanding suburban fringe, and the immigration of low-wage workers directly into suburban communities. See Richard D. Alba, John R. Logan, Brian J. Stults, Gilbert Marzan, and Wenquan Zhang, "Immigrant Groups in the Suburbs: A Reexamination of Suburbanization and Spatial Assimilation," *American Sociological Review* 64, no. 3 (1999): 446–60; William H. Lucy and David L. Phillips, *Confronting Suburban Decline: Strategic Planning for Metropolitan Renewal* (Washington, DC: Island, 2000); Myron Orfield, *Metropolitics: The New Suburban Reality* (Washington, DC: Brookings Institution, 1997). Beginning in late 2007, a national recession driven by the collapse of housing markets deepened the financial troubles of many of the nation's vulnerable suburbs, adding fuel to the fire of suburban decline. These factors have affected different suburbs in different ways. Some suburban communities that formerly enjoyed a high degree of financial stability have become even wealthier, while others experience increasing poverty, mounting unemployment, and unprecedented debt.

These proximate causes have taken effect against a broader economic backdrop that seems to indicate suburban decline is here to stay. As Jason Hackworth points out, in *The Neoliberal City: Governance, Ideology, and Development in American Urbanism* (Ithaca, NY: Cornell University Press, 2007), the private sector has been transferring capital away from suburbs and into gentrifying urban centers for decades, reversing the direction of capital that prevailed in the heyday of postwar suburbanization.

10. Elizabeth Kneebone and Emily Garr, *The Suburbanization of Poverty: Trends in Metropolitan America, 2000 to 2008* (Washington, DC: Brookings Institution, 2010).

11. To make matters worse, many of these communities are ill equipped to address the social consequences of poverty. A growing body of research has shown that the built environment of suburban communities poses distinct problems for low-income households, a problem exacerbated

by broader organizational deficiencies, as suburbs typically lack both the municipal resources and civic institutions that have evolved to address urban poverty. See Elizabeth Kneebone and Alan Berube, *Confronting Suburban Poverty in America* (Washington, DC: Brookings Institution, 2014); Alexandra K. Murphy and Danielle Wallace, "Opportunities for Making Ends Meet and Upward Mobility: Differences in Organizational Deprivation across Urban and Suburban Poor Neighborhoods," *Social Science Quarterly* 91, no. 5 (2010): 1164–86; Alexandra K. Murphy, "The Symbolic Dilemmas of Suburban Poverty: Challenges and Opportunities Posed by Variations in the Contours of Suburban Poverty," *Sociological Forum* 25, no. 3 (2010): 541–69.

12. Eric Klinenberg, *Heat Wave: A Social Autopsy of Disaster in Chicago* (Chicago: University of Chicago Press, 2003).

13. By consulting the Fatality Analysis Reporting System (FARS), a federally administered database that contains details concerning every fatal traffic accident that takes place in the United States, I developed a census of Atlantic County pedestrian deaths, identifying seventy-eight fatal incidents that occurred during the study period. FARS contained a wealth of information, including the specific time and location of each crash, basic demographic data on victims, the type of motor vehicle involved, and any situational considerations (e.g., poor lighting, wet pavement) that police officers regarded as contributing to the incident. I supplemented the FARS data with information gathered from a variety of other sources. Local newspaper articles contributed a considerable amount of biographical detail on victims, and made it possible to identify 71% of the decedents (fifty-five of seventy-eight) by name, age, and sex. I requested and obtained autopsy reports on each of these cases from the county medical examiners' offices. Using the geographic coordinates of each incident and cross-checking the location against newspaper accounts of each crash, I plotted every incident using GIS software.

14. Richard C. Harruff, Anne Avery, and Amy S. Alter-Pandya, "Analysis of Circumstances and Injuries in 217 Pedestrian Traffic Fatalities," *Accident Analysis and Prevention* 30, no. 1 (1998): 11–20; Elizabeth A. LaScala, Daniel Gerber, and Paul J. Gruenewald, "Demographic and Environmental Correlates of Pedestrian Injury Collisions: A Spatial Analysis," *Accident Analysis and Prevention* 32, no. 5 (2000): 651–58; Anastasia Loukaitou-Sideris, Robin Liggett, and Hyun-Gun Sung, "Death on the Crosswalk: A Study of Pedestrian-Automobile Collisions in Los Angeles," *Journal of Planning Education and Research* 26, no. 3 (2007): 338–51.

15. Phyllis F. Agran, Diane G. Winn, Craig L. Anderson, and Celeste Del Valle, "Family, Social, and Cultural Factors in Pedestrian Injuries among Hispanic Children," *Injury Prevention* 4, no. 3 (1998): 188–93; Doug Campos-Outcalt, Curt Bay, Alan Dellapenna, and Marya K. Cota, "Pedestrian Fatalities by Race/Ethnicity in Arizona, 1990–1996," *American Journal of Preventive Medicine* 23, no. 2 (2002): 129–35; Loukaitou-Sideris, Liggett, and Sung, "Death on the Crosswalk."

16. Atlantic County, it turns out, is uncannily similar to the United States as a whole in its demographic composition. Its distribution in terms of age, race, and gender differs by only a couple of percentage points from the national population share in each category. This suggests that local demographics were not skewed toward high-risk categories—one possible explanation for Atlantic County's high pedestrian risk. The young and the elderly, for example, are more likely to be killed in pedestrian incidents, owing to both physical frailty and their overrepresentation among the pedestrian population. But of the seventy-eight pedestrians killed in Atlantic County during this five-year period, only 33% (twenty-six) were below eighteen or above sixty-five years old. This is relatively few, given that approximately 38% of Atlantic County's population fell in these high-risk categories during the time of study, according to the 2010 decennial census. Similarly, a handful of studies have highlighted the role of race and ethnicity in pedestrian risk, as Hispanic and Black residents tend to be overrepresented among pedestrian fatality statistics. But again, Atlantic County's population was similar to that of the United States in its racial and ethnic breakdown, so whether or not race and ethnicity help to explain pedestrian risk locally or nationally, these factors can be discounted as an explanation of the county's exceptionally high risk.

17. Previous research has shown that pedestrians are especially likely to be injured or killed in areas close to bars. See Campos-Outcalt et al., "Pedestrian Fatalities"; LaScala, Gerber, and Gruenewald, "Demographic and Environmental Correlates."

18. In 16% of the fatal crashes in Atlantic County, police records indicate that the driver was alcohol impaired, and in 23% the pedestrian tested higher than 0.08 blood alcohol content, the legal threshold for drunk driving under federal law. These statistics suggest that alcohol played a role in many of the incidents, but the figures are still comparable or lower than the national average for each category during the same time period (15% and 37%, respectively).

19. My analysis echoes the findings of a number of quantitative studies that incorporate the configuration of built space in modeling pedestrian risk: R. Ewing, Richard A. Schieber, and Charles V. Zegeer, "Urban Sprawl as a Risk Factor in Motor Vehicle Occupant and Pedestrian Fatalities," *American Journal of Public Health* 93, no. 9 (September 2003): 1541–45; Loukaitou-Sideris, Liggett, and Sung, "Death on the Crosswalk"; Linda Rothman, Ron Buliung, Colin Macarthur, Teresa To, and Andrew Howard, "Walking and Child Pedestrian Injury: A Systematic Review of Built Environment Correlates of Safe Walking," *Injury Prevention* 20, no. 1 (February 2014): 41–49; Linda Rothman, Andrew William Howard, Andi Camden, and Colin Macarthur, "Pedestrian Crossing Location Influences Injury Severity in Urban Areas," *Injury Prevention* 18, no. 6 (December 2012): 365–70.

20. The incident reports and journalistic accounts I compiled painted a picture of pedestrians who were almost always crossing a road or walking in its shoulder when hit—these behaviors were far more common than in national statistics.

21. More than 83% (sixty-five) of the county's fatal crashes occurred in areas with speed limits 35 mph or above, and of these, a total of forty-seven, more than 60% of the total, occurred in areas with speed limits of 45 mph or above. In both cases, these figures were higher than the national averages (roughly 78% and 50%, respectively). Accident research has found that the likelihood of a pedestrian dying in a traffic accident more than doubles when the motor vehicle is travelling 40 mph rather than 20 mph. Reid Ewing and Eric Dumbaugh, "The Built Environment and Traffic Safety: A Review of Empirical Evidence," *Journal of Planning Literature* 23, no. 4 (May 2009): 347–67.

22. I estimated that 33% of the seventy-eight pedestrians killed in Atlantic County between 2005 and 2013 were killed while walking to a bus stop or immediately after exiting a bus close to a shopping center, a statistic that supports the inference that many of the victims lacked access to a motor vehicle.

23. Although freely available from public sources, the names of victims have been changed out of respect for the privacy of their families.

24. The subjective experience I am attempting to convey here is the opposite of "legibility," a concept associated with the work of environmental psychologist Kevin Lynch (*The Image of the City* [Cambridge: MIT Press, 1960], 2). When the different parts of a city or suburb work together and *make sense* given one's own background and needs, the landscape is legible.

25. Susan Leigh Star, "The Ethnography of Infrastructure," *American Behavioral Scientist* 43, no. 3 (1999): 377–91.

26. Martin Heidegger, *Being and Time*, trans. John Macquarrie and Edward Robinson (Cambridge, MA: Blackwell, 1962). Heidegger notes that we often do not recognize things as things until they fail to be "ready-to-hand," or to do whatever it is that we want to do with them. "When we concern ourselves with something, the entities which are most closely ready-to-hand may be met as something unusable, not properly adapted for the use we have decided upon. . . . When its unusability is thus discovered, equipment becomes conspicuous" (102). At this point, we consciously engage with things, according to Heidegger, and contemplate their nature as objects. Anthropologist Alan Costall expands on Heidegger's idea and links it to affordances, suggesting that things have a principal, or "canonical," affordance, but can also be used in counterintuitive

ways when they do not suit our purposes: Alan Costall, "The Meaning of Things," *Social Analysis* 4, no. 1 (March 1997): 76–85.

27. Erin O'Neill, "NJ Pedestrian Deaths Jump after Years of Decline," *NJ.com*, October 13, 2009, https://www.nj.com/news/local/2009/10/nj_pedestrian_deaths_spike_aft.html; Karen Rouse, "Deaths Jump 33%—NJ Pedestrians More At Risk," *Hackensack Record*, November 10, 2009.

28. Karen Rouse, "New Jersey Highways to Be Made Safer," *Northjersey.com*, December 25, 2009, http://www.northjersey.com/news/transportation/122509_Aid_for_walkers_bikers.html.

29. This typology of social control applies to any person or institution empowered to formulate a response when an object is used in an unanticipated way.

30. Joshua Burd and Jeff Grant, "Rt. 1, 9 Deadly for 20 on Foot," *Home News Tribune*, January 10, 2009.

31. To be fair, the fence was not the NJDOT's only response to pedestrian risk in this area of the state. Middlesex County, where Monmouth Junction is located, was awarded a $95,750 grant to improve pedestrian safety under the governor's 2006 initiative, and pledged to use it for pedestrian education programs. Meanwhile, a broader redesign of this section of Route 1 was underway that would incorporate input from a committee tasked with gathering public feedback. But when the NJDOT installs median fencing, it makes the decision on a case-by-case basis and does not require public input from county officials or local stakeholders.

32. Denville Township, "Rt. 46 and Savage Road Pedestrian Overpass Update," *HUB Times* 10, no. 1 (December 2009): 7.

33. NJDOT, "NJDOT Announces Route 46 Closure to Install Pedestrian Bridge over Route 46 in Denville" (Trenton: NJDOT, February 10, 2009).

34. NJDOT, *Roadway Design Manual 2015* (Trenton: NJDOT, 2015), sec. 5.9.3, "Median Fencing on Land Service Highways," 5-24–5-25, https://www.state.nj.us/transportation/eng /documents/RDM/documents/2015RoadwayDesignManual.pdf.

35. Donna Weaver, "Police Decoys Snare Drivers Who Won't Yield to Pedestrians," *Press of Atlantic City*, June 19, 2013.

36. Martin DeAngelis, "55 in Ventnor Told to Obey Crosswalks," *Press of Atlantic City*, September 12, 2009.

37. Martin DeAngelis, "That Longport Pedestrian May Be a Cop," *Press of Atlantic City*, August 4, 2009.

38. Hidden stoplight cameras can be deployed to similar effect in order to discourage the running of red lights, a textbook case of what Bruno Latour refers to as "substitution." Bruno Latour, "Technology Is Society Made Durable," *Sociological Review* 38, no. S1 (May 1990): 103–31.

39. Sean McCullen, "Police, Public Works Promote Pedestrian Pathways," *Gloucester Township Patch*, June 10, 2011, https://patch.com/new-jersey/gloucestertownship/police-public-works -promote-pedestrian-pathways; Kathryn Burger, "Motorists to Stop, Not Just Yield," *Pascack Valley Community Life*, April 22 2010.

40. Casey Feldman Memorial Foundation, "Feldmans Participate in Press Conferences Announcing New Pedestrian Safety Law—'Casey's Law,'" March 31, 2010, https://www .caseyfeldmanfoundation.org/feldmans-hold-press-conference-for-new-pedestrian-law/.

41. Mariana Valverde, *Everyday Law on the Street: City Governance in an Age of Diversity* (Chicago: University of Chicago Press, 2012). As Valverde compellingly argues, the ability of overarching legal and regulatory frameworks to transcend local jurisdictions is a benefit in cases where blocks, zip codes, or school districts are heavily stratified.

42. Anique Hommels, "Studying Obduracy in the City: Toward a Productive Fusion between Technology Studies and Urban Studies," *Science, Technology and Human Values* 30, no. 3 (July 2005): 3–30.

Chapter 4

1. This informal practice, referred to by conductors as "popping the doors," is meant to discourage door holding, but is not officially endorsed by their employers, the Metropolitan Transit Authority (MTA). Occasionally, during my observations at this time of day, I've seen the doors popped preemptively at stations where large groups of teenagers had boarded the train, a staccato whirring and thunking that evokes the gnashing of a metallic mouth, which, compared with Mr. Pellet's polite request and the door chime, offers a sterner warning that the doors are about to close. An online chat forum devoted to topics related to the subway, Subchat (http://www.subchat.com/subchat.asp), is frequented by former New York subway drivers and conductors, who often post revealing insider accounts of the subjective experiences and informal tactics of subway workers. On June 29, 2006, for example, a poster described door popping on the E train: "I was taught this when posting on the E. We had a 46 and he told me that on the E its critical to get the doors closed first try at stations like 34th, Lex, etc. So, hit the close then open really fast to get the people moving, then close the doors" (Goumba Tony, "Re: Question about Door Chimes," Subchat, June 29, 2006, http://www.subchat.com/read.asp?Id=273694).

2. According to the MTA, a thirty-second delay in closing the doors at one station can delay up to nine or ten subsequent trains. Assuming that each train holds several hundred passengers, this suggests that thousands are routinely delayed by moments of poor individual subway etiquette. For an excruciating, moment-by-moment analysis of a cascading set of delays caused by a technical malfunction, see Robert Kolker's "How a Single Mechanical Failure Sparked 625 MTA Delays" (*New York Magazine*, February 23, 2016).

3. For a review of this debate, and a discussion of these defining qualities of the subway as a social environment, see: Mike Owen Benediktsson, Peter Tuckel, William Milczarski, Farimata Caruso, Michelle DeCurtis, Prahelika Gadtaula, Matt Herman, Nicholas MacDonald, Nicholas Silipo, and Daniell Singh, "The Subway as Fourth Place: Anomie, Flannerie, and the Crush of Persons," *Applied Mobilities* 5, no. 2 (Summer 2020): 103–21.

4. See David A. Snow's "Extending and Broadening Blumer's Conceptualization of Symbolic Interactionism" (*Symbolic Interaction* 24, no. 3 [Summer 2001]: 367–77) for a concise description of this idea. See Herbert Blumer's *Symbolic Interactionism: Perspective and Method* (Englewood Cliffs, NJ: Prentice-Hall, 1969, 11, 20), for its origins in one of the canonical works of symbolic interactionism.

5. The distinction here is both cultural and material and relates to the perceived functional necessity of a behavior. Many forms of social etiquette are, by definition, not seen as necessary. Proper table manners are not required to efficiently or effectively absorb nutrients. As behavioral norms, table manners pertain to *how* one eats, not whether food is able to be collectively consumed by a group of people. In fact, the most polite approach may well be diametrically opposed to the most efficient or the "necessary" one. (See Pierre Bourdieu on this point, in *Distinction: A Social Critique of the Judgement of Taste* [Cambridge, MA: Harvard University Press, 1984]: 195–200.) Importantly, this cultural distinction between the elective and the necessary is not resolved by the material technology involved. There are multiple ways of holding a fork: some are more refined than others, and this distinction is at the heart of social etiquette. In contrast, normative infrastructure as I define it is socially defined as necessary, and its definition as such relates to the perceived functional requirements of a sociotechnical system or a material infrastructure. The informal rule (formal in some systems) that riders on an escalator stand to the right and pass on the left is not widely seen in the United States as a matter of good taste or cultivation so much as a reflection of an efficient arrangement of static and moving human bodies that accommodates heterogeneity in physical capabilities and levels of urgency. This distinction is rooted in the cultural interpretation of a program of behavior, which implies a material technology that reflects and supports this interpretation.

6. Sofya Aptekar, "Social Norms and Resistance on the City Bus," *Metropolitics*, May 5, 2015, https://metropolitics.org/Social-Norms-and-Resistance-on-the.html; David Patrick Connor and Richard Tewksbury, "Social Control on Public Buses," *Journal of Theoretical and Philosophical Criminology* 4, no. 1 (January 2014): 1–13; Stéphane Tonnelat and William Kornblum, *International Express: New Yorkers on the 7 Train* (New York: Columbia University Press, 2017).

7. Interestingly, the forty-five-second constraint appears to have been constant throughout the life of the New York subway. It first appears as early as 1907 and continues to this day. "Two Plans to Stop the Subway Crush," *New York Times*, December 2, 1907; Neil MacFarquhar, "In Test, Courtesy Gains Beachhead in Subways," *New York Times*, February 11, 1997.

8. Emma G. Fitzsimmons, "Crowds and Long Delays Fray Subway System and Riders' Nerves," *New York Times*, March 19, 2015; Michael M. Grynbaum, "Mayor De Blasio Is Irked by a Subway Delay," *New York Times*, May 5, 2015.

9. During the first stage of research, which took place between early October and mid-November 2015, I rode the train and observed platforms and concourses at all times of day and night, gathering observations on passenger behavior under normal conditions. During the second stage of research, from early February to late March 2016, I focused my fieldwork on the busiest lines in the system—the 4, 5, and 6, and the N, Q, and R, concentrating my observations at the system's points of access, particularly station entrances and subway doors, at times (6:15 a.m.—9:00 a.m. and 4:30 p.m.—7:00 p.m.), when the human burden on the system is at its peak.

10. A fascinating branch of social science is devoted to the social construction of technology and takes as its subject matter the process by which social and political context makes its way into technological design. For programmatic statements, see Trevor J. Pinch and Wiebe E. Bijker's "The Social Construction of Facts and Artefacts; or, How the Sociology of Science and the Sociology of Technology Might Benefit Each Other" (*Social Studies of Science* 14, no. 3 [1984]: 399–441), Wiebe E. Bijker's *The Social Construction of Bakelite: Toward a Theory of Invention* (Cambridge, MA: MIT Press, 1987), and Trevor Pinch's "The Social Construction of Technology (SCOT): The Old, the New, and the Nonhuman," in *Material Culture and Technology in Everyday Life: Ethnographic Approaches*, edited by Phillip Vannini (New York: Peter Lang, 2009, 45–58).

11. Roger Silverstone and Leslie Haddon, "Design and the Domestication of Information and Communication Technologies: Technical Change and Everyday Life," in *Communication by Design: The Politics of Information and Communication Technologies*, ed. Roger Silverstone and Robin Mansell, 44–74 (Oxford: Oxford University Press, 1996).

12. This widely repeated quote by Russell Sage is cited by Stefan Hoehne in "The Birth of the Urban Passenger: Infrastructural Subjectivity and the Opening of the New York City Subway" (*City* 19, no. 2–3 [April 2015]: 313).

13. On discipline, see Michel Foucault's *Discipline and Punish: The Birth of the Prison* (New York: Vintage Books, 1995). In applying this idea to the subway, I am following Hoehne, who in "Birth of the Urban Passenger" appropriates Foucault, suggesting that the New York subway "disciplined" its subjects over the first years of its existence.

14. On the telephone, see Claude .S. Fischer's *America Calling: A Social History of the Telephone to 1940* (Berkeley: University of California Press, 1994). On the keyboard, see Everett M. Rogers's *Diffusion of Innovations* (New York: Free Press, 2010, 8–10); on the automobile, see Clay McShane's *Down the Asphalt Path: The Automobile and the American City* (New York: Columbia University Press, 1994, 57–81).

15. Hoehne, "Birth of the Urban Passenger."

16. Under the umbrella of normative infrastructure, I include only those behavioral norms that relate to the material technology of the subway. To be clear, as a social space, the subway requires other, more nuanced social competencies. As Tonnelat and Kornblum compellingly argue in *International Express*, the subway requires specific social skills that help riders peacefully

coexist within an anonymous and diverse social setting. Among these skills is the famous blasé attitude, or "reserve," theorized by Simmel and others: Georg Simmel, "The Metropolis and Mental Life," in *The Urban Sociology Reader*, ed. Jan Lin and Christopher Mele (New York: Routledge, 2005), 23–31. But these competencies do not respond to the material environment but to the social environment in the subway, and they do so in ways that are not unique to the subway: the same reserve, for example, is required on the sidewalk or in the public plaza. For this reason, although they are sociologically important and interesting, I exclude this separate set of skills from consideration here.

17. Coordination games, per game theory, are a class of problems in which the optimal outcome overall requires that the players coordinate their behavior. As an example, it does not matter if ascending passengers stay to the right on the stairs or stay to the left, as long as descending passengers do the opposite.

18. If we compare it to other types of justice—for example, "social," "procedural," or "distributive" justice—it becomes clear that systemic justice differs in that it presumes indirect, "restricted" or "rule" utilitarianism: that if a series of rules is followed, a system will allocate the greatest good to the greatest number. See John C. Harsanyi, "Morality and the Theory of Rational Behavior," *Social Research* 44, no. 4 (Winter 1977): 623–56; Amartya Sen, "Utilitarianism and Welfarism," *Journal of Philosophy* 76, no. 9 (September 1979): 463–89.

19. Observational research suggests that people are not particularly strategic when confronted with the coordination problems that occur in crowded urban space. See, e.g., William H. Whyte, *The Social Life of Small Urban Spaces* (Washington, DC: Conservation Foundation, 1980), 80–81.

20. This argument resonates with Kantian ethics. The distinction between orienting one's behavior on its rational outcome and following a rule is the difference between "consequentialist" and "deontological" reasoning. Thinking in this way also parallels the "dual-process" model of cognition, whereby social actors switch between the slow, deliberative reasoning necessary to gauge the consequences of their behavior, whether they decide to act selfishly or altruistically, and a faster, associational form of reasoning that relies heavily upon cognitive shortcuts such as heuristics and decision rules. Much of the time, I would argue, subway riders rely more on the latter than on the former, not just because they lack the time to ponder the consequences of their behavior, which they undoubtedly do, but also because the systemic impact of individual action in the subway is hidden, which makes deliberating the ethics of following the rules pointless. As a result, subway riders default to an automatic mode of thinking driven by the apparent affordances in a situation. On dual process models, see Omar Lizardo, Robert Mowry, Brandon Sepulvado, Dustin S. Stoltz, Marshall A. Taylor, Justin Van Ness, and Michael Wood's "What Are Dual Process Models? Implications for Cultural Analysis in Sociology" (*Sociological Theory* 34, no. 4 [December 2016]: 287–310).

21. Latour, in *Pandora's Hope: Essays on the Reality of Science Studies* (Cambridge, MA: Harvard University Press, 1999, 304), defines "blackboxing" as follows:

> An expression from the sociology of science that refers to the way scientific and technical work is made invisible by its own success. When a machine runs efficiently, when a matter of fact is settled, one need focus only on its inputs and outputs and not on its internal complexity. Thus, paradoxically, the more science and technology succeed, the more opaque and obscure they become.

22. Clifton Hood, *722 Miles* (Baltimore, MD: Johns Hopkins University Press, 2004).

23. At 191st Street station, a formerly dimly lit, 900-foot subterranean passageway referred to on blogs as the "Tunnel of Doom" connects the platform and the Broadway entrance. At Lexington Ave. and 63rd, passengers ride three long escalators down 155 feet below street level, a depth made necessary by other subway tunnels and underground infrastructure. In contrast, elevated lines in

Brooklyn and Queens require passengers to walk up several flights of stairs before reaching the platform, where they are exposed to the elements.

24. Joan Turner, letter to the editor, "Observations on Subway Etiquette," *New York Times*, September 21, 1935; Paul Schwartzman, "The Great Seat Debate: The Bucket or the Bench?" *New York Daily News*, February 9, 1997.

25. A case in point was the system's longtime adherence to the five-cent fare that was charged at the time of the subway's opening. The fare was both a guarantor of public access to the system and a persevering symbol of the infrastructure's democratic spirit. Although constructed and operated by private authorities, the subway was regarded as a public transit system, and the five-cent fare was fiercely protected by the city transit agency, even as the physical expansion of the system escalated costs for its private-sector operators, rendering the subway increasingly unprofitable. Repeated proposals to increase the fare were aired by the railways, provoking a strong public response each time. In part the fare was buoyed by its materialization in the subway's turnstiles, which were designed to take a nickel, but politics appear to have been more to blame. For forty-four years the five-cent fare held, preserved by elected officials who repeatedly made it a focal point in election campaigns. "The five cent fare is the cornerstone of the edifice we call New York," proclaimed Mayor John Hylan, with no apparent attempt at hyperbole—quoted in Vivian Heller, *The City beneath Us: Building the New York Subway* (New York: W. W. Norton, 2004): 41.

26. In the 1970s and early 1980s, for example, the system hit a low point. Derailments became a semi-monthly occurrence, train doors abruptly opened while trains were in motion, and any given train car could be expected to travel only a few thousand miles before breaking down completely (Roger P. Roess and Gene Sansone, *The Wheels That Drove New York: A History of the New York City Transit System* [New York: Springer, 2013]; Clive Thompson, "Derailed," *New York Magazine*, February 18, 2005, https://nymag.com/nymetro/news/features/11160/). Ridership sank to levels not seen since the 1910s, and crime and vandalism, encouraged by the decline in informal monitoring, or "eyes on the street" (Jane Jacobs, *The Death and Life of Great American Cities* [New York: Random House, 1961]), in the system's sparsely populated trains and stations, reached unprecedented levels.

27. Regional Plan Association (RPA), *Moving Forward: Accelerating the Transition to Communications-Based Train Control for New York City's Subways* (RPA, May 2014); Thompson, "Derailed."

28. Michael W. Brooks, *Subway City: Riding the Subway, Reading New York* (New Brunswick, NJ: Rutgers University Press, 1997): 172–76.

29. The Farce Report, "Keep Your Hands off Subway Doors," YouTube, October 27, 2015, uploaded by Pretty Good Videos, https://www.youtube.com/watch?v=aNy4Ne3oeiw.

30. Herbert T. Wade, "How the Car Doors of the New York Municipal Railway Are Operated," *Scientific American*, January 6, 1917.

31. "Multiple-Unit Door Control on the Interborough Subway Trains," *Electric Railway Journal* 66, no. 12 (September 1925): 433–39.

32. "Interborough Opens Drive on Subway 'Rushes'; Court Fines Five Men for Football Tactics," *New York Times*, May 21, 1926.

33. "Loading Speed a Major Factor in Design of New York Subway Cars," *Electric Railway Journal* 75, no. 6 (June 1931): 294–97.

34. "Contract Awarded for 100 Subway Cars at Cost of $6,390,900—Delivery in 2 Years," *New York Times*, December 6, 1946. Bruno Latour refers to this kind of reallocation as "delegation." See *Reassembling the Social: An Introduction to Actor-Network-Theory* (Oxford: Oxford University Press, 2005), 70, 173–74, 194–95.

35. Richard Levine, "Subway Door-Closing Accidents Lead to Transit Authority Study," *New York Times*, September 11, 1987; Associated Press, "Metro Dateline; Subway Panel Offers Safety Procedures," *New York Times*, February 6, 1988.

36. Levine, "Subway Door-Closing Accidents."

37. Unless otherwise noted, all etiquette advertisements quoted in this section are held by the New York Transit Museum's public archive. All direct quotes are drawn from posters featured in a 2016 exhibition (New York Transit Museum, *Transit Etiquette; or, How I Learned to Stop Spitting and Step Aside in 25 Languages,* Grand Central Terminal Gallery Annex, 2016), or excerpts from the museum's digital archives that were featured on the museum website, https://www.nytransitmuseum.org/ (accessed April 5, 2016).

38. Amelia Opdyke Jones, New York City Transit Authority, "The Subway Sun, Vol. XXIII, No. 12: *Hit Him Again Lady!,*" 1956, XX.2010.606.27, Subway Sun Collection, New York Transit Museum.

39. Amelia Opdyke Jones, New York City Transit Authority, "The Subway Sun, Vol. XVII, No. 3: *Have a Heart for Others—Please Load in Line,*" 1950, XX.2018.4.8, Car Card Collection, New York Transit Museum.

40. Ira Henry Freeman, "Subway Riders to Hear TV Voices with Advice on Safety and Etiquette," *New York Times,* August 21, 1953.

41. "Etti-Cat to Spur Subway Eti-quette," *New York Times,* June 26, 1962.

42. MacFarquhar, "Courtesy Gains Beachhead."

43. This end state is clearly reminiscent of social scientists' attempts to theorize forms of power and social control that rely on the automatic and largely unconscious cooperation of human subjects. See, for example, Antonio Gramsci's "hegemony" in *Prison Notebooks,* vol. 1, edited by Joseph A. Buttigieg (New York: Columbia University Press, 2011), or Steven Lukes's "third dimension" of power in his introduction to *Power: A Radical View* (2nd ed., London: Red Globe, 2005). An important distinction, however, is that the context-specific social norms that I am referring to as normative infrastructure do not necessarily prioritize the interests of one actor over those of another, a key ingredient of social power. On the contrary, if a normative infrastructure is robust, the benefits should be dispersed widely across the users of the material infrastructure with which it is associated. For this reason, a better theoretical analogue might be Michel Foucault's "governmentality," in *The Government of Self and Others: Lectures at the Collège de France, 1982–1983* (New York: Springer, 2010)—a technology of self-governance that corresponds to external objective conditions and institutions, and that reduces friction within a larger social or political system.

But, in any case, grand theorizing here is probably not warranted. For the transit agency, the benefits of social engineering are obvious and justified on practical grounds—if the desired social norms are widely adopted, they will produce greater efficiency and obviate the need for more costly and less efficient measures, such as material or legal/regulatory interventions. What is less obvious and more interesting about the agency's strategy for obtaining passenger compliance is that invoking gains in overall efficiency turned out not to be enough, leading the MTA to resort to an ethical discourse that humanizes and personalizes the ostensible beneficiaries of compliance—elderly women, children, fellow passengers—in order to produce changes in collective behavior. This seems to imply a recognition by the agency that in New York City, at least, the discursive framing of ethical action has to retain the individualistic emphasis of the culture at large, projecting the values and traits at stake—decency, accountability, selfishness—onto specific human subjects in order to moralize collective action.

44. Richard Perez-Pena, "Transit Agency Urges Platform Etiquette to Speed Subways," *New York Times,* November 12, 1996.

45. Henry Alford, "Step Aside? Who, Me?," *New York Times,* November 18, 1996.

46. Phillip Taubman, "Enforcing Subway Etiquette: In New York, Fuhgeddaboutit," *New York Times,* November 16, 1996.

47. Levine, "Subway Door-Closing Accidents." According to Levine, MTA director David Gunn remarked that New York is the only city where he had seen passengers prying open subway doors.

48. Perez-Pena, "Transit Agency."

49. See, e.g., Jen Chung, "Two Stalled Trains + Sick Passenger = Morning Commute Problems on A, B, C, D, F, N, Q and R Trains," *Gothamist*, August 23, 2017, https://gothamist.com/news /two-stalled-trains-sick-passenger-morning-commute-problems-on-a-b-c-d-f-n-q-and-r-trains.

50. J. David Goodman, "Angry about Subway Delays? De Blasio Says Blame Cuomo, and Vice Versa," *New York Times*, May 19, 2017.

51. The *New York Times* reporter Randy Kennedy profiles this strategy in depth in his fascinating book about the culture of the subway *Subwayland: Adventures in the World beneath New York* (New York: St. Martin's Griffin, 2004).

52. Jack Katz, *How Emotions Work* (Chicago: University of Chicago Press, 1999), 18–86.

53. On emotional energy, see Randall Collins's *Interaction Ritual Chains* (Princeton, NJ: Princeton University Press, 2004).

54. Tonnelat and Kornblum, *International Express*.

55. Emma G. Fitzsimmons, "Subway Ridership Declines in New York: Is Uber to Blame?," *New York Times*, February 23, 2017.

Chapter 5

1. Ron's youngest son has been watching a lot of nature programs, and this has raised his expectations when the family goes to the beach. What makes this funny is a piece of background information: Ron is afraid of the water and doesn't swim.

2. "A kiosk does not set itself apart from its environment, but rather becomes an element of the fray, a key accoutrement for a life spent in perpetual motion. One can use it, theoretically at least, without breaking one's flow through space and time"—Ariana Kelly, *Phone Booth* (New York: Bloomsbury, 2015), 10.

3. Sociolinguists Shonna Trinch and Edward Snajdr, studying shop signs in Brooklyn, argue that this basic informational style, which they call "old school vernacular," contrasts with newer linguistic styles associated with urban elites, gentrification, and taste cultures linked to social class. Like a bodega advertising "cold beer" and prominently displaying the prices of popular items in the window, the newsstand typically seeks to inform potential shoppers of pertinent details as quickly and efficiently as possible. It does not traffic in witticisms, double entendres, in-jokes, or cultural references. Shonna Trinch and Edward Snajdr, "What the Signs Say: Gentrification and the Disappearance of Capitalism without Distinction in Brooklyn," *Journal of Sociolinguistics* 21, no. 1 (January 2017): 64–89.

4. Joseph A. Schumpeter, *Capitalism, Socialism and Democracy* (London: Routledge, 1994), 82–83.

5. See "Tempest over a News-Stand; A Nuisance to Property-Owners and a Source of Talk for Alderman," *New York Times*, October 11, 1882; "The News-Stand Privilege," *New York Times*, November 22, 1883; "A News-Stand Ordinance; One Passed by the Board of Aldermen. It Regulates the Placing of Booths under the Stairs of the Elevated Roads—Permits to Cost $10 a Year—Much Talk about Soda Water and Fruit Stands, but Nothing Accomplished—Vice President Windolph's Gavel Kept Busy," *New York Times*, September 4, 1896.

6. See chapter 6 in Mariana Valverde's *Everyday Law on the Street: City Governance in an Age of Diversity* (Chicago: University of Chicago Press, 2012).

7. In 1923, the Municipal Arts Society designed and installed model newsstands that would replace the existing structures—not to push the city to impose standardization but rather to "hint at betterment." After all, the *New York Times* noted, "in most European cities that pride themselves on their good appearance, news booths are standardized and regulated by law" ("Plans Art News Stands to Adorn City Streets; Municipal Art Society Offers Suggestions for Booths to Replace

Makeshift Shelters—News Dealers Join with Artists in Designing Model Structures," *New York Times*, May 27, 1923). In 1929, all of the newsstands in city parks were removed and replaced with green, enclosed stands that concealed the printed matter inside ("Vivid Newsstands to Go; Plain Green Ones, with Neat Display Racks, to Replace Old and Colorful Kiosks," *New York Times*, March 31, 1929).

8. "New News Stand Opened; Moss Officiates at First of the Metal Structures at 34th St.," *New York Times*, August 9, 1934.

9. In 1934, a city task force surveyed the industry in the wake of the public corruption scandal, and found that 15,322 sidewalk newsstands were operating in the city, earning as much as $10,000 to $12,000 per year. "Bills Seek $200,000 in News Stand Fees; Deutsch Proposes $5 to $500 Annual Payments Based on Average Earnings," *New York Times*, November 14, 1934.

10. Douglas Martin, "Bernard Green Dies at 91; Founded Newsstand Chain," *New York Times*, March 1, 2002.

11. Judith Cummings, "City Newsstands Act to End Decline," *New York Times*, August 7, 1979.

12. James S. Rossant, letter to the editor, "Why Fifth Avenue Is in Every Way No Place for Newsstands," *New York Times*, January 18, 1991.

13. Peter L. Malkin and Daniel A. Biederman, letter to the editor, "Manhattan Doesn't Have to Suffer from Newsstand Blight," *New York Times*, February 8, 1991.

14. Robert S. Bookman, letter to the editor, "Stand Owners Not Ignoring Issues of Maintenance," *New York Times*, February 9, 1997.

15. The *New York Times* noted the irony in this, as newsstands were regarded by subway riders as beacons of safety in the subway. "Topics of the Times: Underground Newspapers," *New York Times*, February 22, 1988.

16. "Newsstands Are No Menace," editorial, *New York Times*, June 17, 1988; "Topics of the Times: Underground Newspapers."

17. Jonathan P. Hicks, "Street Newsstands and Bus Stops are Giuliani's Latest Concern," *New York Times*, April 14, 1995.

18. David W. Dunlap, "City Seeking an Exterior Decorator," *New York Times*, June 2, 1996.

19. In the case of New York City, newsstand operators had been prohibited by law from posting advertisements on their stands prior to the city's decision to contract out this space to corporate bidders. Kurt Iveson, "Branded Cities: Outdoor Advertising, Urban Governance, and the Outdoor Media Landscape," *Antipode* 44, no. 1 (January 2012): 151–74.

20. David W. Dunlap, "Street Furniture Designs Stuck in Gridlock," *New York Times*, August 9, 1998; Dunlap, "Commercial Real Estate; A Mayor's Prerogative: Rethinking the City's Street Furniture," *New York Times*, January 28, 1998.

21. Tanzina Vega, "Magazine Newsstand Sales Suffered Sharp Falloff in Second Half of 2011," *New York Times*, February 7, 2012.

22. Sally Goldenberg, "Extra! Fines Soaring," *New York Post*, September 3, 2013.

23. Defining the consequences of economic activity as ancillary to that activity can be a way of deflecting blame, or presenting these consequences as inevitable. This has not been the case regarding the much maligned newsstand, however. Many of the attempts at regulatory reform summarized above can be seen as attempts to manage the negative externalities of the newsstand. If a newsstand clogs a busy pedestrian corridor, or makes a street corner look shabby and disorganized, this is incidental to the activity of selling newspapers, candy, and bottled water. These are negative externalities—undesirable side effects of the object, which have no direct bearing on the economic exchange that comprises its core social function. Like other negative externalities, these consequences fall upon the government to manage, in part because they are not incorporated by market mechanisms: the price of a newspaper is not influenced by the congestion of a sidewalk, or the chipping paint on a wooden kiosk. If it were, then there would be an economic

incentive to address these issues. The social costs of the newsstand would be internalized into the economic exchange itself.

24. Jane Jacobs, *The Death and Life of Great American Cities* (New York: Random House, 1961).

25. In sociologist Mitch Duneier's influential ethnography of street life in the West Village, book vendor Hakim Hasan describes himself as a public character, and Duneier's analysis supports this claim, showing how book and magazine vendors help to keep the peace and provide familiarity and security on an anonymous urban block. Mitchell Duneier, *Sidewalk* (New York: Farrar, Straus, and Giroux, 1999).

26. James Q. Wilson and George L. Kelling, "Broken Windows," *Atlantic Monthly* 249, no. 3 (March 1, 1982).

27. "Topics of the Times: Underground Newspapers."

28. George Watson, "Neighborhood Report: Park Slope; A Newsstand Dies, and with It, a Neighborhood's Hub," *New York Times*, February 25, 2001.

29. Glenn Collins, "Newsstands of Tomorrow Get Mixed Reviews Today," *New York Times*, August 30, 2008.

30. Jessica Flint, "Neighbors Mourn a Beacon Gone Dark," *New York Times*, July 8, 2007.

31. I included only corners on which a newsstand was also not licensed in 2018, in order to exclude temporary interruptions in a newsstand's operation and isolate cases in which a newsstand closed down for good.

32. Criminal complaints are all valid crimes reported to the NYPD, including those reported by police officers who are on patrol—they range from minor violations and misdemeanors to felonies.

33. Mitchell Duneier, "Let New York's Veterans Vend," *New York Times*, January 4, 2004.

34. Martin Gottlieb, "For South Asian Immigrants, Newsstands Fulfill a Dream," *New York Times*, January 3, 1986.

35. Miriam Rozen, "New Networks of Immigrant Entrepreneurs," *New York Times*, September 30, 1984.

36. The World Wide Web has changed all of this. By allowing a vast stockpile of information to be indexed, searched, and disseminated, the Web reduces the transaction costs involved in seeking out information of interest. Blogs, podcasts, and other forms of new digital media allow niche interests and topics to be pursued, while minimizing exposure to unrelated information. The digital version of the sports section has its own freestanding URL that can be bookmarked and visited on a moment's notice. But even this effort is not strictly necessary, as relevant information increasingly comes and finds us, through email alerts, "push notifications," or social media posts on our favorite topics. Digital media minimize friction in a way printed media cannot.

37. This line of argument parallels Elijah Anderson's formulation of a "cosmopolitan canopy" created through and around places of commerce and casual sociability—street markets, public parks, etc. Anderson's discussion focuses on places where the aggregate effect of countless civil interactions across social boundaries creates an environment of tolerance. Here, I suggest that a newsstand in some cases (certainly not all) can create a space of civility, sociability, and tolerance on an otherwise nondescript street corner. Because newsstands are relatively durable, permanent structures, and often keep long hours, the sidewalks where they are located can become reliably and consistently vibrant places. However, this effect, if it happens, is localized—more patio umbrella than canopy. Elijah Anderson, *The Cosmopolitan Canopy: Race and Civility in Everyday Life* (New York: W. W. Norton, 2011).

38. Colin Moynihan, "On a Changing East Village Street, a Source of Continuity Fights for His Job," *New York Times*, January 7, 2014; Rich Schapiro, "City's Tossin' Me Out: Beloved Cooper Sq. Guy Losing Newsstand," *Daily News*, April 2, 2011.

39. Flint, "Neighbors Mourn a Beacon."

40. Asking and giving directions are among the rare social norms that bring strangers into a form of verbal contact that is not transactional, or based around exchange. It is difficult to think of any other kind of social interaction in which it is acceptable for a person to walk up to a complete stranger and begin talking to them. Asking directions involves trust and a degree of intimacy: when we ask directions, we tell a stranger something about ourselves, even if it is just our destination.

41. Michael Sullivan, "Directions," *Places Journal*, June 2018, https://placesjournal.org/article/directions/.

42. A case in point was the urban horse. In the early twentieth century, when the automobile replaced the horse as the primary urban mode of transport, small manufacturers and equestrian enthusiasts, among others, continued to make use of the animals for some time. On the cobblestone streets of New York, the horse remained a mainstay for decades, trotting alongside its motorized technological successors. "The relative slowness of the transition [was] striking," write McShane and Tarr, in their fascinating social history. The disappearance of the horse from American cities varied from "function to function." For specific urban constituencies, the horse continued to be a valuable commodity long after the advent of electric- or steam-powered alternatives (166). The automobile changed transportation, but not for everyone, and not all at once. Clay McShane and Joel Tarr, *The Horse in the City: Living Machines in the Nineteenth Century* (Baltimore, MD: Johns Hopkins University Press, 2007).

43. To be fair, there are rational reasons to link payphones with drug dealing. Payphone calls cannot be legally tapped, and this offers a degree of security to people arranging elicit activity. But both the widespread legitimate uses of payphones long after the popularization of the cell phone and the vehemence with which payphones were targeted in quality-of-life campaigns suggest that arguments against payphones on law-and-order grounds were part of a broader stigmatization of a technology primarily of use to low-income city residents. On reactions to new payphones on the Upper West Side, see Edward Wong's "Neighborhood Report: New York Up Close; More Pay Phones? No Thanks" (*New York Times*, November 21, 1999). On antipayphone campaigns across the country, see Renee Reizman's "What Killed the Pay Phone? It Was More than Mobile Phones: An Object Lesson" (*Atlantic*, February 2, 2017). On the continued usefulness of payphones, see Tanvi Misra's "Why Some Places Still Have Plenty of Pay Phones" (*Citylab*, November 10, 2014, www.citylab.com/life/2014/11/why-some-places-still-have-plenty-of-pay-phones/382454/).

44. Jovana Rizzo, email message to author, September 13, 2018. A spokesperson for the New York City Department of Information Technology and Telecommunications (NYC DOITT) confirmed this for me in personal correspondence.

45. Through a Freedom of Information Legislation (FOIL) request, I was able to obtain eleven months of LinkNYC call data from the NYC DOITT covering 2016 and 2017, shortly after the program began.

46. Even strictly quantitative differences in the output of an object can dramatically change its qualitative social affordances. When the gas lamp made way for the electric streetlight, the most meaningful difference was straightforward: electric lamps gave off more light. But an entire occupation vanished—the lamplighter was no longer needed—and for users, the electric streetlight illuminated urban architecture at night and permitted a wider range of nighttime activity, changing the very temporal rhythms of everyday urban life. See Sandy Isenstadt, "Good Night," *Places Journal*, April 2014. Similarly, in home electronics, the transition from record player to cassette player to digital audio playable on mobile phones has changed the fidelity of recorded sound and the size of the object necessary to play audio tracks. But with portability has come a meaningful qualitative change in social experience, as young people increasingly carry their own background music everywhere they go, living social lives that are, in an important way, mediated by music.

See James E. Katz, Katie M. Lever, and Yi-Fan Chen, "Mobile Music as Environmental Control and Prosocial Entertainment," in *Handbook of Mobile Communication Studies*, ed. James E. Katz. (Cambridge, MA: MIT Press, 2008), 368–76.

Conclusion

1. As an aside, in revisiting my fieldnotes and writing this chapter in mid-2020, I was momentarily taken aback by this detail. I sat down immediately adjacent to an elderly woman I didn't know? Several months after this field visit, proxemics, or conceptions of personal space, were abruptly problematized, as the state designated "social distancing" procedures while in public, intended to prevent the spread of the Covid-19 coronavirus.

2. Jerold S. Kayden, *Privately Owned Public Space: The New York Experience* (New York: John Wiley and Sons, 2000).

3. Kristine Miller, *Designs on the Public: The Private Lives of New York's Public Spaces* (Minneapolis: University of Minnesota Press), 126.

4. Alexander Burns, "Donald Trump, Pushing Someone Rich, Offers Himself," *New York Times*, June 17, 2015.

5. Thomas de Monchaux, "Seeing Trump in Trump Tower," *New Yorker*, October 6, 2016.

6. Paul Goldberger, "Architecture: Atrium of Trump Tower Is a Pleasant Surprise," *New York Times*, April 4, 1983.

7. Ada Louise Huxtable, letter to the editor, "Donald Trump's Tower," *New York Times*, May 6, 1984.

8. K. Miller, *Designs on the Public*, 119.

9. Letter from Trump to Schneider, quoted in K. Miller, 131.

10. Thomas de Monchaux, "Seeing Trump in Trump Tower," *New Yorker*, October 6, 2016, https://www.newyorker.com/culture/cultural-comment/seeing-trump-in-trump-tower.

11. Daniel Miller, *The Comfort of Things* (Cambridge, UK: Polity, 2008).

12. The resemblance between "closest at hand" and Heidegger's "ready-to-hand" is intentional. Heidegger's concept has proven useful to people who study affordances, precisely because it captures the way we unreflectively interact with the material world while pursuing everyday patterns of behavior. His phenomenology accurately schematizes the modes of thought and behavior observed throughout this book and is compatible with the recurring idea of "troublesome" objects that appears here. Martin Heidegger, *Being and Time*, trans. John Macquarrie and Edward Robinson (Cambridge, MA: Blackwell, 1962), 99–103.

13. This might be taken as an endorsement of a theoretical approach to materiality that draws upon pragmatism, symbolic interactionism, or phenomenology, but I do not mean it as such, at least not strongly. Other analytical frameworks for studying material objects were useful to the writing of this book, and are equally valid. (The influence of Bruno Latour and Actor Network Theory, for example, should be evident throughout.) Instead, my argument for immediacy is rooted in the modes of thought and behavior that are associated with being in, and moving through, public space. If my research setting were an art museum, a laboratory, or a church, places in which the relationship of objects to larger, more ephemeral social meanings is deeply and consciously considered, this argument would not hold.

14. In fairness, as noted in chapters 1 and 2, it is far more common for urban planning and design to incorporate the subjectivity of potential users than it once was. Architects and planners now routinely integrate the results of public visioning sessions, town-hall meetings, focus groups, and charettes into their designs. But many material or regulatory interventions, particularly in the area of transportation facilities and infrastructure, continue to proceed without this level of sensitivity to the environmental psychology of use. There is also an important distinction to be

drawn between the desires of a community, as expressed in place-making exercises, and their ongoing, moment-by-moment needs once a new artifact or public space has been put in place.

15. Langdon Winner, "Do Artifacts Have Politics?," *Daedalus* 109, no. 1 (1980): 121–36.

16. This emergent quality may be another important point of contrast between ordinary objects and extraordinary ones, like the nuclear reactors described by Winner in his well-known essay on the politics of material artifacts.

17. Winner, 133–34.

18. Mike Owen Benediktsson, "Where Inequality Takes Place: A Programmatic Argument for Urban Sociology," *City and Community* 17, no. 2 (June 2018): 394–417.

19. David Frisby and Mike Featherstone, eds., *Simmel on Culture: Selected Writings* (New York: Sage, 1997), 146–51.

20. See Terence McDonnell, *Best Laid Plans: Cultural Entropy and the Unraveling of AIDS Media Campaigns* (Chicago: University of Chicago Press, 2016).

21. Thomas Gieryn, "What Buildings Do," *Theory and Society* 31, no. 1 (February 2002): 35–74.

22. A combination of humans and objects, acting on one another within a defined system or place, is an "assemblage" for Christopher Bear, in "Assembling the Sea: Materiality, Movement and Regulatory Practices in the Cardigan Bay Scallop Fishery" (*Cultural Geographies* 20, no. 1 [2013]: 21–41), or a "network" for Bruno Latour, in *Reassembling the Social: An Introduction to Actor-Network-Theory* (Oxford: Oxford University Press, 2005, 129). A coming together of human actors, organizations, and objects is a "lash-up" for Harvey Luskin Molotch, in *Where Stuff Comes From: How Toasters, Toilets, Cars, Computers, and Many Others Things Come to Be as They Are* (New York: Routledge, 2003, 2).

23. In fact, recall that these did occur, as children were burned by playground equipment, and visitors took the park's invitation to the water too literally, scrambling over the boulders and falling into the far-from-salubrious waters of the East River.

INDEX

actor network theory, 211n5, 238n13
affordances, 4–5; concept of, 211–212n7, 213n13; Heidegger's ready-to-hand concept, 238n12; lawn and maintenance, 33; of newsstand, 158–159, 172–175, 202–203; of objects, 237n46; public space requiring open, 202–203; space for neighborhood, 31; term, 4
agora, 223n49
agoraphobia, fear of public spaces, 74–80
American Community Survey (ACS), 219–220n37, 222n31
American Sociological Association (ASA), 211n3
Americans with Disabilities Act (ADA), 134, 137
Anderson, Elijah, formulation of cosmopolitan canopy, 236n37
annihilation, death of things, 183
"a-park-ments", funding of, 28
appearance, of objects, 7–9, 17–18
Apprentice, The (television show), 189
Atlantic City Expressway, 99
Atlantic County: alcohol and drunk driving in, 227n18; fatal crashes in, 227n21; pedestrians in, 227n22; roadways in, 18; United States and, 226n16

Bay Improvement Group, 74, 75–76
bench: disappearance of, 192, 194; flowerpots on, 192; return of, 194; symbolism of, 194–195; Trump Tower, 19, 187, 188; view from, 190
big decisions, 196
Biggie Smalls, 86
blackboxing, 231n21
Black Horse Pike, 18, 98–99, 225n8; affordances of, 202; bus stop along, 107–109; fence installation, 111; pedestrian deaths, 103–104; pedestrians and, 100, 102; symbolic and material fix along, 112, 114; symbolic programming of, 117–119

Black Monday, 179
Blarney Stone, 9
Bloomberg, Michael: connecting city revenue and waterfront park, 28; on newsstand, 167; New York City under, 15; plaza project, 58; on Times Square social interaction, 66
Bloomberg News, anchor Pellett, 121
blue-collar worker, 4
bonus plazas, 59, 62, 189
Borer, Michael, on symbolic meanings of public objects, 9
Boston's Fenway Park, Green Monster, 9
Brand, Stewart, on parks, 52
Bratton, William: on panhandling, 65; on removing plazas, 66
Broadway, as Great Blight Way, 66
broken windows theory: Giuliani and, 166; Kelling and Wilson's, 173; mural project and, 76; policing approach 69
Brooklyn Bridge, 31, 39, 41
Brooklyn Bridge Park (BBP), 16, 191; creation of, 203–204; debate over design of, 198, 201–202; design of, 30, 54; funding plan for, 29; Harbor View Lawn and, 52; ideal version of, 204–205; from imagination to reality, 49–51; inception of planning, 27–29; management of, 29–30; as playground for Brooklyn, 43–46; programming of, 46–48; public lawn as part of, 25; public leisure of, 196; publicness of, 30, 202; single pier opening to public, 48; stakeholders contesting design, 30; Van Valkenburgh as architect, 39–42; as world-class attraction, 41, 42. *See also* public lawn(s)
Brooklyn Bridge Park Corporation, 219n31
Brooklyn Bridge Park Defense Fund (BBPDF), 218n10
Brooklyn Heights, 47; front lawn for, 30–35; park as front lawn, 33; residents supporting park design, 33–34; view from promenade in, 32

A NOTE ON THE TYPE

This book has been composed in Adobe Text and Gotham.
Adobe Text, designed by Robert Slimbach for Adobe,
bridges the gap between fifteenth- and sixteenth-century
calligraphic and eighteenth-century Modern styles.
Gotham, inspired by New York street signs, was designed
by Tobias Frere-Jones for Hoefler & Co.

CPSIA information can be obtained
at www.ICGtesting.com
Printed in the USA
LVHW102020200522
719355LV00011B/68/J

9 780691 174334